Anthropology 1AB3

Introduction to Anthropology: Race, Religion and Conflict

Third Custom Edition

McMaster University

NELSON

NELSON

ISBN-13: 978-0-17-677408-0
ISBN-10: 0-17-677408-4

Consists of Selections from:

Cultural Anthropology: The Human Challenge, 14th Edition
William A. Haviland
Harald E.L. Prins
Bunny McBride
Dana Walrath
ISBN 10: 1-133-95742-0, © 2014

Sociocultural Anthropology: A Problem-Based Approach, Third Edition
Richard H. Robbins,
Maggie Cummings,
Karen McGarry
ISBN 10: 0-17-657016-0, © 2017

Cover Credit:

MILA Zed/Shutterstock

Brief Contents

The Essence of Anthropology

The Anthropological Perspective

Anthropology is the study of humankind in all times and places. Of course, many other disciplines focus on humans in one way or another. For example, anatomy and physiology concentrate on our species as biological organisms. The social sciences examine human relationships, leaving artistic and philosophical aspects of human cultures to the humanities. Anthropology focuses on the interconnections and interdependence of all aspects of the human experience in all places, in the present and deep into the past, well before written history. This unique, broad **holistic perspective** equips anthropologists to address that elusive thing we call *human nature*.

Anthropologists welcome the contributions of researchers from other disciplines, and in return offer their own findings to these other disciplines. An anthropologist may not know as much about the structure of the human eye as an anatomist or as much about the perception of color as a psychologist. As a synthesizer, however, the anthropologist seeks to understand how anatomy and psychology relate to color-naming practices in different societies. Because they look for the broad basis of human ideas and practices without limiting themselves to any single social or biological aspect, anthropologists can acquire an especially expansive and inclusive overview of human biology and culture.

Keeping a holistic perspective allows anthropologists to prevent their own cultural ideas and values from distorting their research. As the old saying goes, people often see what they believe, rather than what appears before their eyes. By maintaining a critical awareness of their own assumptions about human nature—checking and rechecking the ways their beliefs and actions might be shaping their research—anthropologists strive to gain objective knowledge about human beings. With this

anthropology The study of humankind in all times and places.

holistic perspective A fundamental principle of anthropology: The various parts of human culture and biology must be viewed in the broadest possible context in order to understand their interconnections and interdependence.

IN THIS CHAPTER YOU WILL LEARN TO

- Describe the discipline of anthropology and make connections among its four fields.

- Compare anthropology to the sciences and the humanities.

- Identify the characteristics of anthropological field methods and the ethics of anthropological research.

- Explain the usefulness of anthropology in light of globalization.

in mind, anthropologists aim to avoid the pitfalls of **ethnocentrism**, a belief that the ways of one's own culture are the only proper ones.

To some, an inclusive, holistic perspective that emphasizes the diversity within and among human cultures can be mistaken as shorthand for liberal politics among anthropologists. This is not the case. Anthropologists come from many different backgrounds, and individuals practicing the discipline vary in their personal, political, and religious beliefs (Figure 1.1). At the same time, they apply a rigorous methodology for researching cultural practices from the perspective of the culture being studied—a methodology that requires them to check for the influences of their own biases. This is as true for an anthropologist analyzing the culture of the global banking industry as it is for one investigating trance dancing among contemporary hunter-gatherers. We might say that anthropology is a discipline concerned with unbiased evaluation of diverse human systems, including one's own. At times this requires challenging the status quo that is maintained and defended by the power elites of the system under study.

While other social sciences have predominantly concentrated on contemporary peoples living in North American and European (Western) societies, anthropologists have traditionally focused on non-Western peoples and cultures. Anthropologists work with the understanding that to fully access the complexities of human ideas, behavior, and biology, *all* humans, wherever and whenever, must be studied. A cross-cultural and long-term evolutionary perspective distinguishes anthropology from other social sciences. This approach guards against theories about the world and reality that are **culture-bound**—based on the assumptions and values that come from the researcher's own culture.

As a case in point, consider the fact that infants in the United States typically sleep apart from their parents. To people accustomed to multibedroom houses, cribs, and car seats, this may seem normal, but cross-cultural research shows that *co-sleeping*, of mother and baby in particular, is the norm (Figure 1.2). Further, the practice of sleeping apart favored in the United States dates back only about 200 years.

Recent studies have shown that separation of mother and infant has important biological and cultural consequences. For one thing, it increases the length of the infant's crying bouts. Some mothers incorrectly interpret crying as an indication that the baby is not receiving sufficient breast milk and consequently switch to using bottled formula, which has been shown to be less healthy. In extreme cases, a baby's cries may provoke physical

© Documentary Educational Resources

Figure 1.1 Anthropologist Jayasinhji Jhala Anthropologists come from many corners of the world and carry out research in a huge variety of cultures all around the globe. Dr. Jayasinhji Jhala, pictured here, hails from the old city of Dhrangadhra in Gujarat, northwestern India. A member of the Jhala clan of Rajputs, an aristocratic caste of warriors, he grew up in the royal palace of his father, the maharaja. After earning a bachelor of arts degree in India, he came to the United States and earned a master's in visual studies from MIT, followed by a doctorate in anthropology from Harvard. Currently a professor and director of the programs of Visual Anthropology and the Visual Anthropology Media Laboratory at Temple University, he returns regularly to India with students to film cultural traditions in his own caste-stratified society.

abuse. But the benefits of co-sleeping go beyond significant reductions in crying: Infants who are breastfed receive more stimulation important for brain development, and they are apparently less susceptible to sudden infant death syndrome (SIDS or "crib death"), which occurs at a higher rate in the United States than in any other country. There are benefits to the mother as well: Frequent nursing prevents early ovulation after childbirth, promotes weight

---

ethnocentrism The belief that the ways of one's own culture are the only proper ones.

culture-bound A perspective that produces theories about the world and reality that are based on the assumptions and values from the researcher's own culture.

VISUAL COUNTERPOINT

Figure 1.2 **Sleeping Habits across Cultures** Although infants in the United States typically sleep apart from their parents, cross-cultural research shows that co-sleeping, particularly of mother and baby, is the rule. Without the breathing cues provided by someone sleeping nearby, an infant is more susceptible to sudden infant death syndrome (SIDS), a phenomenon in which a 4- to 6-month-old baby stops breathing and dies while asleep. The highest rates of SIDS are found among infants in the United States. The photo on the right shows a Nenet family sleeping together in their *chum* (reindeer-skin tent). Nenet people are Arctic reindeer pastoralists living in Siberia.

loss to shed pregnancy pounds, and allows nursing mothers at least as much sleep as mothers who sleep apart from their infants (McKenna & McDade, 2005).

Why do so many mothers continue to sleep separately from their infants? In the United States, the cultural values of independence and consumerism come into play. To begin building individual identities, babies are provided with rooms (or at least space) of their own. This room also gives parents a place to stow the toys, furniture, and other paraphernalia associated with good and caring childrearing in the United States.

Although the findings of anthropologists have often challenged the conclusions of sociologists, psychologists, and economists, anthropology is absolutely indispensable to those in other disciplines because it is the only consistent check against culture-bound assertions. In a sense, anthropology is to these disciplines what the laboratory is to physics and chemistry: an essential testing ground for their theories.

Anthropology and Its Fields

Individual anthropologists tend to specialize in one of four fields or subdisciplines: cultural anthropology, linguistic anthropology, archaeology, and physical (biological) anthropology (**Figure 1.3**). Some anthropologists consider

archaeology and linguistics to be part of the broader study of human cultures, but archaeology and linguistics also have close ties to physical anthropology. For example, while linguistic anthropology focuses on the social and cultural aspects of language, it has deep connections to the evolution of human language and to the biological basis of speech and language studied within physical anthropology.

Researchers in each of anthropology's fields gather and analyze data to explore similarities and differences among humans, across time and space. Moreover, individuals within

Figure 1.3 **The Four Fields of Anthropology** Note that the divisions among the fields are not sharp, indicating that their boundaries overlap. Note also that all four include the practice of applied anthropology.

BIOCULTURAL CONNECTION

The Anthropology of Organ Transplantation

In 1954, the first organ transplant occurred in Boston when surgeons removed a kidney from one identical twin to place it inside his sick brother. Today, transplants between unrelated individuals are common, so much so that organs are trafficked in the black market, often across continents from the poor to the wealthy. Though some transplants rely upon living donors, routine organ transplantation depends largely upon the availability of organs obtained from individuals who have died. To reduce illegal traffic, several European countries have enacted policies that assume that any individual who is "brain dead" is automatically an organ donor unless the person has "opted out" ahead of time.

A practice like organ transplantation can exist only if it fits with cultural beliefs about death and the human body. The North American and European view—that the body is a machine that can be repaired much like a car—makes a practice like organ transplantation acceptable. But this is not the view shared by all societies. Anthropologist

Margaret Lock has explored differences between Japanese and North American acceptance of the biological state of brain death and how it affects the practice of organ transplantation.

The diagnosis of brain death relies upon the absence of measurable electrical currents in the brain and the inability to breathe without technological assistance. The brain-dead individual, though attached to machines, still seems alive with a beating heart and normal skin coloring. Part of the reason most North Americans find organ transplantation tolerable with the determination of brain death is that personhood and individuality are culturally ascribed to the mind, and thus located in the brain. North Americans' acceptance of brain death has allowed for the "gift of life" through sometimes anonymous organ donation and subsequent transplantation.

By contrast, in Japan, the concept of brain death is hotly contested, and organ transplants are rarely performed. The Japanese idea of personhood does not incorporate a mind–body split; instead, a person's identity is tied to

the entire body rather than solely to the brain. Consequently, the Japanese reject that a warm body is a corpse from which organs can be harvested. Further, organs cannot be transformed into "gifts" because anonymous donation is incompatible with Japanese social patterns of reciprocal exchange.

Organ transplantation involves far greater social meaning than the purely biological movement of an organ from one individual to another. Cultural and biological processes are tightly woven into every aspect of this new social practice.

BIOCULTURAL QUESTION

What criteria do you use for death, and is it compatible with the idea of organ donation? Do you think that donated organs are fairly distributed in your society or throughout the globe?

For more on this subject, see Lock, M. (2001). Twice dead: Organ transplants and the reinvention of death. Berkeley: University of California Press.

---

each of the four fields practice **applied anthropology**, which entails the use of anthropological knowledge and methods to solve practical problems. Most applied anthropologists actively collaborate with the communities in which they work—setting goals, solving problems, and conducting research together. In this book, the Anthropology Applied features spotlight how anthropology contributes to solving a wide range of challenges.

An early example of the application of anthropological knowledge to a practical problem was the international public health movement that began in the 1920s. This marked the beginning of **medical anthropology**—a specialization that brings theoretical and applied approaches from cultural and biological anthropology to the study of human health and disease. The work of medical anthropologists sheds light on the connections between human health and political and economic forces, both locally and globally. Examples of this specialization appear in some of the Biocultural Connections featured in this text, including the one presented on this page, "The Anthropology of Organ Transplantation."

Cultural Anthropology

Cultural anthropology (also called *social* or *sociocultural anthropology*) is the study of patterns in human behavior, thought, and emotions. It focuses on humans as

applied anthropology The use of anthropological knowledge and methods to solve practical problems, often for a specific client.

medical anthropology A specialization in anthropology that brings theoretical and applied approaches from cultural and biological anthropology to the study of human health and disease.

cultural anthropology The study of patterns in human behavior, thought, and emotions, focusing on humans as culture-producing and culture-reproducing creatures. Also known as *social* or *sociocultural anthropology*.

culture-producing and culture-reproducing creatures. To understand the work of the cultural anthropologist, we must clarify the meaning of **culture**—a society's shared and socially transmitted ideas, values, emotions, and perceptions, which are used to make sense of experience and which generate behavior and are reflected in that behavior. These are the (often unconscious) standards by which societies—structured groups of people—operate. These standards are socially learned, rather than acquired through biological inheritance. The manifestations of culture may vary considerably from place to place, but no individual is "more cultured" in the anthropological sense than any other.

Integral to all the anthropological fields, the concept of culture might be considered anthropology's distinguishing feature. After all, a biological anthropologist is distinct from a biologist *primarily* because he or she takes culture into account. Cultural anthropologists may study the legal, medical, economic, political, or religious system of a given society, knowing that all aspects of the culture interrelate as part of a unified whole. They may focus on divisions in a society—such as by gender, age, or class—factors we will explore in depth later in this text. But it is also worth noting the significance of these same categories to the archaeologist who studies a society through its material remains, to the linguistic anthropologist who examines ancient and modern languages, and to the biological anthropologist who investigates the physical human body.

Cultural anthropology has two main components: ethnography and ethnology. An **ethnography** is a detailed description of a particular culture primarily based on **fieldwork**, which is the term all anthropologists use for on-location research. Because the hallmark of ethnographic fieldwork is a combination of social participation and personal observation within the community being studied and interviews and discussions with individual members of a group, the ethnographic method is commonly referred to as **participant observation** (Figure 1.4). Ethnographies provide the information used to make systematic comparisons among cultures all across the world. Known as **ethnology**, such cross-cultural research allows anthropologists to develop theories that help explain why certain important differences or similarities occur among groups.

Ethnography

Through participant observation—eating a people's food, sleeping under their roof, learning how to speak and behave acceptably, and personally experiencing their habits and customs—the ethnographer seeks to gain the best possible understanding of a particular way of life. Being a participant observer does not mean that the anthropologist must join in battles to study a culture in which warfare is prominent; but by living among a warring people, the ethnographer should be able to understand how warfare fits into the overall cultural framework.

The ethnographer must observe carefully to gain an overview without placing too much emphasis on one

© Matt Dyas/Courtesy of Florian Stammler

Figure 1.4 Fieldwork in the Arctic British anthropologist Florian Stammler engages in participant observation among Sami reindeer nomads in Siberia. Specializing in Arctic anthropology, particularly in the Russian far north, Stammler coordinates the anthropology research team at the University of Lapland's Arctic Centre. His interests include Arctic economy, human–animal relations, and the anthropology of place and belonging.

cultural feature at the expense of another. Only by discovering how *all* parts of a culture—its social, political, economic, and religious practices and institutions—relate to one another can the ethnographer begin to understand the cultural system. This is the holistic perspective so basic to the discipline.

The popular image of ethnographic fieldwork is that it occurs among hunters, herders, fishers, or farmers who live in far-off, isolated places. To be sure, much ethnographic work has been done in the remote villages of Asia, Africa, or Latin America, islands of the Pacific Ocean, deserts of Australia, and so on. However, as the discipline developed after the mid-1900s with the demise of colonialism, industrialized societies

---

culture A society's shared and socially transmitted ideas, values, and perceptions, which are used to make sense of experience and which generate behavior and are reflected in that behavior.

ethnography A detailed description of a particular culture primarily based on fieldwork.

fieldwork The term anthropologists use for on-location research.

participant observation In ethnography, the technique of learning a people's culture through social participation and personal observation within the community being studied, as well as interviews and discussion with individual members of the group over an extended period of time.

ethnology The study and analysis of different cultures from a comparative or historical point of view, utilizing ethnographic accounts and developing anthropological theories that help explain why certain important differences or similarities occur among groups.

and neighborhoods in modern cities have also become a significant focus of anthropological study.

Ethnographic fieldwork has transformed from expert Western anthropologists studying people in "other" places to a collaborative approach among anthropologists from all parts of the world and the varied communities in which they work. Today, anthropologists from around the globe employ the same research techniques that were used in the study of non-Western peoples to explore diverse subjects such as religious movements, street gangs, refugee settlements, land rights, conflict resolution, corporate bureaucracies, and health-care systems in Western cultures.

Ethnology

Largely descriptive in nature, *ethnography* provides the raw data needed for *ethnology*—the branch of cultural anthropology that involves cross-cultural comparisons and theories that explain differences or similarities among groups. Intriguing insights into one's own beliefs and practices may come from cross-cultural comparisons. Consider, for example, the amount of time spent on domestic chores by industrialized peoples and traditional food foragers—people who rely on wild plant and animal resources for subsistence.

Anthropological research has shown that food foragers work far less time at domestic tasks and other subsistence pursuits compared to people in industrialized societies. Despite access to "labor-saving" appliances such as dishwashers, washing machines, clothes dryers, vacuum cleaners, food processors, and microwave ovens, urban women in the United States who are not working for wages outside their homes put 55 hours a week into their housework. In contrast, aboriginal women in Australia devoted 20 hours a week to their chores (Bodley, 2008, p. 67). Nevertheless, consumer appliances have become important indicators of a high standard of living in the United States due to the widespread belief that household appliances reduce housework and increase leisure time.

By making systematic comparisons, ethnologists seek to arrive at scientific explanations of cultural features and social practices in all times and places. (The Biocultural Connection you read on page 6 is one of countless examples of anthropological insights gained through comparative research.)

Applied Cultural Anthropology

Today, cultural anthropologists contribute to applied anthropology in a variety of contexts ranging from business to education to health care to governmental interventions to humanitarian aid. For example, anthropologist Nancy Scheper-Hughes has taken her investigative work on the global problem of illegal trafficking of organs and used it to help found Organs Watch, an organization dedicated to solving this human rights issue (see the Globalscape later in this chapter).

Linguistic Anthropology

Perhaps the most distinctive feature of the human species is language. Although the sounds and gestures made by some other animals—especially by apes—may serve functions comparable to those of human language, no other animal has developed a system of symbolic communication as complex as that of humans. Language allows people to create, preserve, and transmit countless details of their culture from generation to generation.

Linguistic anthropology is the branch of anthropology that studies human languages; it investigates their structure, history, and relation to social and cultural contexts. Although it shares data, theories, and methods with the more general discipline of linguistics, it differs in that it includes distinctly anthropological questions, such as, how does language influence or reflect culture? And how does language use differ among distinct members of a society?

In its early years, linguistic anthropology emphasized the documentation of languages of cultures under ethnographic study—particularly those whose future seemed precarious due to colonization, forced assimilation, population decimation, capitalist expansion, or other destructive forces. When the first Europeans began to colonize the world five centuries ago, an estimated 12,000 distinct languages existed. By the early 1900s—when anthropological research began to take off—many languages and peoples had already disappeared or were on the brink of extinction. Sadly this trend continues, with predictions that nearly half of the world's remaining 6,000 languages will become extinct over the next hundred years (Crystal, 2002; Knight, Studdert-Kennedy, & Hurford, 2000).

Linguistic anthropology has three main branches: descriptive linguistics, historical linguistics, and language in relation to social and cultural settings. All three yield valuable information about how people communicate and how they understand the world around them.

Descriptive Linguistics

This branch of linguistic anthropology involves the painstaking work of dissecting a language by recording, delineating, and analyzing all of its features. It leads to a deeper understanding of a language—its structure (including grammar and syntax), its unique linguistic repertoire (figures of speech, word plays, and so on), and its relationship to other languages.

Historical Linguistics

While descriptive linguistics focuses on all features of a particular language at any one moment in time, historical

---

linguistic anthropology The study of human languages—looking at their structure, history, and relation to social and cultural contexts.

Photo by Chris Rainier/Enduring Voices Project

Figure 1.5 **Preserving Endangered Languages** Linguistic anthropologist David Anderson (right) has devoted his career to documenting and saving indigenous languages. He founded and heads the Living Tongues Institute for Endangered Languages and works throughout the globe to preserve languages that are dying out at a shocking rate of about one every two weeks. Here he is recording for the first time the language of Koro, spoken by some 1,000 people in India's remote northeastern state, Arunachal Pradesh. Situated near India's contested border with China, this region is considered a black hole in the study of languages.

linguistics deals with the fact that languages change. In addition to deciphering "dead" languages that are no longer spoken, specialists in this field examine interrelationships among different languages and investigate earlier and later forms of the same language. Their findings make significant contributions to our understanding of the human past. By working out relationships among languages and examining their spatial distributions, they may estimate how long the speakers of those languages have lived where they do. By identifying those words in related languages that have survived from an ancient ancestral tongue, they can also suggest not only where, but how, the speakers of the inherited language lived. Such work shows linguistic ties between geographically distant groups such as the Navajo in Arizona's desert and the Gwich'in above the Arctic Circle in Alaska, or between the Magyars in Hungary and the people of Finland.

Language in Its Social and Cultural Settings

Some linguistic anthropologists study the social and cultural contexts of a language. For example, they may research how factors such as age, gender, ethnicity, class, religion, occupation, or financial status affect speech. Because members of any culture may use a variety of different registers and inflections, the ones they choose (often unconsciously) to use at a specific instance convey particular meanings.

Scientists in this branch of linguistics also look into the dynamic relationship between language and culture—investigating to what degree they mutually influence and inform each other. In this vein, they may investigate how a language reflects culturally significant aspects of a people's environment or values.

Linguistic anthropologists may also focus on the socialization process through which an individual becomes part of a culture, moves up in social status, or takes on a new professional identity. First-year medical students, for example, amass 6,000 new terms and a series of linguistic conventions as they begin to take on the role of a physician. Individuals training for any specialized career, from lawyer to chef, face similar challenges in quickly expanding their vocabularies.

Applied Linguistic Anthropology

Linguistic anthropologists put their research to use in a number of settings. Some, for example, have collaborated with recently contacted cultural groups, small nations (or tribes), and ethnic minorities in the preservation or revival of languages suppressed or lost during periods of oppression by dominant societies. Their work has included helping to create written forms of languages that previously existed only orally. This sort of applied linguistic anthropology represents a trend in mutually useful collaboration that is characteristic of much anthropological research today (**Figure 1.5**).

Archaeology

Archaeology is the branch of anthropology that studies human cultures through the recovery and analysis of material remains and environmental data. Such material products include tools, pottery, hearths, and enclosures that remain as traces of cultural practices in the past, as well as human, plant, and marine remains, some of which date back 2.5 million years. The arrangement of these traces, as much as the traces themselves, reflects specific human ideas and behavior. For example, shallow, restricted concentrations of charcoal that include oxidized earth, bone fragments, and charred plant

---

archaeology The study of cultures through the recovery and analysis of material remains and environmental data.

Figure 1.6 Analyzing Human Remains in a Bioarchaeology Laboratory Bioarchaeology graduate students J. Marla Toyne and Mellisa Lund Valle are conducting a skeletal inventory and checking for pathological conditions in human remains from a 14th-century mass execution and sacrifice site at Punta Lobos in the Huarmey River Valley in northern Peru. Their work is part of a research project directed by Dr. John Verano of Tulane University, New Orleans.

Courtesy of John Verano

remains, located near pieces of fire-cracked rock, pottery, and tools suitable for food preparation, indicate cooking and food processing. Such remains can reveal much about a people's diet and subsistence practices.

In addition to specific questions about a single group of people at a particular place and time, archaeologists use material remains to investigate broad questions, including settlement or migration patterns across vast areas, such as the spread of the earliest humans from Africa or the first peopling of the Americas. Together with skeletal remains, material remains help archaeologists reconstruct the biocultural context of past human lifeways and patterns. Archaeologists organize this material and use it to explain cultural variability and change through time.

Because archaeological research is explicitly tied to unearthing material remains in particular environmental contexts, a variety of innovations in the geographic and geologic sciences have been readily incorporated into archaeological research. Innovations such as geographic information systems (GIS), remote sensing, and ground-penetrating radar (GPR) complement traditional explorations of the past through archaeological digs.

Although archaeologists tend to specialize in particular culture zones or time periods that are connected with particular regions of the world, a number of topical subspecializations also exist. We turn now to these.

historical archaeology The archaeological study of places for which written records exist.

bioarchaeology The archaeological study of human remains—bones, skulls, teeth, and sometimes hair, dried skin, or other tissue—to determine the influences of culture and environment on human biological variation.

Historical Archaeology

Archaeologists can reach back for clues to human behavior far beyond the maximal 5,000 years to which historians are confined by their reliance on written records. Calling this time period "prehistoric" does not mean that these societies were less interested in their history or that they did not have ways of recording and transmitting history. It simply means that written records do not exist.

That said, archaeologists are not limited to the study of societies without written records; they may study those for which historic documents are available to supplement the material remains. **Historical archaeology**, the archaeological study of places for which written records exist, often provides data that differ considerably from the historical record. In most literate societies, written records are associated with governing elites rather than with farmers, fishers, laborers, or slaves, and therefore they include the biases of the ruling classes. In fact, according to James Deetz, a pioneer in historical archaeology of the Americas, in many historical contexts, "material culture may be the most objective source of information we have" (Deetz, 1977, p. 160).

Bioarchaeology

Bioarchaeology is the study of human remains—bones, skulls, teeth, and sometimes hair, dried skin, or other tissue—to determine the influences of culture and environment on human biological variation. Whether mummified (as in the dry deserts of northwestern China, Egypt, or Peru) or not, human remains excavated at archaeological sites provide valuable clues about the lifestyle and health of prehistoric peoples, including information about activity, physiological stress, nutrition, disease, and social rank (Figure 1.6).

For example, mummified skeletal remains from the Andean highlands in South America not only reveal this burial practice but also provide evidence of some of the earliest brain surgery ever documented. In addition, these bioarchaeological remains exhibit skull deformation techniques that distinguish nobility from other members of society.

Some archaeologists specialize in *ethnobotany*, studying how people of a given culture made use of indigenous plants. Others specialize in *zooarchaeology*, tracking the animal remains recovered in archaeological excavations. Still others, maritime archaeologists, may research submerged sites or old sailing vessels sunk to the bottom of a sea, lake, or river hundreds or even thousands of years ago.

Contemporary Archaeology

Although most archaeologists concentrate on the past, some study material objects in contemporary settings, and that includes garbage dumps. Just as a 3,000-year-old shell mound (*midden*) on the seacoast of Denmark, New England, or Tiera del Fuego offers significant clues about prehistoric communities living on mussels, oysters, fish, and other natural resources, modern garbage dumps provide evidence of everyday life in contemporary societies. For large cities like New York, the accumulation of daily garbage is staggering. In just a few centuries, millions of inhabitants have dumped so much trash that this urban area has been physically raised 6 to 30 feet—primarily from discarded newspapers and rubble from demolition and building construction, but also from huge amounts of plastic and household and office supplies and equipment (Rathje & Murphy, 2001).

Among the first anthropologists to study modern garbage was William Rathje, who founded the Garbage Project at the University of Arizona in 1973. The project began with a study of household waste of Tucson residents and later expanded to other cities. When surveyed by questionnaires, only 15 percent of households reported consuming beer, and none reported an intake of more than eight cans a week. Analysis of garbage from the same area showed that 80 percent of the households consumed some beer, and 50 percent discarded more than eight cans per week (Rathje & Murphy, 2001).

Beyond providing data on beer consumption, the Garbage Project has tested the validity of research survey techniques, upon which sociologists, economists, other social scientists, and policymakers rely heavily. The tests show a significant difference between what people *say* they do and what the garbage analysis shows they *actually* do.

Applied Archaeology

The Garbage Project also gives us a fine example of applied archaeology producing useful, thought-provoking information about contemporary social issues. Its program of excavating landfills in different parts of North America, initiated in 1987, produced the first reliable data on what materials actually go into landfills and what happens to them there. Again, common beliefs turned out to be at odds with the actual situation. For example, when buried in deep compost landfills, biodegradable materials such as newspapers take far longer to decay than anyone had expected. This kind of information is a vital step toward solving waste disposal problems. The data gathered from the Garbage Project's landfill studies on hazardous wastes and rates of decay of various materials play a major role in landfill regulation and management today (Rathje & Murphy, 2001).

Cultural Resource Management

While archaeology may conjure up images of ancient pyramids and the like, much archaeological fieldwork is carried out as **cultural resource management**. What distinguishes this work from traditional archaeological research is that it is a legally required part of any activity that might threaten important aspects of a country's prehistoric and historic heritage. Many countries, from Chile to China, use archaeological expertise to protect and manage their cultural heritage.

In the United States, for example, if a construction company plans to replace a highway bridge, it must first contract with archaeologists to identify and protect any significant prehistoric or historic resources that might be affected by this new construction. And when cultural resource management work or other archaeological investigation unearths Native American cultural items or human remains, federal laws come into the picture again. The Native American Graves Protection and Repatriation Act (NAGPRA), passed in 1990, provides a process for the return of these remains, especially human bones and burial gifts (such as copper jewelry, weapons, and ceramic bowls), to lineal descendants, culturally affiliated Indian tribes, and Native Hawaiian organizations.

In addition to working in all the capacities mentioned, archaeologists also consult for engineering firms to help them prepare environmental impact statements. Some of these archaeologists operate out of universities and colleges, while others are on the staff of independent consulting firms. When state legislation sponsors any kind of archaeological work, it is referred to as *contract archaeology*.

Physical Anthropology

Physical anthropology, also called *biological anthropology*, focuses on humans as biological organisms. Traditionally, physical anthropologists concentrated on human evolution, primatology, growth and development, human adaptation, and forensics. Today, **molecular anthropology**, or the anthropological study of genes

---

cultural resource management A branch of archaeology concerned with survey and/or excavation of archaeological and historical remains that might be threatened by construction or development; also involved with policy surrounding protection of cultural resources.

physical anthropology The systematic study of humans as biological organisms; also known as *biological anthropology*.

molecular anthropology The anthropological study of genes and genetic relationships, which contributes significantly to our understanding of human evolution, adaptation, and diversity.

and genetic relationships, contributes significantly to our understanding of human evolution, adaptation, and diversity. Comparisons among groups separated by time, geography, or the frequency of a particular gene can reveal how humans have adapted and where they have migrated. As experts in the anatomy of human bones and tissues, biological anthropologists lend their knowledge about the body to applied areas such as gross anatomy laboratories, public health, and criminal investigations.

Paleoanthropology

Dealing with much greater time spans than other branches of anthropology, **paleoanthropology** is the study of the origins, predecessors, and early representatives of the present human species. Focusing on long-time biological changes (evolution) paleoanthropologists seek to understand how, when, and why we became the species we are today. In biological terms, we humans are *Homo sapiens*, a species in the larger order of primates, one of the many kinds of mammals. Because we share a common ancestry with other primates (monkeys and apes), paleoanthropologists look back to the earliest primates (about 65 million years ago, abbreviated mya) or even to the earliest mammals (225 mya) to reconstruct the intricate path of human evolution. At times, paleoanthropologists take a **biocultural** approach, focusing on the interaction of biology and culture.

Paleoanthropologists compare fossilized skeletons of our ancestors to other fossils and to the bones of living members of our species. Combining this knowledge with biochemical and genetic evidence, they strive to scientifically reconstruct the complex course of human evolutionary history. With each new fossil discovery, paleoanthropologists have another piece to add to the puzzle still far from fully solved. Further on in this text, we discuss how, genetic evidence establishes the close relationship between humans and ape species—chimpanzees, bonobos, and gorillas. Genetic analyses indicate that the distinctively human line split from the apes sometime between 5 and 8 million years ago.

Primatology

Studying the anatomy and behavior of the other primates helps us understand what we share with our closest living relatives and what makes humans unique. Therefore, **primatology**, or the study of living and fossil primates, is a vital part of physical anthropology. Primates include the

Penelope Breese/Liaison/Getty Images

Figure 1.7 Primatologist Jane Goodall Nearly forty-five years ago Jane Goodall began studying chimpanzees to shed light on the behavior of our distant ancestors. The knowledge she has amassed reveals striking similarities with our species. Goodall has devoted much of her career to championing the rights of our closest living relatives.

Asian and African apes, as well as monkeys, lemurs, lorises, and tarsiers.

Biologically, humans are members of the ape family—large-bodied, broad-shouldered primates with no tail. Detailed studies of ape behavior in the wild indicate that the sharing of learned behavior is a significant part of their social life. Increasingly, primatologists designate the shared, learned behavior of nonhuman apes as *culture*. For example, tool use and communication systems indicate the elementary basis of language in some ape societies.

Primate studies offer scientifically grounded perspectives on the behavior of our ancestors, as well as greater appreciation and respect for the abilities of our closest living relatives. As human activity encroaches on all parts of the world, many primate species are endangered. Primatologists, such as Jane Goodall (Figure 1.7), strongly advocate for the preservation of primate habitats so that these remarkable animals will be able to continue to inhabit the earth with us.

Human Growth, Adaptation, and Variation

Some physical anthropologists specialize in the study of human growth and development. They examine biological mechanisms of growth as well as the impact of the environment on the growth process. For example, Franz Boas, a pioneer of American anthropology of the early 20th century (see the Anthropologists of Note feature on the next page) compared the heights of immigrants who spent their

---

paleoanthropology The anthropological study of biological changes through time (evolution) to understand the origins and predecessors of the present human species.

biocultural An approach that focuses on the interaction of biology and culture.

primatology The study of living and fossil primates.

ANTHROPOLOGISTS OF NOTE

Franz Boas (1858–1942) • Matilda Coxe Stevenson (1849–1915)

Franz Boas on a sailing ship, about 1925.

Franz Boas was not the first to teach anthropology in the United States, but it was Boas and his students, with their insistence on scientific rigor, who made anthropology courses common in college and university curricula. Born and raised in Germany where he studied physics, mathematics, and geography, Boas did his first ethnographic research among the Inuit (Eskimos) in Arctic Canada in 1883 and 1884. After a brief academic career in Berlin, he came to the United States where he worked in museums interspersed with ethnographic research among the Kwakiutl (Kwakwaka'wakw) Indians in the Canadian Pacific. In 1896, he became a professor at Columbia University in New York City. He authored an incredible number of publications, founded professional organizations and journals, and taught two generations of great anthropologists, including numerous women and ethnic minorities.

As a Jewish immigrant, Boas recognized the dangers of ethnocentrism and especially racism. Through ethnographic fieldwork and comparative analysis, he demonstrated that white supremacy theories and other schemes ranking non-European peoples and cultures as inferior were biased, ill informed, and unscientific. Throughout his long and illustrious academic career, he promoted anthropology not only as a human science but also as an instrument to combat racism and prejudice in the world.

Among the founders of North American anthropology were a number of women, including **Matilda Coxe Stevenson**, who did fieldwork among the Zuni Indians of Arizona. In 1885, she founded the Women's Anthropological Society in Washington, DC, the first professional association for women scientists. Three years later, hired by the Smithsonian's Bureau of American Ethnology, she became one of the first women in the world to receive a full-time official position in science. Along with several other pioneering female anthropologists in North America, she was highly influential among women's rights advocates in the late 1800s. The tradition of women building careers in anthropology continues. In fact, since World War II more than half the presidents of the now 12,000-member American Anthropological Association have been women.

Matilda Coxe Stevenson in New Mexico, about 1900.

Recording observations on film as well as in notebooks, Stevenson and Boas were also pioneers in visual anthropology. Stevenson used an early box camera to document Pueblo Indian religious ceremonies and material culture, while Boas photographed Inuit and Kwakiutl Indians from the early 1890s for cultural as well as physical anthropological documentation. Today, their early photographs are greatly valued not only by anthropologists and historians, but also by indigenous peoples themselves.

childhood in the "old country" (Europe) to the increased heights reached by their children who grew up in the United States. Today, physical anthropologists study the impact of poverty, pollution, and disease on growth. Comparisons between human and nonhuman primate growth patterns can provide clues to the evolutionary history of humans. Detailed anthropological studies of the hormonal, genetic, and physiological bases of healthy growth in living humans also contribute significantly to the health of children today.

Studies of human adaptation focus on the capacity of humans to adapt or adjust to their material environment—biologically and culturally. This branch of physical anthropology takes a comparative approach to humans living today in a variety of environments. Human beings are the only primates to inhabit the entire earth. Although biological adaptations make it possible for people to live in environmentally extreme regions, cultural adaptations also contribute to our survival in places that are dangerously cold, hot, or of high altitude.

Some of these biological adaptations are built into the genetic makeup of populations. The long period of human growth and development provides ample opportunity for the environment to shape the human body. *Developmental adaptations* are responsible for some features of human variation, such as the enlargement of the right ventricle of the heart to help push blood to the lungs among the Aymara Indians of the Bolivian altiplano—an extensive area of high plateau at the widest part of the Andes. *Physiological adaptations* are short-term changes in response to a particular environmental stimulus. For example, if a woman who normally lives at sea level flies to La Paz, a large Bolivian city in the altiplano at an altitude of 3,660 meters (nearly 12,000 feet), her body will undergo a series of physiological responses, such as increased production of the red blood cells that carry oxygen. These kinds of biological adaptation contribute to present-day human variation.

Genetically based human differences include visible traits such as height, body build, and skin color, as well as biochemical factors such as blood type and susceptibility to certain diseases. Still, we remain members of a single

ANTHROPOLOGY APPLIED

Forensic Anthropology: Voices for the Dead

The work of Clyde C. Snow, Michael Blakey, and Amy Zelson Mundorff

Forensic anthropology is the analysis of skeletal remains for legal purposes. Law enforcement authorities call upon forensic anthropologists to use skeletal remains to identify murder victims, missing persons, or people who have died in disasters, such as plane crashes. Forensic anthropologists have also contributed substantially to the investigation of human rights abuses in all parts of the world by identifying victims and documenting the cause of their death.

Among the best-known forensic anthropologists is Clyde C. Snow. He has been practicing in this field for over forty years, first for the Federal Aviation Administration and more recently as a freelance consultant. In addition to the usual police work, Snow has studied the remains of General George Armstrong Custer and his men from the 1876 battle at Little Big Horn, and in 1985 he went to Brazil, where he identified the remains of the notorious Nazi war criminal Josef Mengele.

Snow was also instrumental in establishing the first forensic team devoted to documenting cases of human rights abuses around the world. This began in 1984 when he went to Argentina at the request of a newly elected civilian government to help with the identification of remains of the *desaparecidos*, or "disappeared ones," the 9,000 or more people who were eliminated by death squads during seven years of military rule. A year later, he returned to give expert testimony at the trial of nine junta members and to teach Argentineans how to recover, clean, repair, preserve, photograph, x-ray, and analyze bones. Besides providing factual accounts of the fate of victims to their surviving kin and refuting the assertions of revisionists that the massacres never happened, the work of Snow and his Argentinean associates was crucial in convicting several military officers of kidnapping, torture, and murder.

Since Snow's pioneering work, forensic anthropologists have become increasingly involved in the investigation of human rights abuses in all parts of the world, from Chile to Guatemala, Haiti, the Philippines, Rwanda, Iraq, Bosnia, and Kosovo. Meanwhile, they continue to do important work for more typical clients. In the United States these clients include the Federal Bureau of Investigation and city, state, and county medical examiners' offices.

Forensic anthropologists specializing in skeletal remains commonly work closely with forensic archaeologists. The relation between them is rather like that between a forensic pathologist, who examines a corpse to establish time and manner of death, and a crime scene investigator, who searches the site for clues. While the forensic anthropologist deals with the human remains—often only bones and teeth—the forensic archaeologist controls the site, recording the position of relevant finds and recovering any clues associated with the remains.

In Rwanda, for example, a team assembled in 1995 to investigate mass murder (genocide) for the United Nations, which included archaeologists from the U.S. National Park Service's Midwest Archaeological Center. They performed the standard archaeological procedures of mapping the site, determining its boundaries, photographing and recording all surface finds, and excavating, photographing, and recording buried skeletons and associated materials in mass graves.[a]

In 1991, in another part of the world, construction workers in New York City discovered an African burial ground from the 17th and 18th centuries.

species. Physical anthropology applies all the techniques of modern biology to achieve fuller understanding of human variation and its relationship to the different environments in which people have lived. Physical anthropologists' research on human variation has debunked false notions of biologically defined races, a belief based on widespread misinterpretation of human variation.

Forensic Anthropology

One of the many practical applications of physical anthropology is **forensic anthropology**—the identification of human skeletal remains for legal purposes. In addition to helping law enforcement authorities identify murder victims, forensic anthropologists investigate human rights abuses such as systematic genocide, terrorism, and war crimes. These specialists use details of skeletal anatomy to establish the age, sex, population affiliation, and stature of the deceased. Forensic anthropologists can also determine whether the person was right- or left-handed, exhibited any physical abnormalities, or had experienced trauma.

While forensics relies upon differing frequencies of certain skeletal characteristics to establish population affiliation, it is nevertheless false to say that all people from a given population have a particular type of skeleton. (See the Anthropology Applied feature to read about the work of several forensic anthropologists and forensic archaeologists.)

forensic anthropology The identification of human skeletal remains for legal purposes.

The excavation of mass graves by the Guatemalan Foundation for Forensic Anthropology (Fernando Moscoso Moller, director) documents the human rights abuses committed during Guatemala's bloody civil war, a conflict that left 200,000 people dead and another 40,000 missing. In 2009, in a mass grave in the Quiche region, Diego Lux Tzunux uses his cell phone to photograph the skeletal remains believed to belong to his brother Manuel who disappeared in 1980. Genetic analyses allow forensic anthropologists to confirm the identity of individuals so that family members can know the fate of their loved ones. The analysis of skeletal remains provides evidence of the torture and massacre sustained by these individuals.

Ground Project provided incontrovertible evidence of the horror of slavery in North America, in the busy northern port of New York City. The more than 400 individuals, many of them children, were worked so far beyond their ability to endure that their spines were fractured.

A decade after construction workers happened upon the African Burial Ground, terrorists attacked the World Trade Center in lower Manhattan. Amy Zelson Mundorff, a forensic anthropologist for New York City's Office of the Chief Medical Examiner, was injured in the September 11 attack. But two days later she returned to work where she supervised and coordinated the management, treatment, and cataloguing of people who lost their lives in the tragedy.

Thus, several kinds of anthropologists analyze human remains for a variety of purposes. Their work contributes to the documentation and correction of violence committed by humans of the past and present.

Researchers used a bioarchaeological rather than a strictly forensic approach to examine the complete cultural and historical context and lifeways of the entire population buried there. Directed by Michael Blakey, the African Burial

[a]Haglund, W. D., Conner, M., & Scott, D. D. (2001). The archaeology of contemporary mass graves. *Historical Archaeology* 35 (1), 57–69.

Anthropology, Science, and the Humanities

Anthropology has sometimes been called the most humane of the sciences and the most scientific of the humanities—a designation that most anthropologists accept with pride. Given their intense involvement with people of all times and places, anthropologists have amassed considerable information about human failure and success, weakness and greatness—the real stuff of the humanities.

Anthropologists remain committed to the proposition that one cannot fully understand another culture by simply observing it; as the term *participant observation* implies, one must *experience* it as well. This same commitment to fieldwork and to the systematic collection of data, whether qualitative or quantitative, is also evidence of the scientific side of anthropology. Anthropology is an **empirical** social science based on observations or information taken in through the senses and verified by others rather than on intuition or faith. But anthropology is distinguished from other sciences by the diverse ways in which scientific research is conducted within the discipline.

Science, a carefully honed way of producing knowledge, aims to reveal and explain the underlying logic, the structural processes that make the world tick. The creative scientific endeavor seeks testable explanations for observed phenomena, ideally in terms of the workings of hidden but unchanging principles or laws. Two basic ingredients are essential for this: imagination and skepticism. Imagination, though having the potential to lead us astray, helps us recognize unexpected ways phenomena might be ordered and to think of old things in new ways. Without it, there can be no science. Skepticism allows us to distinguish fact (an observation verified by others) from fancy, to test our speculations, and to prevent our imaginations from running away with us.

In their search for explanations, scientists do not assume that things are always as they appear on the surface. After all, what could be more obvious to the scientifically uninformed observer than the earth staying still while the sun travels around it every day?

Like other scientists, anthropologists often begin their research with a **hypothesis** (a tentative explanation or hunch) about the possible relationships between certain observed facts or events. By gathering various kinds of data that seem to ground such suggested explanations on evidence, anthropologists come up with a **theory**, a coherent statement that provides an explanatory framework for understanding; an explanation or interpretation supported by a reliable body of data. In their effort to demonstrate links between *known* facts or events, anthropologists may discover *unexpected* facts, events, or relationships. An important function of theory is that it guides us in our explorations and may result in new knowledge. Equally important, the newly discovered facts may provide evidence that certain explanations, however popular or firmly believed, are unfounded. When the evidence is lacking or fails to support the suggested explanations, promising hypotheses or attractive hunches must be dropped. In other words, anthropology relies on empirical evidence. Moreover, no scientific theory—no matter how widely accepted by the international community of scholars—is beyond challenge. That includes the findings of some of anthropology's earliest and most respected scholars.

It is important to distinguish between scientific theories—which are always open to challenges born of new evidence or insights—and doctrine. A **doctrine**, or dogma, is an assertion of opinion or belief formally handed down by an authority as true and indisputable. For instance, those who accept a creationist doctrine on the origin of the human species as recounted in sacred texts or myths do so on the basis of religious authority, conceding that such views may be contrary to genetic, geological, biological, or other explanations. Such doctrines cannot be tested or proved one way or another: They are accepted as matters of faith.

Straightforward as the scientific approach may seem, its application is not always easy. For instance, once a hypothesis has been proposed, the person who suggested it is strongly motivated to verify it, and this can cause one to unwittingly overlook negative evidence and unanticipated findings. This is a familiar problem in all science as noted by paleontologist Stephen Jay Gould: "The greatest impediment to scientific innovation is usually a conceptual lock, not a factual lock" (Gould, 1989, p. 226). Because culture provides humans with concepts and shapes our very thoughts, it can be challenging to frame hypotheses or to develop interpretations that are not culture-bound. However, by encompassing both humanism and science, the discipline of anthropology can draw on its internal diversity to overcome conceptual locks.

---

empirical An approach based on observations of the world rather than on intuition or faith.

hypothesis A tentative explanation of the relationships among certain phenomena.

theory A coherent statement that provides an explanatory framework for understanding; an explanation or interpretation supported by a reliable body of data.

doctrine An assertion of opinion or belief formally handed down by an authority as true and indisputable.

culture shock In fieldwork, the anthropologist's personal disorientation and anxiety that may result in depression.

Fieldwork

Anthropologists are keenly aware that their personal identity and cultural background may shape their research questions, bear upon their factual observations, and even influence their interpretations and explanations. To avoid inadvertent bias or distortion, they immerse themselves in the data to the fullest extent possible through on-location research traditionally known as *fieldwork*.

CHAPTER 2

CULTURE AND MEANING

©Yvette Cardozo/Alamy

As noted in the epigraph by Rupert Ross on the next page, it is nearly impossible to accurately interpret people's acts when we do not understand the meanings they attribute to those acts. This photo of an Inuit woman, dressed in traditional regalia, demonstrates the potential pitfalls of misinterpretation. What do you see when you look at the photo? Is this everyday dress, or is this for a special occasion? What is the significance of her finery? Unless you are well versed in Inuit culture and history, it is likely that your interpretation says more about your own cultural context than that of the Inuit. Understanding human beliefs and behaviours requires a similar attention to meaning in context.

Acts are never merely acts. They are also signals of attitude. Those signals, however, are often culture specific. When acts are seen, but their signal-content misinterpreted, it is impossible to avoid forming inaccurate interpretations of others. Until we understand what particular acts mean *to the other, we will continually ascribe motivations and states of mind that are well off the mark.*

Rupert Ross, Dancing with a Ghost

Problem 1

How can people begin to understand beliefs and behaviours that are different from their own?

INTRODUCTION

The World Behind Everyday Appearances

In **sociocultural anthropology** we strive to look beyond the world of everyday experiences to discover the patterns and meanings that lie behind that world. Take, for example, the typical classroom chair with attached desk.

In our taken-for-granted, everyday world, this piece of furniture is a utilitarian object: something to sit on, or to write on, or even to put our feet on. But for the sociocultural anthropologist, as the epigraph to this chapter suggests, acts are never merely acts, nor are objects, even classroom chairs, merely objects; both are signals whose meaning is culturally specific. The classroom chair tells some interesting tales and poses some interesting questions. For example, why do we have chairs at all? Many societies don't; instead, people sit or squat on the ground or the floor or sit on stools or benches. Historically, the chair likely first appeared in Europe or the Near East, but it wasn't common even in Europe until the 18th century. Another question: Why does the classroom chair take the form it does? One feature of the chair that anthropologists might explore as they try to decipher the meaning of the classroom chair with writing surface is the erect position into which it forces the body, compelling it, in effect, to "pay attention." We might take a clue from the French philosopher Michel Foucault, who refers to the shaping of the human body as a

> **sociocultural anthropology**
> A comparative approach to the study of societies and cultures that focuses on differences and similarities in the ways that societies are structured and cultural meanings are created.

"political anatomy." By this, he means that people's bodies are controlled by others to operate with the necessary speed and efficiency. Political anatomy produces, he says, "docile bodies."

An anthropologist might suggest that the classroom chair with desk is part of the political anatomy of educational settings—part of the system of relations that gives meaning to the classroom. In other words, this piece of furniture forms the body into a shape that prepares it (or forces it) to attend to a teacher and not to others in the same room. Moreover, it is appropriate to its unique setting in the classroom, as are other objects of furniture. Imagine, for example, replacing classroom chairs with bar stools, whose main purpose is to promote bodily mobility and conversation with others.

Once alert to the idea that the classroom chair might serve as an instrument of control, we might notice other ways in which classroom design serves as a mode of discipline. The distribution of people in space, with each person in a particular "spot" in neat, ordered rows, serves to discipline people to "pay attention" to the classroom centre and not to others around them. We might also notice the distinctive ordering of time and the use of clocks, bells, and whistles to control the movement and activities of people in school settings. We can even take our analysis a step further and examine the discipline of the school setting sequentially, from

Sociocultural anthropologists find patterns of meaning even in objects as simple as a classroom chair.

kindergarten through high school. Contrast, for example, the wide-open space of the kindergarten classroom, with its open, movable chairs and tables and teacher's desk set off to the side, with the enclosed, partitioned space of a second- or third-grade classroom, with its neatly arranged desks facing the centred desk of the teacher. This is the evolution of classroom discipline.

Students, of course, do not always obey the subtle commands that direct their bodies to do certain things at certain times. One only has to examine the strange bodily contortions of students as they resist the form into which the classroom chair tries to force them. We also try, occasionally, to resist the isolation imposed by the arrangement of classroom furniture or the timetables set by clocks, bells, and whistles.

The ways in which specific societies order behaviour through the arrangement of space and time is but one small area examined by sociocultural anthropology, but it serves as an example of how, from an anthropological perspective, we cannot take anything about even our own beliefs and behaviour for granted, let alone the behaviour and beliefs of those whose backgrounds and histories differ from our own.

This book is about how sociocultural anthropology can help us see beyond our taken-for-granted world. We will be examining how sociocultural anthropology helps us understand others and, in the process, better understand ourselves. We will also be examining how knowledge of others and ourselves is relevant to careers in social and economic development, public policy and planning, education, medicine, and conflict resolution.

A Multi-faceted Discipline

The term "anthropology" comes from two Greek words: *anthropos*, meaning "human beings," and *logia*, meaning "the study of" or "the knowledge of." This study of, or knowledge of, human beings includes everything that humans do currently or have done

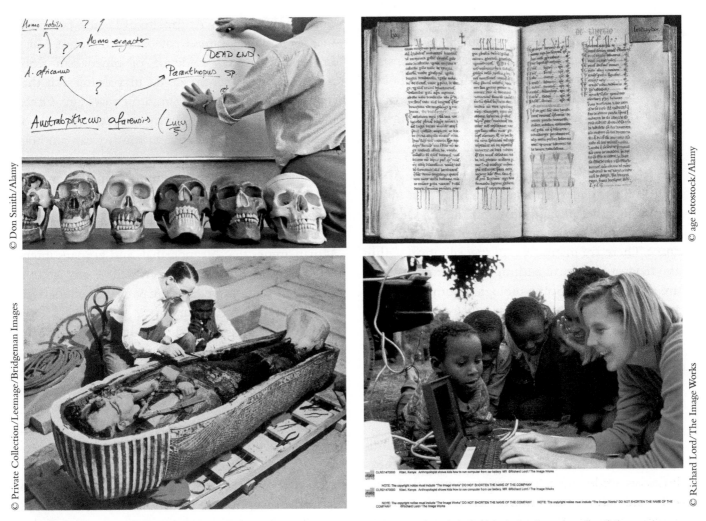

Most anthropologists specialize in one or more of anthropology's four sub-fields. Clockwise, these include biological anthropology, linguistic anthropology, sociocultural anthropology, and archeology.

© Don Smith/Alamy

© age fotostock/Alamy

© Private Collection/Leemage/Bridgeman Images

© Richard Lord/The Image Works

in the past. It also includes collecting evidence of how and when we became human and comparing humans to other organisms in the world. If asked to describe a typical anthropologist, you might envision an intrepid explorer, like Indiana Jones, searching for priceless artifacts or painstakingly excavating ancient fossils. But it would be more realistic to imagine a sociocultural anthropologist equipped with a notebook and a voice recorder rather than a shovel or a trowel. The kind of knowledge about human beings that interests sociocultural anthropologists is acquired by spending time with people, talking to them, observing what they do, and trying

to understand their lives—as anthropologist Bronislaw Malinowski aptly put it—"from the native's point of view" (see section 1.2).

In North America, anthropology is divided into four different approaches to the study of humans. Although these four subdisciplines address some of the same questions about what it means to be human, they focus on different aspects of the anthropological question (hence, the differences among the tools—notebooks versus shovels—used by different kinds of anthropologists). The subdisciplines are biological anthropology, archaeology, linguistic anthropology, and sociocultural anthropology (known as

CULTURE AND MEANING

"cultural anthropology" in the United States and "social anthropology" in Britain; in Canada the discipline is influenced by both these traditions). To understand what makes sociocultural anthropology unique among the subdisciplines (and among the social sciences in general), it is important first to understand the points of convergence and divergence among these subdisciplines.

Biological anthropology, the oldest of the four subdisciplines, focuses on the study of the evolution, function, and health of the human body and our closest primate ancestors across time and space. There are many areas of specialization within the field of biological anthropology, three of which are discussed here. Some biological anthropologists, for instance, specialize in *paleoanthropology*, which is the study of the fossilized remains of the earliest humans, and endeavour to understand the history of human biological evolution. Paleoanthropologists excavate ancient sites of early human activity or habitation, and they study fossil remains in laboratories.

Through close examinations of fossil records in Africa, Europe, and parts of Asia, paleoanthropologists study mostly extinct, transitional species between apes and humans called "hominids." Hominids are bipedal primates that first evolved in Africa ("bipedal" refers to the ability to walk on two feet for extended periods). They subsequently spread throughout the rest of the world. Although the history of hominid evolution is changing rapidly as new fossils are discovered, it is currently believed that hominids evolved over 4 million years ago.

By studying and comparing the anatomy of hominid feet and leg joints, as well as preserved footprints, paleoanthropologists can reconstruct such things as the height, gait, and locomotion patterns of ancient hominids. At the site of Laetoli in Tanzania, for instance, famed paleoanthropologist Mary Leakey discovered evidence of bipedalism from hominid footprints preserved in volcanic ash that date to approximately 3.7 million years ago. Other paleoanthropologists study the cranial anatomy of hominids. Tooth structure and tooth wear can help us reconstruct hominid diets. Reconstructions of the physical structure of hominids can also provide evidence for migrations and ancient interactions of hominids. Based upon his excavation and study of Neanderthal sites, Canadian anthropologist Eugene Morin argues that Neanderthals and humans interacted with each other between 30,000 and 40,000 years ago. This interaction may have included, in some cases, interbreeding.

Other biological anthropologists specialize in *primatology*, or the study of our closest nonhuman relatives. One of the most famous primatologists is Jane Goodall. In 1960, she went to Gombe Stream National Park in Tanzania, where she would begin a lifetime study of the behavioural patterns of wild chimpanzees. Given that humans and chimpanzees are closely related genetically, many primatologists believe that the study of apes can help glean information about the behaviour of early hominids that lived between 4 and 5 million years ago. Today, Goodall continues her research. She has worked tirelessly to help establish safe chimpanzee sanctuaries, and she speaks out against the destruction of their ecosystems.

The newest branch of biological anthropology is *forensic anthropology*, which is the study of human remains for identification and cause of death. Forensic anthropologists can often determine the age, sex, health status, height, and cause of death by examining human skeletal material and its surrounding context. Many forensic anthropologists assist with human rights cases, excavating human bones found buried in mass graves. By excavating remains found in war-torn areas of the world, such as the former Yugoslavia, Rwanda, and Darfur, forensic experts can document cases of mass genocide. This information, in turn, can

biological anthropology
A subdiscipline of anthropology that focuses upon the study of the evolution, function, and health of the human body and our closest primate ancestors across time and space.

be used in international human rights tribunals to establish the guilt or innocence of various parties. In addition, by identifying missing individuals, forensic anthropologists are able to provide many families with a sense of closure through confirmation of the death of a loved one. Other forensic experts work on active criminal investigations in tandem with the police in an effort to identify human remains that may be associated with a criminal case.

Archaeology is the branch of anthropology that studies human history and its artifacts. Archaeologists typically look at the material remains of human groups in order to learn how people lived. Tools, pottery shards, and other artifacts offer clues about the social and cultural lives of societies that existed thousands of years ago. Archaeologists excavate archaeological sites (areas that display evidence of past human activity).

Although archaeologists are often romanticized as treasure hunters within our pop culture, they do not keep any artifacts they find. All artifacts discovered are carefully mapped and recorded at a site to preserve their provenience, or specific location in space. For example, it is important to note where an artifact is found inside a house. Is it in the kitchen, a storage room, a bathroom, or a midden, or refuse area? By mapping out the horizontal location of artifacts, archaeologists can make inferences about the functions of different spaces on a site. Some areas, for instance, might be used for cooking, others for making weapons, and other areas for weaving or producing textiles. When recording provenience, archaeologists also record vertical provenience, or how far below the surface that an artifact is discovered. Often, different layers of soil (called "strata") are connected to different dates of occupation. So, it is important to map both vertical and horizontal provenience to understand spatial functions as well as time periods.

Once an archaeological site is excavated, the artifacts discovered are taken to labs where they are washed and further analyzed. Decorations on pottery, for instance, can help date the pot (and, by extension, the site), and they may also reveal other information about past lifestyles. Occasionally, residue may even be discovered inside an artifact such as a pot. Archaeologist Pat McGovern, for instance, conducts chemical analyses on the residue of ceramic pots. In the process, he has discovered (and re-created) some of the world's oldest alcoholic beverages. In Iran, he found the world's oldest barley beer dating to approximately 3400 BCE, as well as the oldest wine made from grapes, from 5400 BCE. Brewing ancient beverages for modern consumers may sound exciting, but more than that, the ingredients in such beverages can tell us a lot about ancient life. For instance, we can learn about trade routes and migrations of people by examining the ingredients in beer. If a particular ingredient is not locally available, archaeologists can trace its source to other cultural areas and try to understand past human interactions, such as trade, on a wider scale.

Linguistic anthropology involves examining the relationship between language and culture. *Linguistic anthropologists* explore how people use language, both in a physical sense with regard to how communication is structured, and in a historical sense with regard to how different languages have developed and spread throughout history. Linguistic anthropologists are interested in studying all languages across time and space, although most focus on language use within a particular

archaeology
The branch of anthropology that studies human history and its artifacts. Archaeologists typically look at the material remains of human groups in order to learn how people lived.

linguistic anthropology
A study of the relationship between language and culture. Linguistic anthropologists explore how people use language, both in a physical sense with regard to how communication is structured, and in a historical sense with regard to how different languages have developed and spread throughout history.

CULTURE AND MEANING

cultural framework. *Sociolinguists*, for instance, are interested in how various aspects of culture shape how we use language. They may analyze the structure and vocabulary used within speech, the study of accents, and even the study of topics of conversation. Language is informed by a society's views on gender, class, race, and other factors such as the context of speaking. Think, for example, about how you may speak differently (in terms of vocabulary choice, intonation, and conversation topics) when you have a conversation with your grandmother versus your best friend.

An early and famous sociolinguistic study was conducted by American linguist William Labov who studied the speech of sales associates working in department stores in Manhattan. Interested in the connection between social class and speech, Labov (1966) studied speech differences among sales associates at three department stores: S. Klein, which offered low-priced merchandise; Macy's, which appeals typically to middle-class consumers; and Saks, a high-end, expensive retailer. Labov noted that sales associates in each store talked differently, with associates from Saks putting greater emphasis on preconsonantal r's, found in such words as "beer" or "floor." A strong emphasis on the pronunciation of "r" is considered to be a subtle and unconscious form of prestige, and it is an emphasis mainly used in upper-class speech in Manhattan.

Historical linguists study the origins of languages and changes in language over time. For example, Canadian anthropologist John Colarusso received international media attention in 2014 when he deciphered writings on an ancient Greek vase referred to as the "New York Goose Play Vase" in New York's Metropolitan Museum of Art. An expert on the ancient Circassian language, Colarusso translated the meanings of ancient scribbles and graffiti on pottery that dates to over 3000 years ago.

The above examples from the fields of biological anthropology, archaeology, and linguistic anthropology highlight the diversity of interests within anthropology.

Given that anthropologists study all aspects of humanity across time and space, it is not uncommon to find an anthropologist studying ancient Egyptian hieroglyphics, observing homeless people in Toronto, or excavating archaeological sites in Peru.

Although all anthropologists specialize in the study of particular peoples, places, and issues, they also tend to work collaboratively, when necessary, to understand various societies. An archaeologist excavating an ancient site in Turkey, for instance, will most certainly call in biological, or physical, anthropologists when and if skeletal material is uncovered. Similarly, a historical linguist, like John Colarusso, will work with archaeologists or art historians to help decipher writings on ancient pottery. But what, then, is sociocultural anthropology, the primary focus of this text? How do the research interests and methods of sociocultural anthropologists differ from those of other anthropologists?

What Makes Sociocultural Anthropology Unique? *Sociocultural anthropologists* look at how societies are structured and how cultural meanings are created. Although these anthropologists are interested in differences among peoples throughout the world, they also look for similarities in how people construct their own versions of what it means to be human. Sociocultural anthropologists, then, explore both the universal and the particular, moving back and forth between these two levels of inquiry and analysis in their work. They do fieldwork and ethnography among the societies and cultures they study (see Chapter 2), gathering data by talking to people and by participating in and observing their day-to-day lives.

This focus on social structures and cultural meanings, in all their forms, is what makes sociocultural anthropology unique among the subdisciplines. Many people, including some anthropologists, wonder whether sociocultural anthropology should be characterized as a science or as one of the humanities. At its best, sociocultural anthropology incorporates aspects of both: the methodological and analytical rigour of the sciences, and the interpretive insights and nuances of the humanities. Eminent anthropologist Eric Wolf (1964, 88) perhaps put it best when he described anthropology as "the most scientific of the humanities, [and] the most humanistic of the sciences." This combination of versatility and breadth is precisely what makes anthropology such an interesting and dynamic discipline.

Moreover, the unique perspective on humanity provided by sociocultural anthropology is well suited to thinking about the complexity of the contemporary world and the human condition. This book is organized around nine general problems that arise from the human condition—problems such as how to understand people with different beliefs and behaviours; why ways of life change; how people justify violence; and whether solving problems of social inequality is possible. These problems concern everyone, not just sociocultural anthropologists, but definitive solutions are not possible. So the goal, instead, is to achieve a greater understanding of why those problems exist and what might be done to address them. Sociocultural anthropologists can ask specific questions about them, applying their unique disciplinary perspective and methodologies. We will be focusing on these nine general problems in this text. At various points you will be asked to supply your own answers to questions and, perhaps, to discuss your answers with others.

Understanding others requires you to recognize that your behaviours and beliefs, as well as those of people in other societies, are socially patterned and constructed. For that reason, you will find in this text many comparisons between North American life and life in other societies. Whether or not you pursue a career in anthropology or a career that explicitly requires anthropological expertise, learning to approach and understand human beliefs and behaviour from an anthropological perspective is a valuable skill in the contemporary world.

QUESTIONS

1.1 Why do human beings differ in their beliefs and behaviours?

1.2 Is it possible to see the world through the eyes of others?

1.3 How can the meanings that others find in experience be interpreted and described?

1.4 What can learning about other peoples tell anthropologists about their own societies?

1.5 How can an anthropological perspective be used outside academia?

QUESTION 1.1: WHY DO HUMAN BEINGS DIFFER IN THEIR BELIEFS AND BEHAVIOURS?

From an anthropological perspective, members of a society view the world in a similar way because they share the same **culture**; people differ in how they view the world because their cultures differ. What do anthropologists mean by "culture"? A good place to start to understand the concept is with the fact that members of all human societies experience specific life events such as birth, death, and the quest for food, water, and shelter. All societies have what are for them appropriate rules for courtship, ideas about child rearing, procedures for exchanging goods, methods of food production, techniques for building shelters, and so on. But from one society to the next, the meanings people assign these events differ. We learn these meanings from, and teach these meanings to, other members of our culture.

culture
The system of meanings about the nature of experience that are shared by a people and passed on from one generation to another, including the meanings that people give to things, events, activities, and people.

Our working definition of culture, therefore, is as follows: "culture is the system of meanings about the nature of experience that is shared by a people and passed from one generation to another." This definition encompasses the meanings that people give to things, events, activities, and people. Anthropologists have debated—and often disagreed about—the substance of culture and the best ways to study it. Our working definition of culture highlights those aspects of this complicated and contentious term upon which most anthropologists *can* agree: culture is about meaning; cultural meanings must be learned; and, once learned, meanings are shared by members of a particular culture. Culture enables human beings to make sense of their life experiences and to understand those experiences as meaningful in particular ways. Human beings share certain basic experiences: hunger and death, for example. Why, though, do people from different backgrounds understand these experiences in different ways? Thinking about culture begins to suggest an answer to this question.

Attitudes toward death provide one example. For some people, death marks the passage of a person from one world to another. For others, death is an ending, the final event in a life span. Still others view death as part of a never-ending cycle of birth, death, and rebirth. The Kwakwaka'wakw of British Columbia, for example, believe that when a person dies, the soul leaves the body and enters the body of a salmon. When a salmon is caught and eaten, a soul is released and is free to enter the body of another person.

Some societies fear the dead; others revere them. In rural China until recently, each household contained a shrine to the family ancestors. Before any major family decision, the head of the household addressed the shrine to ask the ancestors' advice, thus making the dead part of the world of the living. In southern Italy, by contrast, funeral customs were designed to *discourage* the dead from returning. Relatives placed useful objects such as matches and small change near the body to placate the soul of the deceased and to ensure that it did not return to disturb the living.

A Chinese bride makes an offering to an ancestral shrine.

In some societies, death is accepted as natural and inevitable; in others, death is always attributed to the malevolent act of some person, often involving sorcery. In these societies, every death elicits suspicion and a demand for vengeance. Still other societies require great demonstrations of grief and mourning for the deceased. Thus, the Dani of New Guinea require a close female relative of a recently deceased person to sacrifice part of a finger. When the Wari' of western Brazil still lived independent of Western civilization, they disposed of the bodies of their dead by eating the roasted flesh, certain internal organs, and sometimes the ground bones. They ate the dead not because they needed the meat or because they liked the taste of human flesh, but rather out of a respect and compassion for the dead person and the dead person's family (we will explore this example in section 1.2). In southern Europe, widows were required to shave their heads; at one time in India, widows were cremated alive at their husbands' funerals, a practice known as *sati*. In most North American societies, survivors of the deceased are expected to restrain their grief almost as if it were a contagious disease. To many North Americans, the sight of southern Italian women pulling their hair and being restrained from flinging themselves into an open grave is as bewildering as their own restraint of grief would be to southern Italians.

Food provides another telling example of how a culture takes the "raw materials" of human life and makes them meaningful. All humans need to eat; however, no society accepts all items in their edible universe as "good to eat." Only a relatively few items are so designated. Insects such as grubs, beetles, and ants are acceptable fare in some societies, while people in others are horrified by the thought of eating insects. North Americans generally do not define insects as food (although U.S. federal regulations do allow a certain percentage of insect matter to be included in processed food). Most North Americans like and are encouraged to drink milk, yet some people in China consider milk undrinkable. Conversely, the Chinese raise dogs for meat—something that would horrify most North Americans. North American children who have raised pet guinea pigs would have a hard time accepting the Peruvian practice of raising guinea pigs for food.

Of all the 2 million or so species of living organisms that inhabit Earth, only humans dwell largely in worlds that they themselves have created by giving meanings to things. This creation is what anthropologists mean by the term "culture." Human beings are cultural animals; they ascribe meanings of their own creation to objects, persons, behaviours, emotions, and events and then proceed to act as if those meanings are real. All facets of their lives—death, birth, courtship, mating, food acquisition and consumption—are suffused with meaning.

Clifford Geertz suggests that human beings are compelled to impose meaning on their experiences because without those meanings to help them comprehend experience and impose an order on the universe, the world would seem a jumble, "a chaos of pointless acts and exploding emotions" (1973, 46). Geertz writes that human beings are "incomplete or unfinished animals who complete themselves through culture—not culture in general, but specific forms of it": Balinese, Italian, Ilongot, Chinese, Kwakiutl (known today as Kwakwaka'wakw), Canadian, and so on (1973, 49). When people share the meanings they give to experiences, they share and participate in the same culture.

Differences in culture arise, in part, from the fact that different groups of human beings, for various reasons, create, share, and participate in different realities; as a consequence, they assign different meanings to death, birth, marriage, and food. Objects, persons, behaviours, emotions, and events in a human world have meanings ascribed to them by those who share, use, or experience them. The clothes people wear, the foods they eat (or refuse to eat), even their gender, are defined through the meanings that people give them. Understanding culture, and the culturally situated meanings that flourish in various cultural contexts, is therefore the main object of anthropological study. In the next section, we will explore how anthropologists have approached the study of culture.

EXERCISE 1.1

Mere edibility is not enough to determine what counts as food. Food is a cultural creation; that is, human beings define what is and is not food. Consider, for example, the items listed below, all of which serve as food among one group of people or another. Which of these would you eat, and which would you not eat? If there are any you would not eat, explain why.

	Yes	No
eel		
kangaroo tail		
dog		
guinea pig		
raw squid		
sea urchin (sea slugs)		
ants		
monkey brains		
grubs		
opossum		
rattlesnake		
iguana		
horse		
dolphin		
pickled pig's feet		
haggis (stuffed intestines)		
cow brains		
blood sausage		
raw steak		
rotten meat		
armadillo		

CULTURE AND MEANING

QUESTION 1.2: IS IT POSSIBLE TO SEE THE WORLD THROUGH THE EYES OF OTHERS?

This question lies at the heart of the anthropological enterprise. The anthropologist must be able to look beyond everyday appearance to decipher the often hidden meanings of beliefs, objects, and behaviours, while setting aside her or his preconceptions about what is normal or proper. In addition to that, the anthropologist must also learn one culture and then relate what he or she has learned to members of another culture in order to translate the meanings of one world into the meanings of another. In the process, many anthropologists experience cultural traditions and values vastly different from their own. In this section, we explore the intricacies of two key concepts in anthropology: ethnocentrism and cultural relativism.

How Do People Explain the Beliefs and Behaviours of Others?

Richard Scaglion (1990) is fond of telling the story of his friend, a member of the Abelam tribe of Papua New Guinea, who was looking through an issue of *Sports Illustrated*. The friend, dressed in full ceremonial regalia with a feather through his nose, was laughing uncontrollably at a woman shown in a liquor advertisement. When he managed to stop laughing long enough to explain what he thought was so funny, he said, "This white woman has made holes in her ears and stuck things in them." When Scaglion pointed out that his friend had an ornament in his nose, the reply was "That's different. That's for beauty and has ceremonial significance. But I didn't know that white people mutilated themselves."

Scaglion's friend was confronting a problem that many do when the behaviour or beliefs of others seem to differ from their own, and his response was not unusual. He was both shocked and mystified at the strange behaviour. And this suggests a dilemma: Since there are so many versions of what the world is like, how do we go about trying to understand each of them without making positive or negative judgments? Which version of the world is correct? Are there any such versions we *can* reject or condemn? Can we say, as so many have, that one culture is superior to another?

In the catalogue of human behaviours and beliefs, it is not difficult to find practices or ideas that may seem bizarre or shocking even to trained anthropologists. Sociocultural anthropologists have described the beliefs of the Ilongots of the Philippines, who must kill an enemy to obtain a head that they can throw away in order to diminish the grief

Abelam villager in ceremonial costume.

and rage they feel at the death of a kinsman or kinswoman. They have studied the historical records of the Aztecs in Mexico, who believed that the universe underwent periodic destruction and that the only way to ward off disaster was to pluck the hearts from live sacrificial victims to offer to the gods. They have also studied modern states that routinely engage in or sanction torture, terror, and genocide. How, then, should we react to practices and beliefs such as these?

The Ethnocentric Fallacy and the Relativist Fallacy

If we do condemn or reject the beliefs or behaviours of others, we may be embracing the **ethnocentric fallacy**, or the idea that our beliefs and behaviours are right and true, while those of other peoples are wrong or misguided. Sociocultural anthropologists have long fought against **ethnocentrism**, that is, the tendency to judge the beliefs and behaviours of other cultures from the perspective of one's own. They try to show that what often appears on the surface to be an odd belief or a bizarre behaviour is functional and logical in the context of a particular culture. They find the ethnocentric fallacy *intellectually* and *methodologically* intolerable; if everyone everywhere thinks that they are right and that others must be wrong, an intellectual and social dead end is inevitable. Furthermore, if we, as anthropologists, assume that we have all the right answers, our study of other cultures becomes simply the study of other people's mistakes.

Because of the intellectual and methodological implications of ethnocentrism, sociocultural anthropologists emphatically reject this position. But the opposite pole to ethnocentrism, **cultural relativism**, raises issues of its own. Cultural relativism, simply stated, holds that no behaviour or belief can be judged to be odd or wrong simply because it is different from our own; instead, we must try to understand a culture on its own terms and to understand behaviours or beliefs for the purpose, function, or meaning they have to people in the societies in which we find them. In other words, cultural relativism holds that a specific belief or behaviour can be understood only in relation to the culture—the system of meanings—in which it is embedded.

For example, according to Renato Rosaldo (1989), the ceremonies and rituals accompanying a successful headhunting expedition help the Ilongot psychologically manage their grief over the death of a kinsperson. However, relativism poses a *moral* predicament. Once we concede, say, that it is permissible to rip out the hearts of living human beings, provided that you believe it necessary to save the world, or that it is permissible to subject young girls to genital modification to protect family reputations, we find ourselves falling quickly into the **relativistic fallacy**, or the idea that it is impossible to make moral judgments about the beliefs and behaviours of others. This standpoint, of course, seems morally intolerable because it implies that no beliefs or behaviours can be condemned. So, we are left with two untenable positions: the ethnocentric alternative, which is intellectually and methodologically unsatisfactory, and the relativistic alternative, which is morally unsatisfactory. How do we solve this problem?

ethnocentric fallacy
The mistaken notion that the beliefs and behaviours of other cultures can be judged from the perspective of one's own culture.

ethnocentrism
The tendency to judge the beliefs and behaviours of other cultures from the perspective of one's own culture.

cultural relativism
The effort to understand the beliefs and behaviours of other cultures in terms of the culture in which they are found.

relativistic fallacy
The idea that it is impossible to make moral judgments about the beliefs and behaviours of members of other cultures.

Virginity Testing in Turkey and Cannibalism Among the Wari'

To illustrate further the dilemma of relativism and the difficulty of appreciating the cultures of others without making moral judgments, consider this incident. Some time ago a human rights group based in the United States issued a report condemning the practice of virginity testing in Turkey. Traditionally, young women in Turkey, as in some other cultures, are expected to avoid sexual relations prior to marriage, although the same rule does not apply to men. In this tradition, the bride's virginity is revealed by displaying, the morning after the wedding, the sheet that was spread on the couple's wedding bed with the telltale hymeneal blood stain. The human rights report condemns the traditional testing as well as the reported practice of forcing tests on hospital patients, students, and applicants for government jobs. As anthropologists, we must ask: Is the human rights group being ethnocentric in judging Turkish customs by North American cultural norms, or is it correctly identifying abuses of women that must be corrected? Might it help if we better understood the logic behind the belief?

In her book on Turkish village society, *The Seed and the Soil*, anthropologist Carol Delaney (1991) describes how virginity testing relates to the way in which Turkish villagers conceptualize and explain the reproductive process. They see producing children as analogous to the planting and growing of crops; the man provides the "seed" with his semen, and the woman serves as the "soil" in which the seed germinates and grows. As a metaphor for reproduction, the idea of the seed and the soil provides villagers with a way of thinking about and understanding reproduction. However, the metaphor of seed and soil has at least one important implication; since seeds do not have a limited life span, as we know semen to have, villagers believe that once planted, the seed (semen) may grow at any time. Consequently, if a woman has had sexual relations with a man other than her husband at any time prior to her marriage, the paternity of the child

will be in doubt. Since descent in traditional Turkish villages is closely tied to many things, including property rights, uncertainty about the identity of the true father can have major implications. Thus, in the context of Turkish beliefs about procreation, virginity testing may be said to make sense.

Furthermore, Turkish beliefs about conception are not that far removed from our own, since our language draws from the same agricultural metaphors as those of Turkish villagers to explain reproduction. We talk about women being "fertile" or "barren" and semen "fertilizing" "eggs." "Sowing one's oats," as an expression of sexual activity, is still heard in parts of the United States and Canada. Furthermore, these views are reinforced by religious proscription, legitimized in the Koran and the Hebrew Scriptures. Thus, before we either condemn or accept the Turkish villagers for their treatment of women, we need to examine what their beliefs tell us about our own. Ours may be equally problematical.

But what of cannibalism, such as the Wari' practice of roasting and eating the dead? Surely, there is no way to justify that! Cannibalism, as Beth Conklin (2001) points out in her study of Wari' cannibalism, *Consuming Grief*, pushes the limits of cultural relativism, guaranteeing reactions of revulsion and fascination. But in addition to that, it has political implications: for centuries, cannibalism was the ultimate smear tactic. To accuse one's enemies or people one wanted to degrade or dominate of cannibalism was the ultimate justification for conquest, domination, and exploitation. In 1503, Queen Isabella of Spain decreed that Spaniards could legally enslave specifically those American Indians who were cannibals. Pope Innocent IV, in 1510, ruled that Christians could punish, by force of arms, the sin of cannibalism. By claiming moral superiority in this way, Christians were claiming the right to decide ultimately what is right and what is wrong. Armed with that power, they felt justified in imposing their own views and way of life.

What Queen Isabella and Pope Innocent IV conveniently overlooked, however, was that Europeans at the time practised cannibalism. As Conklin notes, medicinal cannibalism—the consumption of human body parts for curative purposes—had a long tradition in Europe. Up until two centuries ago, European physicians prescribed the consumption of human flesh, heart, bones, and other body parts as cures for such afflictions as arthritis, reproductive disorders, sciatica, warts, and skin blemishes. Human blood was thought to be a cure for epilepsy, and physicians recommended that it be drunk immediately after the supplier died. Physicians also thought that the blood of someone who died violently was particularly effective. Thus, in Denmark, epileptics would stand around the scaffolds, cups in hand, waiting to catch the blood of executed criminals. And almost every apothecary kept dried and powdered human body parts on hand for anxious customers.

The people of medieval Europe accepted in their own lives the same types of practices they condemned in others; furthermore, they failed to understand the practices from the point of view of the others. The Wari' ate their dead, for example, because they believed it was the compassionate thing to do. As Conklin puts it, "More painful than having the corpse eaten would have been to have it *not* eaten" (2001, 81). For the Wari', a corpse left intact was a painful reminder of the deceased. People unrelated to the deceased ate the corpse, even when the smell or taste repulsed them, in the belief that it would help family members come to terms with their loss.

The Western practice of burying the dead (which missionaries and government officials forced the Wari' to do after contact) was almost as horrific to the Wari' as their cannibalism might have been for non-Wari'. "It's cold in the earth," a father who had recently lost a two-year-old son explained to Beth Conklin. "We keep remembering our child, lying there, cold. We remember and we are sad. It was better in the old days, when the others ate the body. Then we did not think about our child's body much. We did not remember our child as much, and we were not so sad" (xv). Burying the body also

violated many fundamental Wari' values. For them, the ground was "dirty" and "polluting." They never sat directly on the dirt, and discarding things on the ground was considered disrespectful. Special ritual objects were never supposed to touch the ground.

Without a deeper understanding of Wari' culture, we cannot know how consuming the dead aligns with the meaning they impose on their world, including how they deal with their emotions. By consuming the dead, Wari' are trying to obliterate the painful memories of their loss. The memory of the body is painful, but equally painful are the material objects associated with the deceased and the very mention of the deceased's name. Thus, the Wari' not only consume the body but also burn the house and personal possessions of the deceased. For months, too, they walk into the forest to find places associated with the deceased— where a hunter made a kill or a woman felled a fruit tree, or where there was something such as a favourite log on which the person liked to sit—cut the vegetation around it, and after it has dried, burn

The Taj Mahal, a monument built to honour a 17th-century Mughal emperor's wife, who died in childbirth.

CULTURE AND MEANING

the spot, changing the appearance of the last earthly places to which memories of the deceased might cling. As they "sweep" (the Wari' term for it), they cry over the memories, but once done, "it is different," "there is not much sadness there." For most North Americans, a dead body is only a shell, its soul or spiritual essence gone. Thus, some societies can prepare the dead to look as they did in life and think of them buried in that way. The Wari', by contrast, want to separate the dead from the living, so obliterating their memories is perfectly logical. And they are not the only group to do so.

There are other aspects of Wari' beliefs about consuming the dead. For example, the Wari' believe that the spirits of the dead ultimately enter the bodies of animals they depend on for food, thus creating a cycle of eating and being eaten. The point, then, is that when we impose our own meanings on practices such as cannibalism and fail to see those practices the way others do, we miss a great deal.

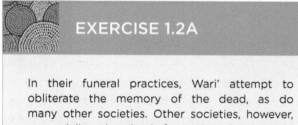

EXERCISE 1.2A

In their funeral practices, Wari' attempt to obliterate the memory of the dead, as do many other societies. Other societies, however, memorialize the dead—forgetting them would be an act of disrespect. Think about your own cultural background and whether or not you are encouraged to preserve the memory of the dead. List the ways you try to keep the memory of deceased persons alive, and speculate as to why you do that instead of trying to forget them. If you are encouraged to forget the dead, how is that accomplished? Why? Compare your beliefs and practices with those of your classmates.

But does this mean that *any* practice or belief, once we understand it from "the native's point of view," is acceptable? Does understanding the cultures of others require that we accept and justify all beliefs and practices?

Objectivity and Morality

For anthropologists, the conflict between ethnocentrism and relativism is not just theoretical. When choosing their research subjects, anthropologists may face this dilemma: Should they maintain a "moral distance" from those they are studying and remain "objective," or should they engage in criticizing behaviour or beliefs they encounter (e.g., virginity testing)?

The contradiction between "objective" anthropology and a politically committed anthropology became apparent to Nancy Scheper-Hughes when she returned as an anthropologist to a shantytown in Brazil where, previously, she had worked as a community organizer. The women with whom she had worked in the past became angry. Why, they asked, was she now, as an anthropologist, so passive, so indifferent to the destruction around her when as a community organizer, she had helped them fight for clean water, decent wages, and protection from police brutality? She tried to explain that as an anthropologist, she was there now to observe, document, and write about their lives as truthfully as she could. The women refused to accept this view of her work and insisted that, if they were to work with her, she would have to work with them to fight for better lives. "What," they said, "is anthropology to us?"

On the basis of that experience, Scheper-Hughes (1995, 416) now argues for a politically committed, morally engaged, and ethically grounded anthropology. "Those of us who make our living observing and recording the misery of the world," she writes, "have a particular obligation to reflect critically on the impact of the harsh images of human suffering that we foist upon the public."

Scheper-Hughes proposes what she calls a more "womanly-hearted" anthropology, one that is concerned with how people treat one another. Moral relativism, she says, is no longer appropriate to the world in which we live, and anthropology, if it is to be worth anything, must be "critically grounded." Anthropologists cannot ignore the massacres and disappearances of vulnerable people that often occur in the communities in which anthropologists work. They must, she insists, serve as witnesses and reporters of human rights abuses and of the suffering of the poor and the oppressed. Witnessing, rather than just observing, therefore, requires not simply that we approach our subjects from a relativist perspective, but rather that we employ **critical cultural relativism**, through which anthropologists engage directly with questions of inequality, ethics, and power.

But serving as a witness for the poor and oppressed can itself lead to moral dilemmas for the anthropologist when the people with whom the anthropologist works engage in behaviour that may appear morally questionable. Scheper-Hughes confronted this question when she discovered and reported that impoverished women in the Brazilian shantytowns sometimes allowed their starving infants to die in the belief that they were doomed anyway. When Philippe Bourgois (2003) studied the world of crack dealers on the Upper East Side of New York City, he worried about the negative images he would be conveying if he reported the personal violence, sexual abuse, addiction, and alienation he witnessed. He recalled the advice of anthropologist Laura Nader, who advised others not to study the poor and powerless because whatever you say will be used against them.

Human rights activists, in particular, are skeptical about cultural relativism. If, they say, we must tolerate the beliefs and practices of other cultures because to do otherwise would be ethnocentric, how can we ever criticize what seem to be violations of basic human rights, such the right to bodily integrity, or the right to be free from torture, arbitrary imprisonment, slavery, and genocide?

critical cultural relativism
An alternative perspective on cultural relativism that poses questions about cultural beliefs and practices in terms of who accepts them and why, who they might be disproportionately harming and benefiting, and the cultural power dynamics that enable them.

Cultural relativism, they say, makes arguments about human rights meaningless by legitimizing almost any behaviour. Critical cultural relativism, on the other hand, might allow us to understand cultural beliefs and practices on their own terms without ignoring the cultural power dynamics that allow them to "make sense" within a given culture.

Take the case of the practice in some areas of India of *sati*, the burning of a widow on her husband's funeral pyre. In 1987, Roon Kanwar, an 18-year-old, was burned alive on her husband's pyre. Women's rights groups protested, but relatives claimed that *sati* is an ancient Indian custom and accused the protesters of being Western imperialists imposing their own cultural standards on them. Although India has outlawed the practice, prosecutors rarely enforce the law because of the difficulty of obtaining evidence. Would it matter if Roon Kanwar committed *sati* voluntarily? What would happen if she objected? Does it matter that only women are burned? Is the purpose of *sati* to deny a widow the inheritance of her husband's family's land?

Elizabeth Zechenter, who makes the argument for universal principles of human rights, says that cultural relativists are right to contend that endorsing or rejecting some foreign customs risks imposing one's cultural prejudices on others. She adds, however, that the idea we can make no judgments without being ethnocentric is illusory: "One simply cannot avoid making judgments when faced with oppression and brutality masquerading under the guise of cultural tradition. Such a nonjudgmental tolerance of brutality is actually an ultimate form of ethnocentrism, if not an outright ethical surrender" (1997, 336).

There is obviously no easy answer to the question of when, if ever, it is proper to judge the beliefs and practices of others to be right or wrong, or when, if ever, it is proper to work to change behaviours or beliefs judged to be wrong. Ideally, our attempts to understand what, at first, seemed puzzling in some cultures, and our arrival at some solution to that puzzle, should lead us to ask ourselves what made the behaviour or belief puzzling in the first place. We also need to bear in mind that when cultures order the world in certain ways for their members, they are, in effect, masking other ways of viewing things. We need to appreciate that there are perspectives different from our own and that our ethnocentric biases may blind us to those alternatives. In other words, while culture provides us with certain meanings to give to objects, persons, behaviours, emotions, and events, it also shields us from alternative meanings. What our culture hides from us may be more important than what it reveals.

EXERCISE 1.2B

Think of a recent story reported in the mass media that challenges your sense of cultural relativism. What aspect of this story is problematic for you, and why? What aspects of your cultural background (e.g., religion, class, and gender) inform the judgments that you are inclined to make in this case? Do you think it is possible for us (as anthropologists and anthropology students) to overcome our ethnocentric biases? Support your opinion.

QUESTION 1.3: HOW CAN THE MEANINGS THAT OTHERS FIND IN EXPERIENCE BE INTERPRETED AND DESCRIBED?

In one Sherlock Holmes detective story, Dr. Watson, Holmes's assistant, decides to teach the great detective a lesson in humility. He hands Holmes a pocket watch owned by Watson's late brother and challenges

Holmes to infer from the watch the character of its owner. Holmes's interpretation: "[Your brother] was a man of untidy habits—very untidy and careless. He was left with good prospects, but he threw away his chances and finally, taking to drink, he died."

Watson, astounded at the accuracy of Holmes's description of his late brother, asks if it was guesswork. "I never guess," replies Holmes.

"I began by stating that your brother was careless. When you observe the lower part of the watch case, you notice that it is not only dented in two places, but it is cut and marked all over from the habit of keeping other hard objects, such as coins or keys, in the same pocket. Surely it is no great feat to assume that a man who treats [an expensive] watch so cavalierly must be a careless man. Neither is it a very far-fetched inference that a man who inherits one article of such value is pretty well provided for in other respects."

"But what about his drinking habits?" asks Watson.

Holmes responds: "Look at the innerplate which contains the keyhole [where the watch is wound]. Look at the thousands of scratches all around the hole-marks where the key has slipped. What sober man's key could have scored those grooves? But you will never see a drunkard's watch without them. He winds it at night, and he leaves these traces of his unsteady hand. Where is the mystery in all this?"

Had Holmes been an anthropologist, he might have been tempted also to draw some inferences about the society in which the watch was manufactured, particularly about its conceptions of time. For example, in some societies, time is task oriented, not clock oriented; time might be measured by how long it takes to cook rice, as in Madagascar. In other societies, time patterns depend on natural events such as the rising of the sun or the ebb and flow of tides. British anthropologist E. E. Evans-Pritchard, in his classic account of the Nuer of the Sudan, noted:

the Nuer have no expression equivalent to "time" in our language, and they cannot, therefore, as we can, speak of time as though it were something actual, which passes, can be wasted, can be saved, and so forth. I don't think they ever experience the same feeling of fighting against time because their points of reference are mainly the activities themselves, which are generally of a leisurely character. Events follow a logical order, but they are not controlled by an abstract system, there being no autonomous points of reference to which activities have to conform with precision. Nuer are fortunate.

An anthropologist might also infer that clocks are instruments of discipline; they tell us when to get up, when to go to bed, when to eat, when to start work, and when to stop work. Our work patterns are defined by clocks, and our wages may depend on the constant repetition over time of a particular task. Historian E. P. Thompson (1967) notes that until the institution of modern notions of time and the need to measure it with clocks, work patterns were characterized by alternating bouts of intense labour and idleness, at least whenever people were in control of their own working lives. He even suggests that this pattern persists today, but only among a few self-employed professionals such as artists, writers, small farmers, and, he suggests, university students.

Watson's brother's watch was a product of Western society, part of its culture. Holmes "read" the watch as if it were a collection of symbols or words, a **cultural text** that revealed the character of its owner. He could just as easily have viewed it as a text inscribed with the symbols that revealed the ideas about time and work that characterized the civilization that produced it.

One way to think about culture is as a text of significant symbols: words, gestures, drawings, natural objects—anything, in fact, that carries meaning. To understand another culture we must be able, as

cultural text
A way of thinking about culture as a text of significant symbols, such as words, gestures, drawings, and natural objects, all of which carry meaning.

© SuperStock/Getty Images

Modern notions of clock-based time tell us a great deal about the culture we live in. What measures of time are most important in your life as a student?

Holmes was with a pocket watch, to decipher the meanings of the symbols that comprise a cultural text. We must be able to interpret the meanings embedded in the language, objects, gestures, and activities that are shared by members of a society. Fortunately, the ability to decipher a cultural text is part of being human; in our everyday lives we both read and maintain the text that makes up our own culture. We have learned the meanings behind the symbols that frame our lives, and we share those meanings with others. Our task in understanding another culture is to take the abilities that have enabled us to dwell in our own culture and use them to understand the cultures of others.

Deciphering the Balinese Cockfight

To illustrate how an anthropologist might decipher a cultural text, imagine yourself coming upon a cockfight on the island of Bali. You see a ring in which two roosters with sharpened metal spurs attached to their legs are set at each other until one kills the other. Surrounding the fighting cocks are men shouting encouragement to their favourites, each having placed a wager that his favourite will kill its opponent.

CULTURE AND MEANING

What do you make of this? Your first reaction might be shock or disgust at the spectacle of the crowd urging the cocks to bloody combat. After a while you might begin to find similarities to events that are meaningful to you, such as some North American sports. But what if, like Sherlock Holmes—or like Clifford Geertz (1972), from whom this example is taken—you want to understand the meaning of what is happening and what that meaning tells you about how Balinese view their world? If you assume that the cockfight is a feature of Balinese culture, a Balinese text filled with symbols that carry meaning about what it is to be Balinese, how might you proceed to read this text?

You might begin by finding out the language the Balinese use to talk about the cockfight. You would no doubt discover that the double-entendre of cock both as a synonym for rooster and as a euphemism for penis is the same for the Balinese as it is for North Americans. The double-entendre even produces, says Geertz, the same jokes, puns, and obscenities in Bali as it does in North America. You would discover that *sabung*, the Balinese word for cock, has numerous other meanings and is used metaphorically to mean hero, warrior, champion, political candidate, bachelor, dandy, lady-killer, or tough guy. Court trials, wars, political contests, inheritance disputes, and street arguments are compared with cockfights. Even the island of Bali is thought of as being cock shaped (in this case, meaning the fowl). You would also find that men give their fowls inordinate attention, spending most of their time grooming them and even feeding them a special diet. As one of Geertz's Balinese informants put it, "We're all cock crazy."

Having discovered the importance of cockfights to the Balinese and the connections they make between cocks and men, you next examine the cockfight itself. You learn that cockfights are public events held in arenas of about 4.7 square metres from late afternoon until after sundown. Handlers, expert in the task, attach sharp spurs to the cocks' legs; for a cock thought to be superior to an opponent, the spurs are adjusted in a slightly disadvantageous position.

In Balinese society, cockfighting is a major sporting event that is closely tied to cultural interpretations of manhood, competition, and status.

© Robert Harding Picture Library Ltd./Alamy

The cocks are released in the centre of the ring and fly at each other, fighting until one kills the other. The owner of the winning cock takes the carcass of the loser home to eat; the losing owner is sometimes driven in despair to wreck family shrines. You discover that the Balinese contrast heaven and hell by comparing them to the mood of a man whose cock has just won and the mood of a man whose cock has just lost.

You find out that while the Balinese place odds on cockfights, there are strict social conventions that dictate the wagering. For example, a man will never bet against a cock that is owned by someone of his family group or village or a friend's family group or village, but he will place large bets against a cock owned by an enemy or the friend of an enemy. Rarely is a cockfight without social significance (e.g., between two outsiders), and rarely do cocks owned by members of the same family or village fight each other. Moreover, the owners of the cocks, especially in important matches, are usually among the leaders of their communities. You might learn that cockfights come close to encouraging open expressions of aggression between village and kingroup rivals, but not quite, because the cockfight is, as the Balinese put it, "only a cockfight."

Given the social rules for betting and the ways in which odds are set, you might reason, as Geertz did, that the Balinese rarely make a profit betting on cockfights. Geertz says, in fact, that most bettors just want to break even. Consequently, the meaning of the cockfight for a Balinese has little to do with economics. The question is what meaning the cockfight *does* have for the Balinese. What is the cockfight really about, if it is not about money?

Geertz concludes that the Balinese cockfight is, above all, about status, about the ranking of people vis-à-vis one another. The Balinese cockfight is a text filled with meaning about status as the Balinese see it. Cocks represent men—more specifically, their owners; the fate of the cock in the ring is linked, if only temporarily, to the social fate of its owner. Each cock has a following consisting of the owner, the owner's family, and members of the owner's village, and these followers "risk" their status by betting on

the cockfight. Furthermore, Geertz maintains that the more a match is between near equals, personal enemies, or high-status individuals, the more the match is about status. And the more the match is about status, the closer the identification of cock and man, the finer the cocks, and the more exactly they will be matched. The match will inspire greater emotion and absorption, and the gambling will be more about status and less about economic gain.

For Geertz, the cockfight is like any art form; it takes a highly abstract and difficult concept—status—and depicts it in a way that makes it comprehensible to the participants. The cockfight is meaningful to the Balinese because it tells them something real about their own lives, but in a way that does not directly affect their lives. They see the struggle for status that is part of everyday life vividly portrayed, even though, in the cockfight itself, no one really gains or loses status in any permanent sense.

A few words of caution are necessary concerning what we might learn about the Balinese from this particular cultural text. First, it would probably be a mistake to assume that the people gain status by being on the winning side or lose it by being on the losing side. The status outcomes of the cockfight do not translate into real life any more than the victory of your favourite sports team increases your status. Instead, says Geertz, the cockfight illustrates what status is about for the Balinese. The cockfight is a story the Balinese tell themselves about themselves. It would also be a mistake to assume that the character of the Balinese can be read directly from the cockfight; any conclusion that the cockfight is indicative of an aggressive, competitive, violent national character would quickly be dispelled. The Balinese are shy about competition and avoid open conflict. The slaughter in the cockfight is not how things are literally, but as they could be. Finally, the cockfight reveals only a segment of the Balinese character, as Watson's brother's watch revealed only a segment of its owner's character. The culture of a people, like the possessions of a person, is an ensemble of texts—collections of symbols and meanings—that must be viewed together to achieve a full understanding.

QUESTION 1.4: WHAT CAN LEARNING ABOUT OTHER PEOPLES TELL ANTHROPOLOGISTS ABOUT THEIR OWN SOCIETIES?

Anthropologists do not limit themselves to the study of cultures that are different from their own. They often apply concepts and techniques that are useful in understanding and interpreting other cultures as a means to understand and interpret their own. One objective of studying other cultures is to help us recognize the meanings we impose on our experiences. When Renato Rosaldo (1989) asked the Ilongots why they cut off human heads, they replied that rage, born of grief, drives them to kill others; by severing the heads of their victims, they are able to throw away the anger born of bereavement. Rosaldo found it difficult to accept the idea that the death of a kinsperson could cause anger or rage and that such rage in itself could drive a person to kill another. He questioned the Ilongots further but could obtain no other reason for their headhunting; he devised other theories to explain it, but none were satisfactory. Only his own experience of grief and anger at the accidental death of his wife, Michelle, while both were doing fieldwork among the Ilongots, helped him realize how grief can generate rage and how grief drove the Ilongots to hunt the heads of their enemies. At the same time that he began to understand the Ilongots, he began to understand his own grief and reaction to death.

A Balinese Anthropologist Studies Canadian Hockey

Whether we approach other cultures as anthropologists, as travellers, or as professionals who need to communicate with people of other cultures, the confrontation with other ways of believing and behaving should cause us to reflect on our way of viewing the world. To illustrate, try to step outside yourself and objectify an experience whose meaning you take for granted. Pretend you are a Balinese anthropologist who suddenly comes upon a spectacle as important in its way to Canadians as the cockfight is to Balinese: a hockey game.

As a Balinese, you might first react to this Canadian text with horror and revulsion at seeing men and women speeding from one end of an ice pad to the other with long wooden sticks in their hands, rudely pushing one another out of the way while thousands cheer them on. As you settled in, however, you would soon find some obvious similarities between the hockey game and the cockfight you are familiar with at home. Both are spectator sports in which the spectators sort themselves into supporters of one side or the other. In fact, in hockey, the sorting is even more carefully arranged, since fans of one team are often seated on one side of the arena and fans of the other on the opposite side.

Your next step (as in interpreting the cockfight) would be to examine the language Canadians use to refer to the hockey game. You discover that they use similar expressions in talking about hockey and fighting, for example, *roughing* and *slashing*. Coaches talk about getting "revenge" for defeats, as generals might talk about getting revenge on battlefields. You conclude that Canadians seem to feel the same way about hockey as they do about fighting. If you attend several hockey games, you will most likely witness players of opposing teams taking off their protective gloves and beginning to punch each other.

You soon discover that winning and losing hockey games is as important to Canadians as winning and losing cockfights is to Balinese. Winners engage in frenzied celebrations called "victory parties," and losers are often despondent in defeat. As anthropologists know, this behaviour is not always the case in other societies. For example, when the Gahuku-Gama of the Highlands of New Guinea started playing soccer, they always played until a committee of elders decided that the score was tied; the match was then considered completed. So you speculate that hockey is also about the meanings that Canadians give to the idea of success. You learn that success in Canada (like status in Bali) is a highly abstract idea; because it is abstract, its meaning is embedded in activities understood by members of the society. You need to find answers to certain questions about the meaning of success in Canadian society: How is success defined? How is it obtained? Why doesn't everyone who follows all the rules for gaining success attain it?

Through your fieldwork, you find that most North Americans believe that "all men are created equal" and that every person has (or at least should have) an equal opportunity to succeed. People compete for success, and they ought to compete on an equal footing, on a "level playing field," as some put it. Success, North Americans believe, comes from hard work, sacrifice, and self-denial. But you wonder why North Americans believe that hard work, sacrifice, and self-denial bring success. Aren't there instances where they do not? How do North Americans explain why women and minorities succeed less often than white males do? Why do some people achieve more success than others? You conclude that it is impossible to prove directly in real life the correctness of this North American success model. Faith in the value of work and self-denial must be generated in other ways. As a Balinese anthropologist studying the Canadian custom of hockey, you conclude, then, that the meaning of Canadian hockey lies in its demonstration of the North American success model as it is supposed to work. But the Canadian game of hockey is more than simply a mirror of society: Canadian hockey is also a ritual that creates meaning.

Rituals do not just reflect society. As Yngve Lithman (2004) suggests, they also draw attention to something and provide an explanation for something. One of the reasons why Canadian hockey has become a national symbol is that it brings Canadians from different parts of the country together with a common focus. During the hockey season, a team from Calgary competes against a team from Montreal, a team from Vancouver plays in the same ice rink as a team from Toronto, and so on.

An anthropologist might suggest that the meaning of hockey, for North Americans, is tied to our cultural understandings of success.

Anthropologist Noel Dyck points out that Canadian hockey "is not only one of Canada's proudest contributions to the world of sport but also a national passion" (2000, 10). Hockey becomes important to children very early in life, and it involves the whole family. Tiny players, called "Tim Bits," sponsored by the Tim Hortons coffee shops throughout Canada, begin their training so young that their mothers or fathers, or even their grandfathers or grandmothers, help them put on their protective clothing in the dressing rooms. Young teams of children are grouped according to age into categories such as novice, atom, peewee, bantam, and midget, all progressing to secondary school and university teams. Those working toward professional play are called "Junior" and progress from Junior D to Junior A. At the other end of the life cycle, older players play on teams for "old timers," which are also grouped according to age.

Canadian hockey is also a ritual that, anthropologists Peter Collings and Richard Condon suggest, helps people adjust to sudden change by providing a way for players to gain status, achievement, and self-esteem. In the Kitikmeot region of the Northwest Territories, society is no longer based on hunting as a way of life, but communities are not yet fully integrated into the North American capitalist economy. In the Canadian Arctic, hockey has become a

CULTURE AND MEANING

recreational activity that helps bridge this gap, and for most communities, it is a passion.

At first, when radio and television were introduced to the Arctic, and to the community of Holman, where Collings and Condon did their fieldwork in the 1980s, children played hockey on the snow-covered streets. Later, when a sporting organization in Yellowknife sent skates to Inuit communities, children began playing hockey on ice ponds. The initial hockey games were played Inuit style, with little emphasis on winning or losing, and were governed by flexible rules. Eventually, however, a league was established, and teams from different communities began to compete with each other.

With the formalization of hockey as a competition, violence became a standard feature of the game. Collings and Condon found that significantly more injuries were sustained playing hockey than during any other activity, including hunting, trapping, or fishing. Furthermore, being injured during a hockey game was a sure way to gain prestige, especially if an injured player returned to the ice before his injury was healed. Collings and Condon argue that the game of hockey, as it is played in Holman, models the values of achievement and self-reliance: "If achievement and self-reliance cannot be expressed in the conduct of everyday life, then it can be expressed on the ice while competing with one's peers. Status and control, so elusive to these young people in real life, become attainable goals when modeled in the context of play" (1996, 258).

Collings and Condon acknowledge the positive aspects of sports. Games such as hockey affirm the value of success, as well as a dramatic set of instructions on how it attain it. The games help build character and teach young people about cooperation. But Collings and Condon (1996) also suggest that there is a "darker side" to hockey. For some people, "games can teach violence, verbal aggression, subterfuge, cheating, poor sportsmanship, and other undesirable traits" (261). At the same time, hockey demonstrates the limits of acceptable violence. When players break the rules of how the game is supposed to be played, they incur penalties, just as citizens are penalized for breaking the laws in Canada. When players score a high number of points, they are rewarded with both prestige and, in the case of professional hockey, wealth. Violence and competition are part of Canadian life, and the game of hockey shows how both are important to Canadians, but both must be controlled.

Anthropologists, therefore, can conclude (as did Collings and Condon) that hockey provides for Canadians, as the cockfight does for the Balinese, a small-scale rendering of concepts too complex to be directly comprehended (status and success for Canadians, status only in the case of the Balinese). The audience for a hockey game is led to believe that if the rules that govern the world of hockey are equated with the rules that govern success outside the rink, then the principles that govern success on the hockey rink must also apply in the outside world. If hard work, dedication, submission to authority, and teamwork lead to success in a game, then surely they will lead to success in real life. The rules by which success is achieved in hockey can also be applied to life to succeed in the real world.

Of course, hockey is also a game that people enjoy. Analyzing it should not reduce our enjoyment of it but rather, should heighten our fascination with it. By looking at hockey from the same perspective that Geertz viewed the cockfight, we should gain an understanding of why the meaning carried by the game is important. Understanding the cockfight heightens our appreciation of the hockey game, but it also helps us see similarities between Canadians and Balinese. If you were shocked by the cockfight, seeing the similarities to hockey should lessen that shock, at the same time making hockey seem just a bit more exotic.

An Anthropologist Looks at a "Happy Meal"

Nothing is too mundane to provide some insights into the culture of which it is a part. Take the "Happy Meal" advertised by one of the many fast-food establishments in North America. It consists of a hamburger, French fries, a cola drink, and a plastic toy, which is often gendered—one chooses a "girl" toy or a "boy" toy. What can we learn about the culture of North America by looking beyond the taken-for-granted quality of this meal? Among other things, we can gain some idea of North American demographic and ecological patterns, agricultural and industrial history, and gender roles.

Why, for example, is meat the centre of the meal? Most cultures have diets centred on some complex carbohydrate—rice, wheat, manioc, yams, taro—or something made from these—bread, pasta, tortillas, and so on. It is the spice, vegetables, meat, or fish that when added to these foods gives cuisine its distinctive taste. Meat and fish are, however, generally at the edge, not the centre, of the meal. And why is beef the main ingredient in the Happy Meal, rather than some other meat, such as pork?

Anthropologists Marvin Harris and Eric Ross note that one advantage of beef is its suitability for the outdoor grill, which became more popular as people moved from cities into suburbs. Suburban cooks soon discovered that pork patties crumbled and fell through the grill, whereas beef patties held together better. In addition, to reduce the risk of trichinosis, pork had to be cooked until it was grey, which makes it tough.

In the United States, beef farmers, as well as the farmers who grew the corn fed to cattle to achieve a desirable fat content, benefited from the definition of a hamburger set by the United States Department of Agriculture: "'Hamburger'" shall consist of chopped fresh and/or frozen beef with or without the addition of beef fat as such and/or seasonings, shall not contain more than 30 percent fat, and shall not contain added water, phosphates, binders, or extenders. Beef cheek (trimmed Beef cheeks) may be used in the preparation of hamburgers only in accordance with the conditions prescribed in paragraph (a) of this section" (Harris 1998, 124).

As Marvin Harris noted, we can eat ground pork and ground beef, but we can't combine them into a patty and call it a hamburger. Hamburgers also cannot be made exclusively of lean beef,

as such patties would fall apart during cooking. Fat must be added as a binder, and the fat must come from beef scraps, not from vegetables or a different animal. This definition of the hamburger protects both the beef industry and the corn farmer, whose income is linked to cattle production. Moreover, it helps the fast-food industry because the definition of hamburger permits the use of inexpensive scraps of fat from slaughtered beef to make up to 30 percent of its hamburger. Thus, an international beef patty that has overcome the "pig's natural superiority as a converter of grain to flesh," as Harris (1998, 126) puts it, has been created.

The cola drink that accompanies the hamburger is the second part of the fat and sugar-centred diet that has come to characterize our culture. People in Canada consume, on average, about 38.6 kilograms of sugar a year. Why so much? Sugar, as anthropologist Sidney Mintz (1985) suggests, has no nutritional properties, but it provides a quick and inexpensive energy boost for hard-working labourers with little time for a more nutritious meal. Sugar also serves as an excellent complement to the fat in hamburgers: it has what nutritionists call "go-away" qualities that remove the fat coating and the beef aftertaste from the mouth.

From the Happy Meal, we can also learn that the fat-and-sugar diet is highly environmentally destructive. Beef raising is among the most environmentally inefficient and destructive forms of food raising. For example, the amount of water used to produce 4.5 kilograms (10 pounds) of steak equals the household consumption of a family for an entire year. Thirty-three times more water is needed to produce a kilogram of beef protein than an equivalent amount of plant protein.

Cattle raising is playing a major role in the destruction of tropical forests in Brazil, Guatemala, Costa Rica, and Honduras, where forests have been levelled to create pasture for cattle. Since most of the forest is cleared by burning, the creation of cattle pasture also creates carbon dioxide and, according to some environmentalists, contributes significantly to global warming.

Sugar is no less destructive a crop. Sugar production alters the environment in a number of ways. Forests must be cleared to plant sugar, wood or fossil fuel must be burned in the evaporation process, waste water is produced when sucrose is extracted from the sugar cane, and more fuel is burned in the refining process. Contemporary sugar production in Hawai'i has destroyed forests, and waste products from processing have severely damaged marine environments. "Big Sugar," as the sugar industry is called in Florida, is largely responsible for the pollution, degradation, and virtual destruction of the Everglades.

Thus, one of the "texts" that anthropologists can read from a Happy Meal relates to the extent to which consumption patterns associated with our culture create waste and environmental damage. Because of these consumption patterns, the average child born in Canada or the United States will, in the course of his or her lifetime, do twice the environmental damage of a Swedish child, 3 times that of an Italian child, 13 times that of a Brazilian child, 35 times that of an Indian child, and 280 times that of a Chadian or Haitian child.

And what of gendered toys—dolls for girls and toy cars for boys? Clearly, there is a message about the definition of gender roles, as dolls are expected to be chosen by girls and cars by boys. But, if you look closely enough, you can deduce even more about our culture from this meal.

EXERCISE 1.3

We have examined some of the lessons we can learn about our culture from the Happy Meal. There are obviously others. See what you can deduce about the following dimensions of life in North America from the Happy Meal.

1. What can you say about gender roles in North America?
2. What can you deduce about race relations?
3. What can you say about the physical attributes of people favoured in North America?

QUESTION 1.5: HOW CAN AN ANTHROPOLOGICAL PERSPECTIVE BE USED OUTSIDE ACADEMIA?

What Can You Do with a B.A. in Anthropology?

Students taking anthropology classes often say, "I like anthropology, but what can I do with it?" A more or less typical response is "Anything that you can do with any liberal arts major." That doesn't get us very far, though. Being a professional anthropologist—teacher, researcher, consultant—generally requires an advanced degree. However, an anthropological perspective and methodology can be invaluable in all sorts of career areas. In 2011, for instance, national newspaper *The Globe and Mail* identified ethnography as "the new buzzword in marketing." This buzz about ethnography does not necessarily mean that you will see scores of job postings looking specifically for candidates with an anthropology degree. However, the demand for candidates with ethnographic skills is on the rise. In 2015, a LinkedIn search using "ethnography" as a keyword yielded many hits that included jobs at Netflix, Skype, Microsoft, VISA, and Google. These examples are all from the corporate world, but many anthropologists are employed in the public sector or by nongovernmental organizations (NGOs), as well. Why are these companies looking for ethnographers? Anthropology, like any discipline, deals with problems and questions. In the contemporary lingo of human resources departments, ethnographers "add value" to the companies they work for by bringing a unique perspective to bear on the problems and questions they address. They often have distinctive insights and are able to suggest innovative solutions that accountants, marketers, doctors, or lawyers cannot. In particular, students of anthropology should graduate equipped with at least three problem-solving "tools" unique to the discipline:

- anthropological methods, especially close observation and detailed description and documentation of behaviour, as discussed in Chapter 2
- anthropological concepts, which help in understanding and comparing what observed behaviours, such as rites of passage (Chapter 6), kinship (Chapter 5), and reciprocity (Chapter 7), mean to the people studied
- anthropological theories, which aim to explain why human beings organize their experiences into meaningful categories in the ways that we do

Culture, our core disciplinary concept, is a tool that enables anthropologists to go beyond describing what people do and what it means to them to explain the deeper significance of *why* people do what they do. What kinds of problems can anthropologists help solve with their anthropological "toolkit"? People in management must address the problem of how to structure relationships among staff; people in government must address problems involved in designing public policy initiatives, such as reducing juvenile crime. Someone in a medical field may face the problem of how to educate the young regarding sexually transmitted disease, while someone employed in the tourist industry must address the problem of how to minimize the negative consequences of tourism for local populations. The solutions to all of these and other problems can benefit from an anthropological perspective because all involve ways that people give meaning to their experiences. Throughout the remaining chapters of this book, we will examine various examples of how anthropological perspectives are applied to real-world problems by anthropologists working both within and outside academia.

The best way to understand what anthropology is and how ethnographic insights have problem-solving potential is to look at what anthropologists and ethnographers do and at how they approach various kinds of social problems. The examples of applied anthropology discussed below demonstrate the important ways in which anthropological knowledge and ethnographic expertise matter in the real world. They also begin to suggest some (but certainly not all) of the ways that anthropology can be put to use outside the academy.

Applied Anthropology

Applied anthropology is the subdiscipline of anthropology that specializes in putting anthropological knowledge into practice outside academia. Sociocultural anthropology is, in part, about social and cultural differences, whether they occur from one country to another or within a single classroom. The fact that different peoples assign different meanings to events, objects, individuals, and emotions is a source of considerable conflict, miscommunication, and misunderstanding. Anthropologists seek to explain this diversity, to help people understand one another better, and, in the process, to apply their experience and knowledge to solving social, economic, educational, business, and political problems encountered in our diverse and increasingly interconnected world.

Applied anthropologists therefore work in a variety of topics and settings, and almost anything of interest to academic anthropologists might also be the focus of applied anthropologists. In practice, some branches of anthropology or areas of study lend themselves particularly well to applied anthropology: these include indigenous issues, political anthropology, environmental anthropology, medical anthropology, and corporate ethnography. The majority of applied anthropologists practise their trade with these.

Indigenous Issues

Julia Harrison and Regna Darnell (2006), scholars of the history of Canadian anthropology, have argued that, although the growth of anthropology

CULTURE AND MEANING

in Canada has been influenced by the French, British, and American scholarly traditions, one thing that marks the Canadian disciplinary tradition as distinct is the strong focus on Indigenous peoples. They also suggest that an emphasis on applying research findings in order to serve the needs of the Indigenous communities that have been studied—that is, applied anthropology—has been a defining feature of the discipline in Canada.

Edward Hedican writes that more and more First Nations band administrations are employing anthropologists to conduct research in areas that the bands themselves find useful, such as research that helps to document the validity of First Nations land claims. Such collaborations makes anthropological research easier because, as Hedican suggests, "people will certainly be more willing to cooperate with researchers if they are able to see that the work has some direct relevance to their lives" (2008 [1995], 253).

Dawn Martin-Hill is a Canadian anthropologist and filmmaker of Mohawk ancestry whose work with the Lubicon Cree is discussed in detail in Chapter 8. Much of her research has focused upon exploring the lingering effects of colonialism upon First Nations groups. She also has a particular interest in understanding the historical and cultural basis of First Nations land claims. In her 2008 film, *Sewatokwa'tshera't: The Dish with One Spoon*, she documents and lends her support to the Haudenosaunee, who are involved in disputes with the federal and Ontario governments over land claims.

In February 2006, in what would come to be known as the Grand River Land Dispute, Haudenosaunee from the Six Nations of Grand River began public protests and road blockades. Their goal was to bring greater public awareness to a 40 hectare plot of land near Caledonia that was granted to them in 1754. The protests were sparked by the impending threat of the development of the land into a residential suburban area by Henco Industries Ltd., which claimed to have purchased the land in 1841 from what was then called "Canada West." The dispute is ongoing, and

it is relevant to note that throughout the ordeal, the Haudenosaunee have been portrayed in the mainstream media as violent, irrational, aggressive, and potentially dangerous. Such depictions function to garner public support and sympathy for the developers, and to delegitimize the validity of Haudenosaunee land claims.

In response to overwhelmingly negative mainstream media representations, Martin-Hill has organized numerous peaceful protests. Many of these have included not only Haudenosaunee protesters but also supportive members of the academic community. Such initiatives draw attention to the ways in which the agency and legal rights of Haudenosaunee community members have been threatened, if not delegitimized by both government and corporate interests.

Another way that anthropologists working with Indigenous peoples often apply their knowledge and insights is through efforts to influence and improve relevant public policy. One prominent example is the government-commissioned Hawthorne-Tremblay Report, published in two volumes in 1966 and 1967, which was the largest applied research project in Canadian anthropology. Titled *A Survey of the Contemporary Indians of Canada: Economic, Political, and Educational Needs and Policies*, the report was the result of a collaborative project that involved 35 researchers, both faculty and graduate students, who conducted interviews and surveys in Indigenous communities. The study differed from more traditional scholarly projects in several ways: it was written in readable language rather than academic jargon; it was expressly intended to address the concerns of bureaucrats and government officials rather than scholars; and it provided 151 recommendations with the potential to be implemented by the federal government (Dyck 2006, 82–83). As Dyck states:

> *Although the discussion of the report was preempted by the abortive White Paper proposals of 1969, it did popularize the concept of "citizen plus," a formulation firmly endorsed by*

provincial and territorial Indian organizations in their opposition to the Trudeau government's new Indian policy (83).

Today, making contributions to land claims and to public policy pertaining to Indigenous peoples is a high-demand field for applied anthropologists. The Firelight Group, based in British Columbia, is a research cooperative that provides community-based research and technical support, most often to First Nations clients, on projects that are designed to support reconciliation between indigenous and non-indigenous interests, or to facilitate the inclusion of indigenous perspectives in decision making and public policy. The anthropologists employed by the Firelight Group work on a range of projects that include social, economic, and cultural impact assessments and traditional knowledge and land use studies.

Legal Anthropology

Another important branch of sociocultural anthropology involves the area of law and society, sometimes called "legal anthropology." Sally Falk Moore describes this approach as one that "inquires into the context of enforceable norms: social, political, economic, and intellectual. This includes, but goes farther than, what Western governments and courts define as law. In anthropology, while the 'socio-legal' includes formal juridical institutions and their social surroundings, it also encompasses law-like activities and processes of establishing order in many other social domains, formal and informal, official and unofficial, in our own society and in others" (2005, 1).

Anthropologists who study legal issues in a particular place ask questions about power, such as "who makes the rules, who can undo them, how are they normalized and enforced, and how are they morally justified" (Moore 2005, 2). These questions were first asked in egalitarian societies where legal institutions, such as courts and police, were absent; anthropologists tried to understand what prevented

total chaos. Other questions are now being asked in relation to the possible lasting effects of colonialism on "native laws," as the colonial powers enforced their own sense of what was right and just.

In his book *Culture and Power*, Stanley Barrett argues that globalization has increased conflict throughout the world and that anthropology's interest in the political is likely to grow. He suggests that "power, authority, influence, manipulation, and coercion (or force) constitute the basic terms in this field of inquiry" (2002, 19). With these concepts in mind, anthropologists have extended their interest in legal issues to include, for example, intellectual property issues and global human rights. They also look at global issues that involve international labour, immigration patterns and obstacles, and development schemes, continually asking: "Who is in control? Whose interests are being served?" We will touch on many of these issues in the chapters that follow.

Rosemary Coombe possesses both anthropology and law degrees, and much of her career has focused upon questions pertaining to the relationship between law, ethics, and culture. How do we come to believe that our systems of rules, regulations, and laws are "right," or natural? Moreover, how is our legal system changing in response to globalization and other phenomena?

Anthropologists such as Coombe are beginning to explore the volatile world of intellectual property law. In an increasingly globalized, digitized, and mediated world, where the flow of images of celebrities and commodities is unimpeded by geographical borders, Coombe's work (see Coombe 2013) asks how changing notions of ownership and authorship are understood in different societies. How, for instance, are representations of athletes or movie stars appropriated for different political causes or by advertisers? In the process, how do meanings of their bodies change, and who owns the appropriated images? In these contexts, differing cultural understandings of "ownership" have legal implications. In order to affect change and to educate current policymakers about the cultural implications of changing notions of intellectual property rights, Coombe conducts workshops with lawyers, law societies, government officials, and law schools. Through these efforts, she seeks to bridge the gap between theory and practice. For instance, if practising lawyers do not possess an understanding of the theoretical underpinnings of cultural notions of appropriation and ownership, then it becomes difficult, if not impossible, to represent the diverse needs of clients or to create culturally sensitive and appropriate legislation.

Political Ecology

A relatively new branch of sociocultural anthropology that is gaining popularity is *political ecology*, defined by Blaikie and Brookfield (1987, 17) as a field of study that "combines the concerns of ecology and a broadly defined political economy." One of the directions this approach has taken has involved challenging dominant explanations for environmental degradation and contesting some of the popular solutions to environmental problems (Paulson, Gezon, and Watts 2003, 205). Analyzing the politics of environment may uncover the interests of powerful elites that profit from directing public inquiry away from their activities and toward those of less powerful peoples, such as indigenous groups, who are forced into parts of the rainforest, where they clear plots of land to grow subsistence products.

Although political ecology usually focuses on land scarcity and access to material resources, two anthropologists at McMaster University have included community identity in their study of peri-urban political ecology. Tina Moffat and Beth Finnis combine a focus on access to land with access to education in a "squatter" community of 300 people called Nayabasti, in Kathmandu, Nepal. As in many such communities, most of Nayabasti's people lack both sewers and indoor plumbing and build houses out of rudimentary materials. The people of Nayabasti were given the land informally by the municipal government more than 30 years ago, but they have no legal documentation, and the only improvement that has been made is the partial installation of indoor toilets (unconnected to sewers) by a Danish nongovernmental organization (NGO). When the community was first formed, there were few others close by. However, the area now includes monasteries that were built by Tibetan refugees, as well as the homes of wealthy urbanites who have moved from the core of Kathmandu to the outskirts because the land is cheaper and the air is cleaner. The arrival of these newcomers, who have clear title to their land, has placed the community of Nayabasti at even more risk.

Moffat and Finnis discuss the difficulties the community has faced in its efforts to provide education for local children. In 1998, the residents pooled their resources and set about searching for a place to build their own school. After a period of negotiation with the municipal government, a plot of land was found. The community provided almost all the labour to build the school, with Lumanti, a local NGO, providing financial support. Moffat and Finnis caution that it is still uncertain whether the school will be sustainable in the long term, but the project did reinforce community identity, and the community's "ability to get this far is evidence of the incredible capacity of slum and squatter dwellers" (2005, 465).

Medical Anthropology

Medical anthropology is another branch of anthropology in which anthropologists are able to put their ethnographic skills and perspectives to good use. According to the Society for Medical Anthropology, it is "a subfield of anthropology that draws upon social, cultural, biological, and linguistic anthropology to better understand those factors which influence health and well being (broadly defined), the experience and distribution of illness, the prevention and treatment of sickness, healing processes, the social relations of therapy management, and the cultural importance and utilization of pluralistic medical systems" (http://www.medanthro.net/blog/about-the-blog/).

This area of anthropology has moved in many directions. Medical anthropologists may analyze the politics of healthcare access, local interpretations and experience of health and illness, the cultural and historical context of contemporary medical practice and policies, or perceptions and experiences of risk and stigma related to various illnesses.

Naomi Adelson is a medical anthropologist who has done fieldwork with the James Bay Cree of northern Quebec. In her ethnography, *Being Alive Well*, she notes that the Cree do not have a word that readily translates into what we call "health" in English. Rather, they talk about *miyupimaatisiiun*, or "being alive well." For the Cree, being alive well has less to do with individuals and physiology than with social and political relations. Adelson's informants asked, rhetorically, "If the land is not healthy, then how can we be?" (2000, 1). The Cree understanding and experience of health is grounded in what it means to "be Cree," which is itself grounded in connections to the land and to the past (25). Once, the James Bay Cree travelled and hunted across a vast swath of land in northwestern Quebec, but today many live in the village of Whapmagoostui at the mouth of the Great Whale River, hunting in the bush only on weekends. Since the 1970s, the Cree have been fighting with the provincial government of Québec over the appropriate uses of the land and its resources, most famously in the building of the James Bay I hydroelectric dam and the failed James Bay II project. While the Québec government saw the land as underused and underpopulated and as an untapped source of wealth and power, the Cree knew that the projects would drastically alter the ecosystem surrounding Whapmagoostui, changing the migration and survival patterns of land and sea mammals, fish, and birds. What would it mean to be Cree in the face of such changes? How could they manage to "be alive well"? Adelson (2000, 1) argues that "all definitions of health ... are laden with ideological nuances and can never be separated from cultural norms and values."

Since Adelson conducted her initial fieldwork, there has been a fusing, at the local level, of health and politics. Adelson distributed copies of her research to local political and health authorities, and her use of "being alive well" to explain Cree understandings of health has been incorporated, via *The James Bay Experience: A Guide for Health Professionals Working Among the Cree in Northern Quebec*, into the vocabulary of doctors, dentists, and other healthcare workers in the area (115).

In her work on the social determinants of health among migrant farm workers in Ontario who come to Canada under the Seasonal Agricultural Workers Program (SAWP), anthropologist Janet McLaughlin (2009) bridges the gap between scholarly and applied anthropology. Her work exemplifies the potential overlap between several of the branches of anthropology we have described here, addressing concerns of medical anthropology, political ecology, and legal anthropology. McLaughlin notes that although health, or at least access to the highest attainable standard of health, is a human right, transnational migrant workers are in a paradoxical position when it comes to exercising this right. Although human rights are meant to be universally applicable, "they are also primarily premised on the relationship between individuals and the obligations of the state to respect, protect and fulfill the rights of citizens. What then are the implications for people who live and work in nations in which they are not citizens?" (McLaughlin 2009, 1). The health of migrant workers is shaped by a number of factors related to the nature of their employment, including the work they do, their working conditions, their access to healthcare, language barriers, and the type of housing in which they stay while in Canada. Yet they are also more vulnerable and neglected in terms of their healthcare needs because of the temporary nature and precarity of their employment, their transnational mobility, and their status as non-citizens. In addition to writing about these migrant workers for audiences that include other anthropologists and scholars of development, McLaughlin applies and disseminates her knowledge and findings beyond academia by writing policy papers and newspaper articles and working with several community groups that address the needs of migrant workers. Beyond that, she is the co-founder of the Migrant Worker Health Project (www. migrantworkerhealth.ca), a website that houses a collection of resources and information for healthcare workers to assist them in providing care to migrant workers.

Corporate Ethnography

Increasingly, corporations recognize that anthropologists possess many unique and beneficial skills that can assist with the marketing and advertising of key products. Specifically, anthropologists possess excellent qualitative research skills (discussed in Chapter 2), a commitment to cultural relativism, problem-solving skills and approaches unique to the discipline, and a focus on cross-cultural and multicultural understandings of the world. As such, corporations realize that anthropologists can often assist them in marketing particular products to people of specific demographics. If McDonald's, for example, is experiencing low revenue on the sale of a particular product in Norway, they may hire an anthropologist to go to Norway and interview potential consumers to understand why the product is not meeting target sales goals. The anthropologist may learn that the product does not appeal to Norwegian food preferences, that the product is perceived as too expensive, or that the advertising campaign is, perhaps for cultural reasons, unsuccessful at appealing to its target demographic.

The relationship between consumerism, culture, and "taste" (in terms of cultural preferences for certain foods, clothing styles, or particular aesthetic trends) is explored by Canadian anthropologist, corporate ethnographer, and blogger Grant McCracken (see McCracken 2005). McCracken has conducted fieldwork for a wide variety of corporations, including Nike, Ikea, and the Ford Foundation. McCracken's goal is to harness the unique perspectives and fieldwork methods of sociocultural anthropology for analyses of consumer trends. He is hired by large corporations to ask and answer questions such as these: How and why do consumers make the purchases that they do? Why is a particular product not meeting sales expectations? How can a product be re-designed to make it more appealing to the consumer? By interviewing consumers about their shopping and consumption habits, and synthesizing this information with analyses of broader cultural trends with respect to consumption, McCracken is hired to increase the net sales and revenue of large companies.

The alignment of anthropology with corporate interests, however, raises a number of ethical problems. As we will learn in Chapter 2, anthropologists have a primary ethical responsibility to ensure that their work does not harm their informants. But many people, including many anthropologists, would argue that the ultimate purpose of marketing and advertising is to manipulate people into mindless consumerism. From this perspective, the use of ethnography to increase corporate profits is harmful to those consumers who are being studied. Moreover, as we will discuss in Chapter 8, the rampant consumption that characterizes contemporary capitalism has global consequences that are often unseen, or at least not considered, by consumers, including environmental degradation, increased global inequality, and poor working conditions for those people who produce the goods we are encouraged to consume. Is it ethical to use our ethnographic problem-solving skills for corporate ethnography, when consumer culture might itself be considered a problem?

On the other hand, it is worth considering that not all anthropologists who work as corporate ethnographers try to increase sales of soft drinks or cars or sneakers. Some corporate ethnographers work in fields of design, urban development, education, or healthcare.

One example that confounds easy adjudications of the ethics of corporate ethnography is the work conducted by Lisa Reichenbach and Amy Maish (2006) on how pharmaceutical companies might best meet the needs of Type 2 diabetics, while simultaneously maximizing their benefits as a business. They argue that ethnography, with its focus on lived experience, is the best way to improve and encourage patient-focused healthcare and pharmaceutical interventions. In their ethnographic work on Type 2 diabetes patients as healthcare clients, they discovered that the key to understanding the illness experience was to realize that coping with diabetes entails a series of life transitions—from healthy to ill, and from dependent patient to self-care practitioner (through the self-administration of insulin).

The theorization of life transitions, as they are facilitated by what anthropologists call "rites of passage" (which we discuss in Chapter 6), is an example of the way in which these corporate ethnographers are able to bring the unique tools of anthropology to bear on interrelated problems that are of interest to patients and healthcare practitioners: how to improve the experience of taking insulin, and how to increase patient compliance. Of course, this work also addresses a problem for pharmaceutical companies: how to sell more insulin. Reichenbach and Maish suggest that the insights gleaned during their research might ultimately benefit both patients and pharmaceutical companies, though perhaps not necessarily to the same degree. The key question, they say, when addressing the issue of business opportunities is not just "What is your overall opportunity as a brand?" but also, "How do I realize that opportunity in the real and often painful world of the diabetic?"

CHAPTER 3

CONSTRUCTING IDENTITIES

© Mark Anthony Jacobson

From the moment we are born, interactions with others are shaped by their perceptions of us. Such interactions, as shown in the painting above by Mark Anthony Jacobson, are part of the "Celebration of a New Life." According to Goffman, quoted in the epigraph on the next page, we use our bodies in unconscious and conscious ways to communicate information about ourselves to others. Through our speech, clothing, gestures, postures, and other phenomena, people make assumptions and often judgments about our character and our place in the world. Similarly, we often consciously manipulate our bodies to show others who we think we are. These aspects of what we call "identity"—both individual and collective—form the subject of this chapter.

When an individual enters the presence of others, they commonly seek to acquire information about him or to bring into play information about him already possessed. They will be interested in his general socioeconomic status, his conception of self, his attitude toward them, his competence, his trustworthiness, etc. Although some of this information seems to be sought almost as an end in itself, there are usually quite practical reasons for acquiring it. Information about the individual helps to define the situation, enabling others to know in advance what he will expect of them and what they may expect of him. Informed in these ways, the others will know how best to act in order to call forth a desired response from him.

Erving Goffman

Problem 6

How do people determine who they are, and how do they communicate who they *think* they are to others?

INTRODUCTION

As human beings, we are not born knowing who we are or what our place is in the social landscape; we must learn our **social identity**: who we are and how we stand in relation to others. To appreciate the importance of the self as a social identity, try to imagine a society in which every person is physically indistinguishable from every other person. How would people in such a society know how to behave toward one another? Whenever we interact with another person, the interaction must be based on some idea of who the other is: Friend? Stranger? Family member? Teacher? At the same time, the other must have some idea of who *we* are, a conception of the relationship that exists between us. The need to know the social identity of others is apparent whenever two strangers meet and, directly or indirectly, seek to elicit information about each other. Each tries to place the other in some identity at some spot on the social landscape.

Imagine next a society in which every person is utterly unique. In this case, every interaction would be different, and there would be no way to learn from one situation how to behave in another similar situation.

social identity
The view that people have of their own and others' positions in society. These learned personal and social affiliations may include gender, sexuality, race, class, nationality, and ethnicity. Individuals seek confirmation from others that they occupy the positions on the social landscape that they claim to occupy.

Each person would need to have an infinite variety of behaviours with which to interact with people of an infinite number of types. We avoid this situation by categorizing people, placing them in groups so that not everyone in our social universe is unique. We group them into categories based on criteria such as gender (female, male, or some other gender), ethnicity (Irish, Italian, Chinese), personal characteristics (short, tall, husky, thin), and so on.

Try to imagine, also, a social landscape in which no person acknowledges any other person or communicates in any way who she or he thinks the other is. This scenario, too, would represent an impossible situation. People would have no way of acquiring from others confirmation that they occupy the social identities they think they occupy. In reality, our social identities are constructed in large part by others, who, by their behaviour toward us, confirm that we occupy the spot on the social landscape we claim to occupy. Put another way, nobody is anybody except in relation to somebody.

Finally, try to imagine a social landscape in which everyone communicates to everyone else that they occupy the wrong spot on the landscape. Every person actively disagrees with every other person about who they are. This situation would be, if not impossible, chaotic.

QUESTIONS

6.1 How is identity, and one's sense of self, learned?

6.2 How does the concept of personhood vary from society to society?

6.3 How do societies distinguish individuals from one another?

6.4 How do societies mark changes in identity?

6.5 How do individuals communicate their identities to one another?

6.6 How do people form identities through collective struggles?

To examine how people in a society determine who they are and communicate who they think they are to others, in this chapter we will explore the ways different societies define the person, the ways individuals are differentiated from others, the ways they find out who they are and convey to others who they are, the ways they mark transitions from one social identity to another, and the ways they form collective identities.

QUESTION 6.1: HOW IS IDENTITY, AND ONE'S SENSE OF SELF, LEARNED?

Learning Identities

Hugh Brody begins his book *The Other Side of Eden: Hunters, Farmers, and the Shaping of the World* (2000) with a description of a baby Inuit girl:

> *Imagine the darkness of the far north. Not as something in which the adventurous traveller moves in awe. But as a beginning, for those for whom the Arctic is home. Imagine the inside of a skin tent, or a snowhouse, or a government-regulation low-rental prefab. In this home, an Inuit baby girl wakes in the night. She is held, fed, cuddled—and talked to …*
>
> *In these words, the child is given the sounds of love, and can know that she is safe. Not safe just to feed, to sleep, but safe to do these things as and when she wants. For she is a baby who carries atiq, the spirit and name of her late grandmother. She is the adored baby; she is also her mother's mother, her grandfather's wife. Her grandmother is alive again in the baby. This means the baby is doubly and trebly loved. And she must be treated with respect. (2000, 11–12)*

Is this Inuit baby born with an identity? Or is her identity something she must learn? It is certainly clear to others in her Inuit community that she is the reincarnation of her grandmother, but how long will it take the baby to understand what that means?

Learning to Belong

Hugh Brody suggests that the Inuit baby begins to know that she is an important member of her family almost the moment she is born and that this knowledge expands daily as she interacts with others. As people tell her stories about her land and its creation, she builds up an image of her world and of her place in it. She learns that she is connected to her land and to all the other creatures that share the land with her.

Stories present people of all ages with ways of knowing about who they are and where they came from. Storytelling is also a way of communicating information from one generation to another (Ridington 1990, 14). No one censors Inuit stories, and children's understanding grows as they grow. Brody describes the Inuit child's experiences with stories told by her grandfather and other adults: "The small child listens for as long as she wishes—she is, after all, also her own grandmother. And she discovers that stories are always a mystery, for they have much that cannot be understood, and much that comes from knowledge and experience beyond understanding" (2000, 13).

As this child grows, she recognizes stories that are told over and over, with the same main characters and events. She also learns that no one understands everything in the stories, and she keeps her sense of wonderment about the world.

Brody's example highlights a key point about identity: we are not born knowing who we are or what our places are on the social landscape; we *learn* to be Canadian or Japanese, husbands or wives, Andrea, Gavin, Homa, Natasha, or Sebastian. We learn how we relate to others as sons, daughters, students, friends, or lovers. Both consciously and unconsciously, individuals form various identities so that they can relate to others and cultivate

a space for themselves within their social landscape. At the same time, identities are political and collective, formed around struggles against such threats as colonialism or the state. As we become who we are, we learn how we stand in relation to others.

Identities such as gender, sexuality, race, ethnicity, and national identity, to name a few, are not natural or biological. We are not born knowing instinctively what it means to "be Canadian," for instance. Our sense of Canadianness, like any other identity, is cultivated and learned through various agents of **enculturation**. These are sociocultural forces and institutions that teach us, consciously or unconsciously, about what it means to be a Canadian citizen. Agents of enculturation may include the mass media, parents, peers, school, and the government.

Think about the ways in which children are enculturated into the norms of "Canadian identity," for example, in many public school systems across Canada. In elementary school, most children learn how to sing the national anthem, and because provincial governments control the content of the school curriculum, students learn a government-sanctioned version of Canadian history. Students must demonstrate their successful acquisition and knowledge of this history on tests and papers in order to advance to the next grade. Even as they graduate and get older, Canadians continue to learn about Canada through participation in Canada Day parades and other public spectacles, or by watching the national news on Canadian television stations such as the CBC (Canadian Broadcasting Corporation). In Canada, the mass media play an important role in shaping ideals of Canadianness through their depictions of sport, for instance. Hockey, in particular, has long been promoted as a component of a distinctive

enculturation
The process through which individuals learn an identity. It can encompass parental socialization, the influence of peers, the mass media, government, and other forces.

CONSTRUCTING IDENTITIES

Canadian identity; however, hockey's participants and spectators are mostly white, middle-class, and male (Gruneau and Whitson 1993; Hartman 2009). As such, it is a sport that (perhaps unintentionally) promotes a dominant, or normative, ideal of Canadian identity as white, middle-class, and male. Given that Canada is officially a diverse, multicultural nation in which no particular gender, sexuality, or ethnic or racial identity should be privileged as "more Canadian" than any other, this image is a problem. In this context, hockey's iconic status as a national symbol is ironic, for it excludes a large portion of the nation's multicultural population and promotes hierarchies of Canadianness. To be "truly" Canadian, we learn, is to consume and participate in hockey. In recent years, the sport has been trying to connect with the nation's increasingly multicultural and multilingual population base. Beginning in 2007, for instance, the CBC began broadcasting hockey games in Punjabi; even after hockey moved from the national public broadcaster to Rogers Media in 2014, Punjabi broadcasts were maintained on the private broadcaster's multicultural OMNI television stations.

Despite the problematical nature of hockey as a "Canadian" identity marker, it is important to note that shared experiences, such as sports and other mediated events, are often used to cultivate a sense of **imagined community**. This term, coined by political scientist Benedict Anderson in 1983, suggests that identities, including national ones, are culturally constructed through shared experiences, even in the absence of face-to-face contacts. So, even though a Canadian living in Halifax may never have visited Toronto, Regina, or Whitehorse, a shared sense of "Canadianness" is created through mediated experiences: watching and listening to stories about Canadian successes at the Olympics; attending Canada Day spectacles and ceremonies; following the national news on television, radio, and the Internet or in newspapers; and so on. Because this process of enculturation often begins when we are young, we often fail to see how various cultural forces shape our identities. Thus, we often view our identities as natural, primordial, or biologically

Canadians playing hockey.

based. Think of the many people who are willing to "sacrifice" themselves or die for their country, for instance. Often, individuals are willing to go to such lengths only if they feel that their identification with their nation is somehow instinctual and, by extension, natural.

Over the past century, anthropologists have engaged actively with precisely these sorts of debates. We live in a pop culture that privileges natural explanations for human behaviours. This has been the case since the late 1800s, with the rise of the **nature versus nurture** debate in academia. In 1874, British naturalist Sir Francis Galton, inspired by the principles of Darwinian evolution, coined

imagined community
A term coined by Benedict Anderson in 1983. It refers to the fact that even in the absence of face-to-face interactions, a sense of community (e.g., nationalism) is culturally constructed by forces such as the mass media.

nature versus nurture
A phrase, coined by Sir Francis Galton in 1874, that references a long-standing scholarly debate concerning whether or not human behaviours and identities are the result of nature (biological and genetic factors) or nurture (learned and cultural factors).

the term "nature versus nurture." Galton (whose work on race we discuss in Chapter 7) was a eugenicist who felt that some people, by virtue of their class, race, or other factors, were better suited to reproduce as they were more "fit" to survive in society. Galton believed that many human differences, including intelligence, were rooted in biology, or "nature." His ideas spawned wildly inaccurate assumptions and research on the part of academics throughout the late 19th and 20th centuries. At the time, many scholars felt that many of our identities, such as race and class, are genetic and thus "natural"—that we are born the way we are.

One of the first anthropologists to engage ethnographically with the nature versus nurture debate was Margaret Mead. In 1926, Mead set out for American Samoa to conduct research that would challenge widespread ideas among scientists that acts of teenage rebellion and experimentation were the result of hormonal or other physical changes brought on by puberty (or "nature"). Such behaviour was commonplace among American teenagers; Mead wondered whether similar behavioural patterns existed in other cultures. Under the direction of her doctoral supervisor, Franz Boas, she travelled to the island of Ta'u to study the behaviour of teenage girls. She observed that their experiences of adolescence were completely different from the experiences of American girls. In Samoa, girls were given a lot of freedom to experiment with their sexuality and did not go through periods of torment with parents. Samoan culture, she argued, did not possess the same Judeo-Christian ideals of sexual morality; this, in turn, contributed to different behaviours and attitudes toward sexuality. Mead thus argued that the experiences of adolescents varied depending on the culture in which they were raised. She therefore emphasized the role of culture or "nurture" in human behaviour.

Mead's methods and research findings would subsequently be disputed, but her continued ethnographic work on the "nature/nurture" debate in 1935 should be noted. Mead visited three tribes along the Sepik River in Papua New Guinea to

American anthropologist Margaret Mead in the Admiralty Islands.

explore differences in gender roles. She found that, in each tribe, men and women took on different responsibilities based on their gender. She was thus able to suggest, once again, that human behavioural differences (in this case, gendered divisions of labour) were the result of culture, not biology.

Research that seeks to link biology with human behaviours and identities is potentially dangerous, for it can provide powerful justifications for social inequalities in society. Back in 1968, for instance, Washburn and Lancaster sought to argue that women, for biological and evolutionary reasons, were better "nurturers" of children—an argument that has since been disputed by feminist scholars. But think of the consequences of this type of research. If women can be "proven" to be naturally better "nurturers," then it becomes easy to argue that a woman's place is in the domestic sphere. This information could then inform government policies relating to daycare funding, affirmative action, and other social issues.

Most anthropologists, on the other hand, would be quick to point out the significance of nurture when it comes to the explanation of gender identity, which, in all cultures, is one of the key aspects of personhood and identity. All societies use gender to divide their members into meaningful categories, yet the way in which this is accomplished varies widely

CONSTRUCTING IDENTITIES

from culture to culture and throughout history. In North America, gender assignment begins at birth with the announcement "It's a girl" or "It's a boy," conveniently ignoring the 4 percent of births in which the infant has various combinations of male and female characteristics (e.g., an infant with one testis and one ovary, an infant with one testis and aspects of the female genitalia, or an infant with ovaries and some aspect of male genitalia). Once the announcement of gender is made (or after a surgical procedure in which the infant is "corrected" to fit into either the male or female category), the infant is given a gender-appropriate name, dressed in properly designed or coloured clothing, and spoken to in gender-appropriate language. Parents and other caregivers then teach male children that it is manly to endure pain, to be strong and tough. Male children are discouraged from expressing discomfort and encouraged when they can withstand it. Female children, on the other hand, are comforted when they hurt themselves. Although gender stereotypes are changing, many North American boys are still encouraged to be aggressive and competitive; they learn to compete in games and play with toys that require aggressive behaviour. Girls are still taught to be caring and helpful; they are given toys such as dolls that encourage "feminine" behaviour. As we discuss in greater detail in Chapter 7, gender differences, regardless of whether they are understood as biological or cultural, often serve as a key form of social inequality.

Anthropological fieldwork in various societies has shed light on the problems associated with viewing all human identities in terms of "nature." Yet the development of genetic behavioural research and the ways in which such research is often discussed by laypeople continue to link identities with nature. Think of the ways in which some scientists are actively searching for specific genes that they believe are the cause of particular behaviours. We live in a society that valorizes the "gene" and that is fascinated by ongoing research on the so-called "gay gene" or the "selfish gene." Often, this fascination is more a reflection of popular cultural concerns than it is an accurate reflection of the science. As anthropologist Roger Lancaster (2003) has shown, science journalists misinterpret complex scientific findings in ways that imply that the diversity of human behaviours can be reduced to biology, that ignore the role of culture in shaping identities such as race, gender, and sexuality, and that serve to obscure the fact that many individual behaviours, such as selfishness, may be the result of complex interplays of culture and biology.

Recent developments in genetics suggest, however, that today, there is much more middle ground in the nature versus nurture debate. The consensus that is building among geneticists is that genes are not immutable, nor are genetics destiny. Rather, one's environment (including culture) has a profound effect on one's genes. Any effort to understand the relationship between genes and behaviour must take the cultural environment into account; similarly, geneticists argue that some, if not all, cultural behaviours (propensity to smoke cigarettes or drink alcohol, for example) may very well have important genetic underpinnings.

EXERCISE 6.1

Find a recent newspaper or magazine article that deals with the "nature/nurture" debate. For example, the mass media are always reporting on the latest "scientific" discoveries, which often seek to confirm a biological basis for certain identities—the "gay gene," for example. Outline some of the problems associated with this article from an anthropological perspective. How and why do scientists often overlook the "nurture," or cultural and learned, aspects of our identities?

Now that we have explored how anthropologists tend to emphasize the learned, culturally constructed nature of our personal and collective identities, in the next section we examine in greater detail how a sense of self or personhood is shaped by various cultural forces.

QUESTION 6.2: HOW DOES THE CONCEPT OF PERSONHOOD VARY FROM SOCIETY TO SOCIETY?

The Importance of Self

Of all the products of our culture, the one we most take for granted is our self.

In all societies a personal name is an intimate marker of a person, differentiating one individual from another. Names also can reveal how people conceive of themselves and their relations to others. For many North Americans, names are perhaps the most enduring aspect of the self. Assigned at birth, our names remain with us throughout our lives and represent the self. How much of the self is revealed by a name varies by culture and situation. University students meeting for the first time exchange personal names, rarely bothering with family names. Their sense of self is independent of any group or past. When North American businesspeople meet, they exchange first names, last names, and business titles. Businesspeople are linked to their organizations more than geographical location. In contrast, when Moroccans from different towns meet, the names they offer to others include not only the names of their families but the names of the towns they are from. The Moroccan self is embedded in family and place of origin. Among the Tsimshian of British Columbia, the names people use depend on their social position; when they enter adulthood, get married, or assume a higher rank in Tsimshian society, they change their names. The Tsimshian self is inseparable from one's position in society.

Jorge Chimbinda (2006) has explored the process of "naming" children among the Umbundu of Angola, where there are two ways of naming a child. The most common way is to name a child after a relative who is either alive or dead (an ancestor). The second way is to give

Some contemporary Tsimshian children continue to follow tradition by wearing traditional shawls and will change their names upon entering adulthood.

© Wolfgang Kaehler/CORBIS

a child a new name that refers to some unusual circumstance that was present during the child's birth. For example, a child born during a severe drought will be given a name that refers to the drought and keeps the memory of the suffering alive. The child of a mother who dies in childbirth will be given a name that keeps the memory of the mother's suffering and death. The result of this way of naming is that each child has a last name of his or her own. At the same time, the Umbundu naming system is a historical version of cultural values, such as identity, kinship, geography, folktales, stories, and proverbs. From the Umbundu perspective, names are tools with which people reward the life they have received from their relatives and their world. Names serve to perpetuate the wide kinship web and stress the concept of extended family. Each child represents one of his or her living relatives or ancestors. All relatives and ancestors on both the father's side and that of the mother have equal value because each of them has contributed to the existence of the child. These names also inscribe the imprint of lived experiences on children, so that children named after unusual circumstances embody the meaning of the experiences.

Jorge Chimbinda also explores the effects of colonialism on his people. When Angola became a Portuguese colony, the colonial administrators

CONSTRUCTING IDENTITIES

found it too difficult to keep track of Umbundu people because the naming system did not group people in ways that the administrators understood. For the Portuguese, as for most Europeans, last names were shared among members of families and made family identification orderly. Thus, one of the first ways that the Portuguese colonizers tried to destroy Umbundu identity was to force people to discard their Umbundu names and to use Portuguese names instead.

The differences in naming practices among different societies reveal the different ways societies conceptualize what a person is and how that person relates to the group. Many North Americans believe that individuals are stable, autonomous entities who exist more or less independently of whatever situations or statuses they occupy. Even as they move from status to status or place to place—from student to husband or wife, to employee, to father or mother—they believe themselves to be the same persons. Otherwise, each time they changed situations or statuses they would in effect become different people and would have to change their names. In this regard North Americans are highly individualistic. In other societies, however, individuals are not seen as entities distinct from their social position or group. In societies such as the Umbundu, the relationship between the person and the group, or the person and his or her social position, is holistic; the person cannot be conceived as existing separately from society or apart from his or her cultural beliefs and values.

EXERCISE 6.2

If you were an Umbundu and lived in Angola, which of your ancestors would you choose for the name of your first child? Why would you make this particular choice? In other words, what are the qualities in your ancestors that you would want to transfer to your child? What about your second child and your third?

The Egocentric Self and the Sociocentric Self

Differences between the individualistic and holistic conceptions of the self led Richard A. Shweder and Edmund J. Bourne (1984) to delineate two distinct ways in which the person is conceived in different societies: the **egocentric** and the **sociocentric** views of self. Note that these terms are ideal types, or generalizations about the nature of self in different societies. There will, of course, be exceptions to these patterns, especially given the increasing influence of globalization in constructing our identities. So it is important to recognize that there exist multiple, often overlapping interpretations of self, even within the generalized contexts of the societies described below.

In the *egocentric* view, typified in many ways by the Western view adopted by North American societies, each person is perceived to be capable of acting independently from others, and the locus of motivations and drives is thus internal. For Westerners, the individual is the centre of awareness, a distinct whole set against other wholes. Social relations are regarded as contracts between autonomous, free-acting beings. Individuals are free to negotiate their places in society, and the dominant idea is that each individual is responsible for *what* and *who* he or she is. Moreover, individuals possess intrinsic qualities such as generosity, integrity, and beauty. The egocentric view of the person places a high value on individualism, self-reliance, and freedom of choice, such as the ability to select one's own marriage partner.

egocentric
A view of the self that defines each person as a replica of all humanity, as the location of motivations and drives, and as capable of acting independently from others.

sociocentric
A context-dependent view of self. The self exists as an entity only within the concrete situations or roles occupied by the person.

Keeping in mind that factors such as poverty and ethnicity may make individualism and self-reliance difficult to achieve, it is worthwhile to explore the beliefs associated with this view of the individual. Robert Bellah and his co-authors of *Habits of the Heart* (1984) examined ideas of the individual in the United States that seem to apply equally to Canada. The self in the United States, they say, seeks to work out its own life plot by individually pursuing happiness and satisfying its wants. Unlike individuals in some other societies, many Americans seek to cut themselves off from the past, especially from their parents. They each seek to become their own person, to find their own self. Young men and women need to demonstrate that they can stand on their own two feet and support themselves. This emphasis on self-reliance and independence underpins the belief Americans hold that success is the outcome of free and fair competition among individuals in an open market. Most successful Americans, say Bellah and his associates, claim that they achieved success through their own hard work, seldom acknowledging the contributions made by their families, their schooling, or their positions as members of the upwardly mobile middle class. The only way they can say they deserve what they have achieved is by succeeding through their own efforts.

Because of this dominant perspective of self, many people who were raised within Western, industrialized societies are inclined to view those afflicted with, for instance, eating disorders such as anorexia nervosa or bulimia, as suffering from an individual pathology. It is as if eating disorders were the result of an individual's "problem." Helen Gremillion (2003) conducted 14 months of ethnographic research at a small inpatient eating disorder clinic in the United States. She discovered there that the various cultural forces that have contributed to increases in diagnoses of eating disorders are being ignored in favour of "individualistic" explanations. For example, Gremillion and others often point out that mass media advertising plays a role in constructing normative expectations of an impossibly ideal femininity. Increasingly, the feminine ideal is being defined by physical appearance—in particular, by representations of predominantly white, youthful, slender, "beautiful" women. In this way, advertising on television and the Internet, in magazines, and on billboards is playing a powerful role in shaping Westerners' sense of self. Yet its images of ideal femininity have themselves been constructed and manipulated by computer technologies, which remove wrinkles or fine lines, minimize fat, and reshape facial features. Gremillion argues that many eating disorder treatment plans fail to recognize the role of culture in shaping the self. Such treatment plans replicate Western notions of individualism through the inclusion of careful daily monitoring of weight and patient "progress." These principles of egocentrism, of the individual monitoring of the body—and, by extension, the self—have led to a proliferation of eating disorders.

In contrast to the egocentric view, the *sociocentric* view of the self is context dependent. The self exists as an entity only within the concrete situations or roles occupied by the person. From a sociocentric perspective, there is no intrinsic self that can possess enduring qualities such as generosity, integrity, and beauty. These qualities can apply only to concrete social situations. Instead of saying that a man is generous, a sociocentric perspective would be that "he gives money to his friends." Instead of saying that a woman is principled, the perspective would be that "she does not give away secrets."

It may be the case, as some anthropologists have argued, that, in reality, most societies understand selfhood as both egocentric *and* sociocentric, and that the differences between the societal views of selfhood might lie less in which view they subscribe to than in how they see and practise the interrelationship between the two. For example, Anne E. Becker (1995) characterizes the relationship between body, self, and society in Fiji as one in which the relation of one's body to one's self is mediated through the relation of one's self to one's community (37). The cultivation of one's body (its shape and health, for instance) is understood mainly as a community, rather than a personal, enterprise; this view of the self and body

CONSTRUCTING IDENTITIES

may be more sociocentric than we are familiar with in North America, but it does not mean that Fijians do not also possess an egocentric view. Indeed, during subsequent fieldwork in Fiji, Becker (2004) discovered that the introduction of broadcast television, and specifically Western programming (along with other socioeconomic changes related to globalization), seemed to cause a dramatic shift away from the centrality of the sociocentric self and towards seeing the body as a personal project. As a result, the incidence of eating disorders among school-aged girls, previously almost unheard of, skyrocketed. However, as Gremillion's work above demonstrates, even in North America, the underlying logic of eating disorders must also be understood as sociocentric, even if our common-sense reaction to, and treatment of, these disorders privileges egocentric selfhood.

Personhood in Japan

Some anthropologists attribute a sociocentric view of the self to people in Japan. Anthropologist Christie Kiefer (1976) explained that the Japanese are more likely to include within the boundaries of the self the social groups of which the person is a member. Japanese children are not trained to rely solely on the self, as many North American children are. They are taught that interdependence between the person and the family or group is more important than independence.

Robert Smith (1983) noted that the Japanese view of the self is expressed in their language. For example, Japanese language does not include anything resembling English personal pronouns. In English, children quickly learn to use the two personal referents, *I* and *you*; Japanese boys, on the other hand, must learn six, and girls must learn five. The personal referent used in Japan depends on the speaker's relationship to the listener. It expresses how the self is defined relative to a specific social interaction.

In addition, wrote Smith, the Japanese language contains vocabulary that is very conscious of status. It is characterized by what the Japanese call *keigo*, or

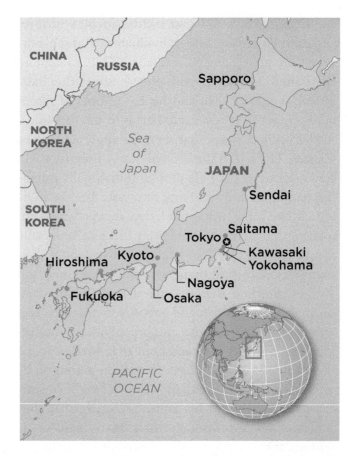

"polite speech." *Keigo* has the effect of establishing at the outset of a conversation the relative social standing and degree of intimacy of speaker and listener. Japanese speakers use different forms of address depending on their social position relative to the person to whom they are speaking. Since the Japanese language is status based, people must be careful of the linguistic forms they use in conversations. When conversing with someone in a superior social position, a speaker must linguistically acknowledge the social difference between speaker and listener. Japanese advertisers have a problem with *keigo* because actors should not give imperative commands (e.g., "Drink Coke") for fear of offending people. They solve the problem by using low-status people who are nonthreatening (e.g., clowns, coquettish women, or children) to issue the commands.

The sociocentric Japanese differ also in their approach to social interactions. Most North Americans believe it is desirable to assert themselves to stand out, and to take charge. The Japanese believe that social interactions should be characterized by restraint or reserve, traits they identify as *enryo*. With *enryo*, the giving of opinions is avoided; this attitude is summarized by the Japanese proverb "the nail that sticks up shall be hammered down."

EXERCISE 6.3

1. The contemporary popularity of social media and attendant forms of virtual selfhood poses some interesting challenges to a strictly dichotomous view of egocentric versus sociocentric selfhood. Many users of sites such as Facebook and Twitter use social media to present idealized versions of their "egocentric" selves. However, these sites also rely upon a more sociocentric sense of self, created through one's social network. Is a person really "on" Facebook if he or she has have no friend connections? Think about the way you construct yourself on social media (or in other virtual forms). Is your social media self described best as egocentric or sociocentric? Why?
2. In your opinion, how accurately does your virtual self reflect your physical self? Is one more real or true than the other?
3. Does your online self ever affect your virtual self? If so, in what ways?
4. How might social media use differ between North America and societies that are considered to have a more sociocentric view of the self?

Yet the Japanese *do* conceive of themselves as separate entities. They are as attached to their personal names as North Americans are, if not more so. Moreover, they believe in self-development. But for them, the autonomy of the individual is established, not in social situations where they actively distinguish themselves from others, but *away from* society, where self-reflection and introspection are legitimate. Through introspection the Japanese find their true heart (*kokoro*) and are put in touch with their true nature—their *hara* ("belly") and *jibub* ("self").

In *Crafting Selves*, an ethnography of Japanese factory workers, Dorinne Kondo (1990) approaches the sociocentric versus egocentric question from a slightly different perspective. She questions whether it is accurate to refer to selfhood, in Japan or elsewhere, as singular. Perhaps, she suggests, it would be better to think about how people craft *selves* through the practices of everyday life. From this perspective, personhood is not static or fixed, but processual and ongoing. According to Kondo, the way that Japanese factory workers craft selves is the result of how they envision and practise their belonging (or lack thereof) to entities such as company and family; selves are therefore crafted in relation to power and hierarchies. Rather than possessing a singular, decisively sociocentric "Japanese self," Kondo suggests that her informants adopt "multiple, infinitely graded, layers of selfhood," often described as oscillating between two ends of a continuum: *omote*, the front, formal side; and *ura*, the back, intimate side. This is not a straightforward dualism: what counts as *omote* or *ura* is always shifting, and the tension between the two is never fully resolved (Kondo 1990, 31).

In the remainder of this chapter, we will look at the self less from an egocentric perspective and more from a sociocentric perspective, as something contingent and relative to the situation. Our focus will be on that part of the self that is defined by social relations and social processes and that is subject to change and redefinition.

QUESTION 6.3: HOW DO SOCIETIES DISTINGUISH INDIVIDUALS FROM ONE ANOTHER?

Differences and similarities among persons are the materials from which we construct our social landscapes. Those materials allow us to distinguish individuals from one another or assign them to one

CONSTRUCTING IDENTITIES

group or another. From these similarities and differences we construct our social identities. However, all societies do not use the same similarities and differences to construct a social code, nor do they use these similarities and differences in the same way. Some characteristics of persons—some tools in the "identity toolbox," so to speak—are used almost universally to differentiate people or to group them together. For example, most societies use family membership, gender, and age as categories within a social code. But other characteristics figure prominently only in some societies—ethnic group membership, skin colour, and wealth, for example.

In many societies, the most important characteristics for defining the self are related to kinship and family membership. In these societies, kinship is the central organizing principle—the main determinant of a person's social identity. Anthropologists working with these societies are often "adopted" by a family. This act is a signal of acceptance, but it also serves the practical purpose of assigning an outsider a social identity through which she or he can be approached by others. To have no kinship label or designation in such a society is to have no meaningful place on the social landscape.

Language is another important identity marker, one sometimes viewed as essential for the maintenance of group identity. Language is often tied strongly to a national identity, and many countries have established institutions to oversee the "purity" of the national language. The Académie française has, for centuries, been charged with keeping the French language free of foreign borrowings, such as "le hot dog" or "le weekend." Sometimes, language becomes a flashpoint in political conflicts over collective identity. In Quebec, for example, efforts of one group to preserve French as the official language of the province, and thus protect what it sees as essential to group identity, have led to a movement for independence from the English-speaking remainder of Canada.

The Québécois, however, argue that Québec identity is not based solely on language. As they see

Continuing his support of Québec's Quiet Revolution, French president Charles de Gaulle declared, "Vive le Québec libre!" in his historic 1967 speech at Montreal's town hall.

it, their history in Canada is one of "slights, assaults, yet survival" (Eller 1999, 297). The conflict between British and French settlers in Canada has been ongoing since both arrived on North American shores. In 1759, the English drove the French Acadians out of eastern Canada; and after the Battle of the Plains of Abraham, outside the walls of Québec City, the Treaty of Paris gave Canada to the English. In 1791, two separate societies were formed: Lower Canada was French and Upper Canada was English, and each had its own culture, religion, stories, political views, and language. Then, in 1841, the Act of Union joined the two societies together, but this union was uneasy: Canada East was still French and Canada West, still English. Canadian Confederation, set out in the *British North America Act* of 1867, created two provinces out of the former Province of Canada: Québec for the French and Ontario for the English. Even so, the two were part of a single entity, Canada, and that entity was ruled by the English.

In the 1960s, during what is often referred to as the "Quiet Revolution," Québec began building its own sense of nationalism, which saw Québec as a "homeland" in which the French were "masters in their own house" (Eller 1999, 327). That "house" was no longer inhabited by French Canadians, or francophones; rather, it was the house of the Québécois—people who were ready to take control of their own lives and separate from the rest of Canada, if necessary.

QUESTION 6.4: HOW DO SOCIETIES MARK CHANGES IN IDENTITY?

Identities are not static, and people are constantly changing their identities as they move through the life cycle. These changes in identity are announced in myriad ways. Many societies have particular ceremonies or rituals that mark a change in a person's status or role in society. Most societies hold religious events, such as baptisms, confirmations, bat/bar mitzvahs, and secular events, including birthdays and graduations, to mark significant changes in an individual's status in society. In this section we explore cross-cultural examples of these phenomena.

The Transition to Adulthood

In a 1908 book now considered a classic of anthropology, Arnold van Gennep introduced the concept of **rites of passage**. The term refers to a category of rituals that mark a person's passage from one identity to another, in the same way that a person's progress through a house might be marked by entering one room after another. Van Gennep identified three phases in a rite of passage: separation, liminality, and reincorporation. First, the ritual separates the person from an existing identity; next, the person enters a transition phase; finally, the changes are incorporated into a new identity. These phases of rites of passage are not equally elaborated in all ceremonies. The separation phase, for example, is a major part of funeral ceremonies designed to help the living let go of the deceased; transition is a major part of initiation ceremonies marking the passage of a person from, say, childhood to adulthood; and incorporation

is emphasized in marriage ceremonies, which, in most societies, mark the transfer of a person from one social group to another.

Rites of passage are visible in Canadian society. For instance, a young man or woman who joins the military is required to undergo "boot camp." Geographically and spatially sequestered from mainstream society, the new recruit lives with other recruits in a dormitory. He or she marks this sense of separation by undergoing physical changes, such as cutting one's hair and wearing a uniform. These acts standardize physical appearances and visually mark an individual as a newcomer or initiate. Recruits then undergo a period of transition, or liminality, where they are expected to perform physically and emotionally draining tasks, such as running long distances when sleep deprived, or enduring verbal insults. Finally, a recruit who is able to endure the stresses of boot camp re-enters mainstream society with a new status: soldier. This period of reincorporation is marked by a new uniform and by a ceremony where the initiate is reintroduced to family and friends with the new status.

Prominent in most societies around the world are ceremonies that mark the transition of a male from boyhood to manhood. Most such ceremonies involve a test of courage. According to anthropologist David Gilmore (1990), one reason why so many societies incorporate tests of masculinity and tortuous initiation rituals for males is that the male identity is more problematical than the female identity. For every individual, there is at the beginning of life a subliminal identification with the mother, and men must make greater efforts to differentiate themselves from their mothers. Consequently, societies incorporate rituals that symbolically separate the boy from his mother, while at the same time incorporating him into manhood.

rites of passage
The term coined in 1908 by Arnold van Gennep to refer to the category of rituals that accompany changes in status, such as the transition from boyhood to manhood, living to dead, or student to graduate.

Victor Turner (1967) used van Gennep's model of rites of passage to describe the move from boyhood to manhood among the Ndembu of Zambia. When Ndembu boys reach puberty, they are taken, as a group of age mates, away from their mothers and out of the village (separation), to live in the forest (transition). There, the boys shave their heads and remove anything from their bodies that might identify them as individuals. While in the forest, the young Ndembu are circumcised and taught all of the special knowledge that Ndembu men know. But in the forest, they have no identity: they are no longer boys, but they are not yet men. In Turner's words, they are "betwixt and between." Once their circumcisions heal and the lessons are completed, the young men return to the village (reintegration) as new persons with new identities. These men, who made the transition to manhood together, will remain in close association throughout their lives as age mates, a category that cuts across kinship groups and that has special tasks in many societies, such as herding animals among pastoralists.

QUESTION 6.5: HOW DO INDIVIDUALS COMMUNICATE THEIR IDENTITIES TO ONE ANOTHER?

Both consciously and unconsciously, we make statements about our identity—who we think we are, or who we want to be—with objects and material things. The clothes we wear and the things we possess are used to display an identity that we desire or that we think we have. In North America, think about how designer clothing, shoes, and bags are coveted as markers of class and status.

Similarly, clothing can also express gender, sexuality, ethnicity, or religious affiliation. In some cases, clothing marks some individuals as "Other" even within their own society. Women who wear the Muslim veil in North America, for instance, have often been identified as "the enemy within," especially since 9/11. Some Muslims in Canada have dealt with this by removing visible signs of their Muslimness, particularly with regard to their dress. Still others have tried to show Canadians that the stereotype that all Muslims are terrorists is not only wrong but completely illogical.

In a study conducted by Homa Hoodfar (2003), young Muslim women in Canada reported that wearing the veil was not something their parents forced them to do. This finding contradicts the claims made by some North American feminists that banning the veil will free women from Islamic patriarchal oppression (2003, 15). In fact, most of the women Hoodfar talked to said they had had to fight with their parents in order to wear it. When Hoodfar and her research assistants asked young women why they wear the veil, one woman said that doing so "allowed her to be a 'person' rather than an object of male scrutiny" (2003, 17–18). Other women explained that they took up the veil when they began university because wearing it communicated certain values. In Hoodfar's words, "By taking up the veil, they symbolically but clearly announce to their parents and their community that, despite their unconventional activities and involvement with non-Muslims, they retain their Islamic mores and values. They are modern Muslim women who want to be educated and publicly active, but not at the cost of their moral principles" (2003, 21). In the same sense that "a picture is worth a thousand words," they believed that wearing the veil communicated identity in a way that saved them from having to explain why they behaved in certain ways. It is also worth noting that there are different interpretations as to what constitutes proper "Islamic dress." For example, some women wear a head scarf and a long dress over their clothes to cover the body completely and sometimes conceal part of the face; others believe that a head scarf suffices to fulfill the requirements of their faith. Still others do not believe that they need to wear a veil in order to maintain their Muslim identity.

While some Muslim women in Canada choose to wear veils or other garments to emphasize their modesty and to divert attention from the contours of their bodies and their sexual appeal, people in some societies may want to *highlight* their sexuality so that it is immediately visible to others. Men in some groups in New Guinea, for example, wear penis gourds. And in 17th-century Europe, men wore codpieces to emphasize their male anatomy.

Sexual identification is an important identity marker, but there are other signals that people use to display their identity. In some parts of Africa, people from different villages have different hairstyles; in North America, teenagers encode their schools or teams by the jackets they wear. People signal their connectedness to others by holding hands, by wearing rings, or by feasting and drinking together.

Rituals of Gift Giving and Hospitality

One of the most influential works in the history of anthropology is *The Gift* (1925), by Marcel Mauss. In it, Mauss identifies what he calls the **principle of reciprocity**: the giving and receiving of gifts. His main point is that gifts, which in theory are voluntary, disinterested, and spontaneous, are, in fact, obligatory. The giving of the gift creates a tie with the person who receives it and who, on some future occasion, is obliged to reciprocate. To Mauss, what matters is not what is given but the relationship that is maintained or established by the gift. The types of things given and received signal the identities of the participants in the exchange and the kind of relationship that exists between them. If the gifts are roughly of equal value, the relationship is one of equality. But if the gifts are unequal in value, the person who gives the more valuable gift is generally of higher status than the receiver.

A well-known example of gift giving in the anthropological literature is the *kula* **ring** of the Trobriand Islanders. The seagoing Trobrianders leave their homes on islands off the eastern coast of New Guinea and travel from island to island, visiting and trading. Noteworthy in their travels is their pattern of gift giving. Each man has trading partners on the islands he visits, and these partnerships are signalled with gifts of red shell necklaces or white shell armbands. As a man travels and trades objects, he gives and receives necklaces and armbands. A man who receives either an armband or a necklace does not keep it but passes it along to another trading partner. There is a set pattern to the exchange: necklaces travel from island to island in a clockwise direction, while armbands move counterclockwise. The time between exchanges and the distances between the islands are so great that it may take two to ten years before the necklaces and armbands make a complete circle.

principle of reciprocity
According to Marcel Mauss, gift giving involves reciprocity. The idea is that the exchange of gifts creates a feeling of obligation, in that the gift must be repaid.

kula **ring**
A system of inter-island gift exchange documented by anthropologist Bronislaw Malinowski in the Trobriand Islands. It involves the exchange of shell necklaces and armbands. According to Malinowski, the *kula* ring serves, among other things, to create alliances and social ties among individuals living on different islands.

© I. DeVore/Anthro Photo

Trobriand Islanders define and maintain their social identities by participating in the *kula* ring, a ritualized pattern of gift giving involving the exchange of necklaces and armbands.

The *kula* ring serves as a concrete representation of ties among individuals. Any change in the pattern of gift giving reflects a change in the nature of the social ties. Special gifts that are individually owned are also circulated, and the owner's status and renown grow as the goods he owns circulate along predetermined paths. A successful *kula* operator participates in many such exchanges and can profit from them by keeping items for as long as he can before passing them along. Of course, if he keeps them too long, others will be reluctant to exchange, so a good deal of social skill is required to take successful part in a *kula* ring.

Anthropologist Margaret Anderson has devoted many years to studying another famous example of gift giving: the **potlatch** ceremony of the Indigenous peoples of the Northwest Coast of British Columbia. Among the Tsimshian, the potlatch is typically a feast that legitimates a change in social relations, such as a funeral. Someone who dies is vacating a spot on the social landscape—or, more specifically, leaving a name empty. The Tsimshian are organized into matrilineal clans or houses. Each house has associated with it a fixed number of personal names, and each name has associated with it specific spiritual powers, honours, and objects of wealth. The man with the highest ranking name is recognized as the owner of the house. The name a Tsimshian holds when he dies is vacated until it is claimed by or given to someone else. If the name vacated belongs to a chief, the feasting will begin with his death and end with the acceptance of a new chief, who is usually the eldest son of the deceased chief's eldest sister. A person who disgraces his name by doing something wrong (such as having an automobile accident or being put in jail) must give a feast to "clean the name."

The potlatch feast, however, does more than allow a Tsimshian to obtain a new name and identity. It also serves to symbolically reorder and validate the names and, hence, the social positions of everyone at the feast through the distribution of gifts. Members of the house of the deceased generally serve as hosts to members of the deceased's father's house. The guests are feasted for the services they have performed (preparing the corpse, carving a pole) and as repayment for the gifts they formerly gave the deceased to help him acquire his name. When the guests are seated, the hosts announce the gifts they are giving to the guests, along with the name of the person from the host group who has contributed the gift. Higher ranking guests receive more gifts at a potlatch than lower ranking guests. Consequently, the seating

potlatch
A celebration, usually involving elaborate feasting and the redistribution of gifts, found among many indigenous Northwest Coast groups, such as the Tsimshian. The potlatch is a means of creating a new identity or of reinforcing social status within a group.

arrangements and the value of the gifts given to guests at the feast serve to announce or publicly notarize the social position or identity of each guest.

Anderson (2004) argues that, although the potlatch has changed since Christianity was introduced in 1857 (when William Duncan of the Church Missionary Society came to Fort Simpson), its meaning and symbolic value have remained, in part, because as long as the feasts began with a prayer, Duncan considered them respectable.

Exchanges that convey recognition of identities need not be limited to material goods. The exchanges also may consist of emotion and sentiment. Hawai'ians, for example, define a desired identity in part by expressions of gregariousness and hospitality. The emotional qualities of a person's relationships are one criterion by which others judge, interact with, and respond to that person. For example, if you accept an offer of hospitality in Hawai'i, it is a signal that you recognize the generous nature of the offer and that you wish to maintain the social link. If you reject the offer of hospitality, it is seen as a hurtful sign that you do not recognize the generous nature of the person making the offer and do not wish to maintain the relationship. Hawai'ians try to keep social pathways open through altruistic exchanges of love (*aloha*), sincerity, feeling (with heart, *na'au*), and warmth (*pumehana*).

Gifts and Commodities

An important characteristic of traditional *kula* and potlatch goods is that they have histories. A Trobriander who receives a necklace or armband can probably recite the history of the object, sometimes from its creation through all the persons who possessed it at one time or another. These goods are similar to heirlooms in our own society, whether it is the family wedding ring that has been worn by brides for three generations, the watch that was owned by a great-grandfather, or the quilt that was made by a great-aunt. The histories of these objects, especially when the objects are given as gifts, are vital to the identity of the person who gives them. They say something

special about the relationship between the giver and the receiver of the gift. The same is true to a lesser extent of gifts that are *produced* by the giver: these carry a special meaning apart from the object itself. A lamp made and given as a gift is often far more meaningful than a lamp purchased at a department store. However, we often must choose the gifts that we give from among thousands of mass-produced, largely impersonal goods available in department and chain stores. Herein lies a dilemma.

James Carrier, in his book *Gifts and Commodities: Exchange and Western Capitalism Since 1700* (1995), argues that since the 16th and 17th centuries, the production and distribution of goods has become impersonal, and that the spread of industrial and commercial capitalism has meant the spread of alienated objects and relations. In earlier times, commodities were personalized in various ways. The relationship between the producer and the seller of goods was a personal one between relatives or friends; the buyer knew who made and sold the object purchased. Even when stores replaced home trade and markets, the buyer knew the store owner, who further personalized the goods by buying them in bulk and individually packaging and displaying them. The buyer–seller relationship was further personalized by the extension of credit from seller to buyer and by the customer loyalty expressed by the buyer to the seller. Today the buyer knows neither the producer nor the seller, and if the item is bought on credit, it is through a credit card issued by some distant bank based on the filing of an impersonal application, with the transaction accomplished completely by mail. Eyes never meet.

Carrier labels goods that carry no special meaning as **commodities**, to distinguish them from

commodities
Traditionally, commodities are items that involve a transfer of value and a counter-transfer: *A* sells something to *B*, and the transaction is finished. As is typical of capitalist market-exchange systems, a long-standing personal relationship between buyer and seller is not established.

what he calls "possessions." Gifts, says Carrier, must be possessions before they can carry meaning in an exchange. Commodities involve a transfer of value and a counter-transfer: *A* sells something to *B*, and the transaction is finished. But in a gift exchange, a more or less permanent link is established between giver and receiver. Gifts are inalienable, that is, they are bound to people after the presentation; commodities are independent of their sellers (or producers). It is easy to return, destroy, or give away a commodity; it is a dilemma to do any of those things with a gift.

As noted, for North Americans the contrast between commodities and gifts poses a special problem. Most of the items we give as gifts are store-bought commodities, often mass produced. Their history is brief and undistinguished: an item of clothing was probably assembled in some factory in Mexico or Indonesia by a young woman earning perhaps a dollar an hour; a sports item was probably assembled in some factory in South America, shipped to a warehouse in Toronto or Chicago, and sold through a mass-produced catalogue; a radio, iPod, or mobile phone, assembled in Korea and distributed by a Japanese company, was probably sold in a North American chain store. These are commodities, not gifts.

For Carrier, the problem is how, in a world filled with impersonal, alienated commodities—goods without history, so to speak—we can turn these things into personal items with meaning and history, into possessions that carry something of the buyer's identity. In gift giving, how do we turn commodities into items that say something about the relationship between the giver and receiver? How do we make commodities meaningful?

We convert commodities into possessions and gifts, says Carrier, through a process of appropriation. For example, when a person takes an impersonal space—a dorm room, say, or a rented apartment—and decorates and modifies it, he or she has appropriated it and given it meaning. When a person buys an automobile, one virtually identical to thousands of others of the same make, model, year, and colour, and comes to think of it as unique, as an expression of his or her identity, that person has appropriated an object and made it a possession. Shopping itself, says Carrier, is a way of appropriating commodities; "wise shoppers" choose what is "right" for them or what is "right" for the recipient of the gift.

Gift Giving and the Christian Celebration of Christmas in North America

The dilemma of converting commodities into gifts is especially acute during the Christian Christmas holiday season, when most gift giving takes place in North America. Christmas as Christians know it did not really emerge until the height of the Industrial Revolution. Its precursors included the traditional end-of-year festivities that took place in England, where gifts consisted of food or feasts given by superiors to their dependants. In the 1770s in New York City, people began celebrating 6 December, the day of St. Nicholas, instead of the New Year. This celebration was actually something anti-Christmas; St. Nicholas was Dutch, and the colonists were celebrating things Dutch to protest British rule over what had been New Amsterdam before British colonization. Not until 1809 did the holiday begin to spread and did St. Nicholas turn into Santa Claus giving gifts of candy to children. The appearance of Clement Moore's *A Visit from St. Nicholas* in 1823 (or '*Twas the Night Before Christmas*, as it later became known) marked the movement of the holiday to the end of the year. At this point children began to receive toys rather than food. Even then, Christmas was celebrated largely on New Year's Day and in the industrial northeast.

The next major step in the evolution of Christmas was the appearance of Charles Dickens's *A Christmas Carol* in 1843. The story was an immediate sensation, especially with its victory of Bob Cratchit and Tiny Tim and their world of the home over Scrooge and the cold, impersonal world of work. By 1865, Christmas had been declared a national holiday, and in 1862, the Thomas Nast image of Santa Claus began appearing in *Harper's Weekly*, completing his construction as a fat, jolly, old man dressed in fur-trimmed robes (inspired, Nast later admitted, by the fur-trimmed clothing of the wealthy Astor family). By the 1880s, writers were beginning to complain about the commercialization of Christmas.

Most social scientists who have written about the Christian celebration of Christmas agree that it is largely a celebration of the family, serving especially to distinguish the world of the family from the outside world of work. Christmas serves to affirm the identity of Christians all over the world as members of specific family groups, and the circle of kin with whom gifts are exchanged defines the boundaries of the family. In one study conducted in a midwestern American city, 90 percent of all gifts exchanged at Christmas were exchanged with family members. Christmas heightens a person's sense of family identity, expressing how warm the family is and how cold the world outside may be.

Thus, it is within the family that the Christmas gift is most important. The question is how to resolve the problem of using commodities as family gifts, how to transform commodities to make them suitable as statements of the special role that family and family relations play in defining our identity. This problem, apparently, is not new. The dilemma of giving gifts that are manufactured and sold in stores existed as early as the mid-19th century, when department stores tried to convince buyers to purchase their gifts in stores by advertising them as "special Christmas stock." Even today, through Christmas decorations, music, and special attractions, such as the ever-present Santa Claus, retailers try to inject the spirit of Christmas into their stock of goods.

But there are other ways that consumers try to appropriate commodities and turn them into Christmas gifts. First, we may simply say that

In North American societies, the yearly ritual of Christmas shopping provides a means of converting impersonal commodities into personalized gifts that show one's love for family members and close friends.

the nature of the gift is immaterial, that "it's the thought that counts." A second way is to purchase things that aren't very useful, giving frivolous or luxurious gifts, or items that are Christmas specific, such as Christmas tree decorations or clothing with Christmas decorations on it. Third, and very important, there is the wrapping rule: Christmas gifts must be wrapped. The wrapping itself converts the commodity into a gift. Difficult-to-wrap presents (e.g., a piano, a horse, a bicycle) must be decorated with a bow. The only categories of things that needn't be wrapped are items made by the giver, such as breads or jams. These items need only a bow and a card.

Finally, says Carrier, there is the shopping itself, the time we spend getting the "right" gift for the "right" person. Why, he asks, do we go through all of this? It is onerous, it is stressful, and it is expensive. Yet one-third of all retail sales are made in November and December, most of them accounted for by Christmas shopping. One-sixth of all retail sales are related to Christmas. People complain about the materialism of Christmas and Christmas shopping. Yet people shop intensely for Christmas.

In the face of this bother and complaint, why do North Americans, even devout Christians, spend

CONSTRUCTING IDENTITIES

so much effort in Christmas shopping? Why not give homemade gifts? Indeed, why give presents at all? Why not give a Christmas card instead? It is true that the giving of purchased gifts reflects a number of motives, ranging from displays of affluence to a desire to shower a loved one with lovely things. However, these more commonly recognized motives do "not explain the intensity of Christmas shopping and people's ambivalence towards it" (Carrier 1993, 62).

Carrier suggests that the answer to this riddle lies in the fact that shopping in itself is a method of appropriation, of converting a commodity into a gift: we exercise a choice from among the mass of commodities presented to us. As Carrier (1993, 63) puts it, "Christmas shopping is an annual ritual through which we convert commodities into gifts. Performing this ritual indicates that we can celebrate and recreate personal relations with the anonymous objects available to us, just as it strengthens and reassures us as we undertake the more mundane appropriations of everyday life during the rest of the year."

Christmas shopping also demonstrates to people, says Carrier, that they can create a world of family, a world of love, out of the impersonal commodities that flood the world "out there." The Christian celebration of Christmas is a time when North Americans make a world of money into a world of family, a time of contrast between the impersonal world of commodities and the personal world of possessions and gifts.

EXERCISE 6.5

These days, gift cards for stores, restaurants, spas, or other goods and services are popular holiday gift items. After reading about Carrier's work, discuss how gift cards might fit into his discussion of commodities and gifts. How can gift cards, as commodities, be turned into gifts? Is this even possible?

QUESTION 6.6: HOW DO PEOPLE FORM IDENTITIES THROUGH COLLECTIVE STRUGGLES?

As this chapter's epigraph suggests, the formation of identity is a cultural process that involves the lived experiences and everyday practices of people. This cultural construction of identity creates both the individual and the collectivity, which we think of as society. In this section, we focus on the collectivity and ask how identity is produced through collective struggles.

The Meaning of "Indigenous"

After examining **Indigenous peoples** of Asia, Africa, Meso- and South America, North America, Eurasia, and Europe, Bruce Miller strives to arrive at a definition of what "Indigenous" means. He concludes his book *Invisible Indigenes* (2003) by looking at the common elements in the various ways the term has been used in different parts of the world. One common factor in all the societies Miller encountered is the association of indigenousness with both the presence and the absence of certain traits. The most critical element in the various definitions is that indigenes are recognized because they live in some clearly identifiable way that maintains their own distinct culture, and that they have been living exactly the same way since they were encountered by the colonizers. Furthermore, people are defined as indigenous because "broadly, definitions have come to focus on difference—the

Indigenous peoples
Groups of people whose ancestors predate the arrival of European or other forms of colonialism, who share a culture and/or way of life that they often identify as distinct from "mainstream" society, and who often feel that they have a right to self-government.

CHAPTER 4

SOCIAL HIERARCHIES

© Paulo Ito

This mural, by graffiti artist Paulo Ito, was painted as a form of protest to the 2014 FIFA World Cup, hosted by Brazil. Through his representation of a starving child eating a soccer ball, Ito draws attention to pervasive social hierarchies (like class and race) within nation-states like Brazil. While large-scale sporting events are normally represented as celebratory events and viewed as opportunities to showcase the host country's "strengths," this mural highlights how massive expenditures on sporting spectacles often obscure pervasive social problems like poverty and ignore and/or exacerbate social inequalities.

Although it may never be possible to quantify the degree of racism that exists in a given society, the evidence unmistakably reveals that racism widely distorts the attitudes of white Canadians toward Aboriginal peoples. Whether blatantly or covertly, many Canadians still believe that Aboriginal people are inferior; as a result, these people believe that there is a sound, rational basis for discriminating against Aboriginal persons at both the individual and institutional level.

James S. Frideres and René R. Gadacz

Problem 7

Why are modern societies characterized by social, political, and economic inequalities? How are certain gender, class, racial, and other identities privileged or marginalized in various social contexts?

INTRODUCTION

The Rationale for Social Inequality

The maldistribution of wealth, status, power, and privilege is a significant problem throughout the modern world. To North Americans it is visible in the starving faces that stare out from our television screens in documentaries and on the evening news, interspersed with advertisements for luxuries such as automobiles, cosmetics, and household appliances. Some people can purchase the finest amenities, while others lack the necessities of life, such as food, shelter, and healthcare. There are few, if any, modern nations in which one part of the population does not in some way enjoy privileges that other parts do not share.

Anthropologists use the term **social hierarchy**, or *social stratification*, to refer to the ordering and ranking of individuals within a society. This ranking is normally based on pervasive systems of inequality that privilege particular classes, castes, races, or genders over others.

Social hierarchy is not an inevitable feature of human societies. For example, although groups such as the Ju/'hoansi and

> **social hierarchy**
> The ordering and ranking of individuals within society, also known as *social stratification*. Those at the top of the hierarchy are generally afforded more power, wealth, prestige, or privileges in a society. Hierarchies can be based on race, gender, class, caste, ethnicity, national affiliation, or other factors.

the Inuit are not totally egalitarian, people go out of their way not to appear better than others. Moreover, there does not seem to be a universal inclination to rank people by one criterion or another; in some societies, skin colour makes a difference, while in others, it does not. In some societies, men are accorded far greater status than women; in others, there is little, if any difference in gender rank. Even the use of age as a criterion of rank varies from society to society. The only general rule seems be that as societies become more complex and more populous, their propensity for social stratification increases.

Some people contend that the hierarchical ordering of people and groups is unavoidable. In their view, scarce resources, occupational specialization, and the power of an elite group to control the behaviour of others inevitably result in some form of social stratification. Others maintain that stratification is not only avoidable but also counter to human nature. According to anthropologist Thomas Belmonte, "since the emergence of stratification, man's[1] history (his changing ways of relating to nature and other men) has stood opposed to his humanity. The emergence of power-wielding elites … laid the basis for a new kind of anti-collective society whose vastly accelerated growth was founded, not on the reconciliation of antagonisms between men, but on their origination and amplification in slavery, caste, and class" (1989, 137).

Those who support Belmonte's view note that in societies such as those of Ju/'hoansi and Inuit, there are no "poor," "rich," "inferior," or "superior" people; nonetheless, these societies are not totally egalitarian, or equal — even in small-scale societies, valued statuses are not available to some members. The question at hand, though, is why modern societies are characterized by extremes of poverty and wealth.

It is worth noting here that poverty is not random. Indigenous populations, minorities, and women are the social categories of people most at risk for poverty. For instance, according to data collected by Statistics Canada, in general, poverty rates (measured by low income) decreased by 2.6 percent between 1981 and 2010. However, recent immigrants, Aboriginal peoples, racialized communities, and people with disabilities have been the least likely to benefit from this decrease; they are also more likely than other groups to remain poor for the long term. The poverty rate for all Canadians in 2010 was 9 percent, but it stood at 17.5 percent for recent immigrants, 18.7 percent for Aboriginal families, 42.8 percent for unattached Aboriginal people, and 13.6 percent for people with disabilities (Citizens for Public Justice 2012). Although the low income rate for women ages 18 to 64 in Canada was only slightly higher than average at 10.3 percent, children in single-parent households headed by women experience poverty at the disproportionately high rate of 21.8 percent (Statistics Canada 2013).

How do we explain the distribution of poverty, power, prestige, status, and wealth based on race, indigenous status, and gender, among other factors?

In this chapter we examine how societies construct social hierarchies and why some groups erect social edifices based on social dominance and submission, high and low status, and oppressors and oppressed. We examine why most people in stratified societies—both those at the top and those at the bottom—consider social ranks to be "the nature of things." We go on to discuss how social hierarchies such as race, gender, and class are intertwined in Canada, particularly in the experiences of immigrants who are also members of visible minorities. We also explore whether a relatively non-stratified community can exist within a large-scale society. Finally, we explore how an anthropological perspective can be applied to alleviate the effects of inequality.

---

[1] Note that Belmonte's use of "man," "men," and "his" in reference to humankind, including both men and women, is no longer accepted practice, especially in scholarly writing, as this usage is considered to be an example of gendered bias in language (see section 7.3 for a longer discussion of the relationship between gender, language, and social hierarchy).

7.1 How do societies use class and caste to rank people in social hierarchies?

7.2 How do people come to accept social hierarchies as natural?

7.3 How is gender a form of social hierarchy?

7.4 How are different forms of social hierarchy interwoven with each other?

7.5 Can a non-stratified community exist within a large society?

7.6 How can anthropology be applied to alleviate the effects of inequality?

QUESTION 7.1: HOW DO SOCIETIES USE CLASS AND CASTE TO RANK PEOPLE IN SOCIAL HIERARCHIES?

Social hierarchies in different societies vary along several dimensions: the criteria used to differentiate people into one level of society or another; the number of levels that exist; the kinds of privileges and rights that attach to people at different levels; and the strength of the social boundaries that separate the different levels. In Canada and the United States, for example, people are stratified by income and personal possessions into a social **class** (e.g., lower class, middle class, and upper class). They are classified by cultural or family background into ethnic groups (e.g., Italian, Jewish, Hispanic, or white Anglo-Saxon Protestant), or by physical appearance or skin colour into racial categories or visible minorities (e.g., black or white). They are also classified by gender and age, as well as by standards such as education. People in Canada and the United States may move from class to class, and they may choose to emphasize or de-emphasize their ethnic group membership, but generally, their racial category and gender are perceived as fixed.

Remember that social hierarchies are based on people's perceptions of others. Below is a list of personal attributes. Your task is to rank them by number from most to least important to you in judging a person's social or personal worth. No ties are allowed. If there is an attribute not included in the list that you wish to add, do so. What are some of your reasons for your rankings? Why are some attributes more important to you than others? What do your rankings tell us about our society?

Rank

____ Personal appearance

____ Income

____ Gender

____ Age

____ Religion

____ Ethnic or community origin

____ Family background

____ Intelligence (as indicated by school performance)

____ Athletic ability

____ Personal possessions (e.g., clothes, car)

____ Personality [Fill in your description of type of personality.] _____

Class as a Form of Social Hierarchy

Social class refers to perceptions of an individual's standing or status in society, normally based on economic criteria, status, or other factors, which may vary from society to society. Max Weber argued that social class can be based on economic wealth or "status class": prestige, honour, educational or occupational achievements, or religious or spiritual affiliation. In North American societies, for instance, we tend to place particular value on some occupations

class

A form of identity informed by perceptions of an individual's economic worth or status. It is also a form of social hierarchy.

that require years of post-secondary schooling over more "hands-on" professions such as construction work and trades. Although many tradespeople earn sizable incomes, their professions lack the "status" associated with medicine or law. Beyond that, we live in a commodified, consumer-driven society in which material possessions, such as cars, houses, and clothing of certain brands, are often perceived as markers of an individual's class background and, by extension, his or her access to wealth, power, and prestige.

Unlike social identities, such as race, which is normally perceived as an ascribed status, or one that is fixed or unchanging, class in North American society has long been viewed as a more fluid social identity. In other words, it can be either an **ascribed status** or an **achieved status**. An individual may be born into a life of wealth, power, and high status as a Rockefeller or a Massey; or alternatively, he or she may, through hard work and determination, overcome the odds and achieve a higher class status. The growing wealth gap between the rich and the poor in North America, and the decreased likelihood of upward class mobility, suggests that the former occurs much more frequently than the latter, and class comes to look, in reality, much more like an ascribed status. This popular myth that class is an achieved category is enshrined in American fiction (F. Scott Fitzgerald's *The Great Gatsby*) and in real life (Barack Obama). By suggesting that class identity is the result of a **meritocracy**, however, these stories overshadow the ways in which class intersects with other identities, such as gender and race.

In many ways, stories of opportunity, available for all, privilege a white male, middle- or upper-class perspective. As discussed earlier, ethnic minorities and women, for instance, are often positioned at the bottom of many social hierarchies, making it difficult for them to have the same opportunities or access to tools, such as post-secondary education, training, or other resources, which are needed to "achieve" a higher class status. The idea of North America as a meritocracy discounts the fact that

there is no "level playing field" when it comes to class, race, and gender. Unfortunately, when we think of class solely as an achieved status, too often we tend to blame the poor for their own fate.

Caste as a Form of Social Stratification

In a **caste system**, individuals are assigned at birth to the ranked social and occupational groups of their parents. A person's place in the social order is fixed; there is no mobility from one caste to another. This lack of mobility is one feature that distinguishes the notion of caste from class. Castes are also separated by strict rules that forbid intermarriage and other forms of interaction, such as eating together, speaking to one another, or working together. In other words, caste systems are endogamous, or closed.

Caste systems exist in societies all over the world (for instance, the Balinese, discussed in depth in Chapter 1, have a caste system). However, India presents the most well-known and paradigmatic example of a caste system of social stratification.

In any stratified society, people's access to jobs, wealth, and privilege is determined largely by

ascribed status
An identity that is perceived as fixed and unchanging because a person is believed to be born with it. In Canadian society, race is often assumed to be ascribed at birth.

achieved status
An identity that is believed to be in flux and that is dependent upon the actions and achievements of an individual.

meritocracy
A social system in which individuals are rewarded and resources are distributed according to achievement, effort, and ability.

caste system
A form of social stratification and identity where individuals are assigned at birth to the ranked and endogamous social and occupational groups of their parents.

their position in the hierarchy. In India, where the population is stratified into hundreds of different castes, these groups are based on traditional occupational roles and Hindu ritual categories of purity and pollution, for example. According to this traditional classification system, the Brahmins, the priestly caste whose lives were devoted to worship and teaching, occupied the top of the hierarchy. Directly under them was the Kshattriya caste, whose members comprised the soldiers, politicians, and administrators. Next was the Vaisya caste, made up of farmers and merchants. At the bottom of the hierarchy was the Sudra caste, whose members were devoted to the service of other castes. Although, traditionally, castes are occupational, they do not so much determine one's occupation as they exclude one from a certain job. Not all Brahmins are priests, nor are all members of the Vaisya caste farmers and merchants, but *only* Brahmins can be priests and *only* Vaisya can be farmers.

Beneath the religious hierarchy were the Harijans, "untouchable" or "unclean" persons, whose occupations were believed to be ritually polluting to others. Members of the Harijans caste have recently changed their name to *dalit*, which means "oppressed" or "ground down." *Dalit* include washermen, tanners, shoemakers, and sweepers—people whose occupations require them to come into contact with animal or human wastes.

For many years, debates about the practice of caste in India centred on which was the more important aspect of the caste system: concrete concerns with occupation roles or more abstract, symbolic issues of purity and pollution. However, rapid social and economic changes in contemporary India have required anthropologists to rethink how and why caste continues to be a salient social category there, and to what extent it continues to work as a justification and method of social stratification. For instance, no traditional caste rankings apply to modern professions such as pilots, call-centre operators, factory workers, or medical doctors. Furthermore, as Isabelle Clark-Decès (2011, 8). argues, "Nowadays ideas of relative purity

do not matter as much as they did in the past, [and] equality and democratic values have undermined the practice of caste ranking."

Yet caste still plays an important role in social hierarchy in India, even if it now overlaps with a newer hierarchy of class; nonetheless, the way in which caste links occupation to hierarchy has changed. Many traditional occupations continue to be filled by members of certain castes to the exclusion of all others, but, as Robert Deliège (2011, 47) has pointed out, "[t]oday everyone aspires to a better life and as a result, the struggle for attractive occupations has become a major issue in contemporary caste struggles." Today, many Indians think of members of other castes as rivals and as different, but not necessarily as inherently inferior or superior to themselves. The contemporary case of the *dalit* and their caste "rivals" provides an interesting example.

The Indian government has in its constitution outlawed discrimination against the *dalit*, or anyone else, based on caste membership. Although these legal measures did not lead to a sudden end to untouchability, they did have important consequences. Untouchables could now go to temple, attend school, apply for jobs, take the same buses and trains as anyone else, and so on. Deliège's *dalit* informants told him they did not find concerns about pollution to be particularly relevant to their lives, and although most people refused to do scavenging work within the village, they would be happy to find jobs as *municipal* scavengers if these jobs were salaried with benefits (2011, 54).

The *dalit* have also been able to use their designation as a "scheduled caste" to their collective socioeconomic advantage. As members of the scheduled caste, the *dalit* have been the recipients not only of constitutional protection against discrimination, but affirmative action in job allotments and higher education, as well as resources and benefits to bridge the socioeconomic gap with other groups. According to Deliège, the consolidation of the category "scheduled caste" has solidified the formerly ill-defined and somewhat fluid line between untouchable and non-untouchable. If you are within the *dalit* category, you are entitled to protection from the state; if you are outside, you are not. This solidification of categories has had drastic consequences, especially at the lower end of the caste hierarchy.

What, for instance, is the difference between an agricultural worker from a scheduled caste and another from a non-scheduled caste? Both earn similar wages and live in similar conditions. It may well be that members of a scheduled caste are insulted from time to time, but members of the non-scheduled caste may also be despised, even if no derogatory caste names are thrown at them. Moreover, the government usually gives non-scheduled communities fewer opportunities to improve their lot. All things being equal, then, it is often (but not always) better to be a member of a scheduled caste (Deliège 2011, 56). Clearly, caste continues to play a significant role in contemporary India; however, as Deliège's work shows, castes, especially those in similar socioeconomic circumstances, often see each other as rivals in a country where socioeconomic class hierarchies are becoming increasingly prevalent.

QUESTION 7.2: HOW DO PEOPLE COME TO ACCEPT SOCIAL HIERARCHIES AS NATURAL?

Race as a Form of Social Stratification

Sociocultural anthropology is about seeing behind the façade of everyday appearances to what lies behind those appearances. Understanding how societies construct rationales to justify and legitimize social discrimination is one of the most important and, to some extent, the most difficult tasks in anthropology. Franz Boas, a founder of

anthropology, was among the first social scientists to discredit racist and sexist theories and ideologies that sought to legitimize the marginalization of people based on race, religion, gender, and ethnicity: see Boas (1940). Part of the problem is that racist and sexist theories exist not only in popular culture but also in science. It will be useful, then, to examine how such theories are constructed and often taken for granted, and how they are used to justify the ranking of people within the social hierarchy.

Constructing the Ideology of Racism

As discussed earlier, in Canada and the United States the ideology of class is based on the assumption that a person's position in the class hierarchy is determined largely by achievement or individual effort; that is, individuals who work hard and dedicate themselves to their work will succeed. Yet there is also the attempt to justify social position by a person's innate, biological makeup—largely by race, innate mental ability (intelligence), and other factors. Thus, the hierarchical ordering of society is seen as an expression of a natural law that some people are born better able to lead and succeed than others.

The term **race** is used here to refer to the presumed genetic, natural, heritable characteristics of a group of people, normally based on physical attributes such as skin colour, eye colour, or hair type. We live in a society that views race as a natural, ascribed category; it is something we believe we are born with. Unlike class, then, race in many industrialized societies (such as Canada) is seen as a fixed, unchanging form of identity.

race
A culturally constructed form of identity and social hierarchy, *race* refers to the presumed hereditary, physical characteristics of a group of people. These physical, or phenotypic, differences are often erroneously correlated with behavioural attributes.

Franz Boas (1858–1942) was one of the founders of anthropology and one of the first anthropologists to challenge racism and sexism in popular culture.

Both scholars and the general public have been conditioned to viewing human races as natural and separate divisions within the human species based on visible physical differences. With the vast expansion of scientific knowledge in this century, however, it has become clear that human populations are not unambiguous, clearly demarcated, biologically distinct groups. Evidence from the analysis of genetics (e.g., DNA) indicates that most physical variation, about 94%, lies within so-called racial groups. Conventional geographic "racial" groupings differ from one another only in about 6% of their genes. This means that there is greater variation within "racial" groups than between them. In neighbouring populations there is much overlapping of genes and their phenotypic (physical) expressions. Throughout history whenever different groups have come into contact, they have interbred. The continued sharing of genetic materials has maintained all of humankind as a single species.

Anthropologists and other scholars, however, maintain that there is no scientific basis for positioning different groups of people into discrete "races" on the basis of physical features—no population of individuals anywhere in the world is morphologically distinct. In other words, for a "race" to scientifically exist, a certain physical feature (e.g., skin colour) would have to be demonstrated as occurring consistently and uniformly within a particular population. But no group of people, anywhere in the world, fits this criterion. Simply put, there is too much physical diversity within specific populations. The Executive Board of the American Anthropological Association (1998), the largest professional

These days, most academics view race as a culturally constructed form of identity. In other words, they view race as a byproduct of cultural beliefs, not biology. Race may not exist from a strictly scientific perspective, but it remains an important topic for anthropologists to explore. In Canada, we live in a society in which the myth that race is natural or biological, as opposed to a cultural category, prevails. Because of this, race has had a variety of social consequences. Over the years, for instance, race has been conflated with behavioural characteristics, resulting in **racism**, or systems of prejudice based on the stratification of physical differences, which are erroneously thought to correlate with behavioural, physical, or intellectual differences in certain

racism
Refers to the discrimination and mistreatment of particular "racial" groups.

populations. We tend to think of racism today as a practice limited to ill-educated or ill-meaning individuals against other individuals, but looked at from an anthropological perspective, it can be seen, rather, as a societal or systemic problem.

For centuries, European and North American societies have been characterized by racial stratification. In these societies, membership in certain racial or ethnic groups has been enough to place people in particular positions in a hierarchy that defines their social, political, and economic worth. In the United States, for example, one's position in the racial hierarchy has often determined whether a person can vote, hold political office, pursue a particular occupation, live in a certain area, use certain public facilities, attend certain schools, or marry a particular person.

Although most Canadians consider themselves to be far less racist than their southern neighbours, racism has a long history in Canada, and groups have been formed on the basis of white supremacy in both countries. The Ku Klux Klan, for instance, was founded in Tennessee in 1865 to terrorize newly freed slaves who questioned white supremacy. By the 1920s, the Klan was well established in Canada. When it arrived from the United States, it added French Canadians and Catholics to its list of inferior peoples. In the 1960s, the Canadian Nazi Party and the Edmund Burke Society, the forerunner of the Western Guard, openly supported racism. Ten years later, the Nationalist Party and the Aryan Nations took their place among the radical right. The common belief shared by these groups was that the "white race" was superior and that it was on the verge of being "wiped out" by the "dark-skinned races." As Stanley Barrett (2002, 92) put it, "according to white supremacists, interracial mixing, or as they preferred, mongrelization, was more dangerous to humankind than the atomic bomb, because without the genetic purity of 'the master race' the world could not survive."

African Canadians are not the only ones to experience racism in Canada. Racist beliefs about Aboriginal peoples are deeply rooted in Canadian history. James Frideres and René Gadacz call this "structural racism" (as opposed to prejudice and discrimination by individuals) because it is embedded in Canadian social institutions. Frideres and Gadacz argue that the Indian reserve is "an internal colony" in which "Canadians are seen as the colonizing people, while Aboriginal persons are considered the colonized people" (2001, 4).

Stratification by race has existed for a number of reasons. It was economically profitable to people who could buy black slaves or obtain workers from among groups legally or socially barred from anything but low-paying jobs. It was advantageous, also, to those who did not have to compete for jobs with people who were socially or legally barred from them. However, stratified societies often claim that the ranking of people by race and ethnicity is natural and that social hierarchies are not socially constructed. In the case of racial stratification, some proponents claimed that it was the Christian God's will that some persons were inferior to others; others claimed that God created different races as He created different species of animals, and furthermore, that the Bible says the species are to be kept apart. Others claimed that members of one race or another were intellectually or morally superior to members of other races. Generally, of course, it was the race of the person making reference to the Christian God or the Bible that was somehow superior.

Canadians assisted fugitive slaves, as depicted in the Charles T. Webber painting *The Underground Railroad*.

Most people had little trouble constructing an ideology to justify racial stratification, especially since it was reinforced by state and religious authorities. Even the supposedly objective findings of scientists assisted in building a racist ideology. In the 19th century, reputable scientists devoted much time and energy to proving that the racial stratification of society was "in the nature of things." Indeed, many contemporary forms of racism emerged out of 19th-century scientific studies of race. Both misguided and ethnocentric by today's standards, they functioned to maintain what Peggy McIntosh refers to as **white privilege**—the positioning of "white" individuals at the top of racial hierarchies. Science thus became a tool for naturalizing the power, authority, and privileges afforded to individuals with white skin. Their research findings supposedly proved that members of one race (usually whites or Europeans) were intellectually superior to members of another race (usually blacks or Asians).

Samuel George Morton was a respected scientist and physician who began in the 1820s to collect and measure skulls from all over the world. When he died in 1851, he left a collection of some 6,000 skulls. Like many in the 19th century, Morton believed that a person's intelligence was related to the size of his or her brain; the larger the brain, the more intelligent the person. Since the size of the brain could be determined by the size of the skull, he believed that a ranking of the races could be objectively achieved by a ranking of skull size.

Morton first measured the size—more specifically, the cranial capacity—of skulls by filling them with mustard seed and then pouring the seed into a container to measure the skull's volume in cubic inches. Dissatisfied with the inconsistency of measurements obtained with mustard seed, he later used 1/8-inch-diameter lead shot. He concluded

white privilege
Refers to the fact that, in many societies, "white" people have access to greater power, authority, and privileges than non-white people.

from his measurements that "white" skulls had a mean value of 92 cubic inches, "American Indian" skulls 79 cubic inches, and "black" skulls from America, Africa, and Australia 83 cubic inches. Among "white" skulls, the largest were those of Germans and English people; in the middle were those of Jews; and at the bottom were those of Hindus. Thus, the social hierarchy of whites at the top, with the English and Germans at the top of the top, and blacks on the bottom, was said to be supported by the evidence of brain size and intelligence.

Morton concluded from all this that "whites" (specifically, northern European "whites") were not only socially superior but also biologically superior. He believed he had provided objective evidence that the distribution of status and power in 19th-century North America accurately reflected not merely social, but biological merit.

When Stephen Jay Gould, a Harvard paleontologist, re-examined Morton's published data, he concluded that Morton's summaries were a "patchwork of fudging and finagling" (1981, 54) to reach conclusions that supported the socially constructed hierarchy. Gould found no evidence of conscious fraud. He concluded that Morton had simply selected or rejected certain data to ensure that the results confirmed what he and most other Americans believed: that whites were naturally more intelligent than the people they called "Indian" or "black."

Working with the same skulls Morton had used more than 150 years earlier, Gould discovered that the sample of 144 Native American skulls included proportionally more small-brained Inca skulls from Peru and fewer large-brained Iroquois skulls. This choice naturally produced a lower mean cranial capacity for indigenous Americans than would have occurred had Morton correctly adjusted for this discrepancy. Moreover, Gould discovered that Morton's failure to include the small-brained Hindu skulls with his "white" skulls had produced a higher average cranial capacity for white skulls. When Gould corrected for Morton's sample biases, he discovered that there was no difference between

SOCIAL HIERARCHIES

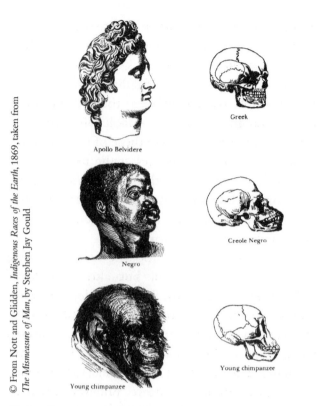

© From Nott and Glidden, *Indigenous Races of the Earth*, 1869, taken from *The Mismeasure of Man*, by Stephen Jay Gould

Nineteenth-century scientists attempted to "prove" that whites were naturally superior to other races. In this illustration from an 1868 racist tract, the proportions of the skulls were distorted, giving the impression that blacks might even rank lower than the apes.

Euro-American and indigenous American cranial capacity. As for comparisons between "white" and "black" skulls, Gould discovered that Morton had ignored the facts that brain size is related to body size and that male skulls are larger than female skulls. Examination of Morton's black skulls indicated that the group included proportionally more female skulls and fewer male skulls. When Gould remeasured the "black" and "white" skulls, he discovered that the mean cranial capacity of black males was slightly higher than the mean for white males, while the mean for white females was slightly higher than that for black females.

Gould did not believe that Morton consciously manipulated his skull measurements to prove that whites were intellectually superior to Native Americans or blacks. Rather, he thought that Morton had simply assumed what his measurements would prove and set about achieving the results he expected.

For example, Gould observed that when Morton used mustard seed to measure cranial capacity, he obtained even greater differences between his "white" and "black" skulls than he had obtained using lead shot. Gould concluded that because mustard seeds are smaller and lighter than lead shot, Morton, probably unconsciously, packed more mustard seed into "white" skulls to obtain a greater difference in cranial capacity between "blacks" and "whites." Unfortunately, while Morton's measurements were obviously in error, as was his assumption that cranial capacity reveals intelligence, and though his conclusions were dictated by the socially constructed hierarchy of his day, they were used well into the 20th century to support the ideology that the racial ranking of persons in society could be justified on natural rather than social grounds.

Class, Race, and the Social Construction of "Intelligence"

Morton's experiments were just one example of the efforts in North America and Europe to show that people somehow deserve their ranking in society: that it is not the result of chance or family privilege but, rather, the result of innate attributes. To believe otherwise would threaten a key assertion of North American ideology: that everyone in Canada and the United States enjoys an equal opportunity for success. Moreover, there are serious political and economic consequences to believing otherwise. If poverty and a low ranking in society are not the fault of the poor, then they must be the result of some failure of society. Such an admission provides a strong reason for governments to enact social and economic policies such as affirmative action, programs of economic redistribution, and laws barring racial and other forms of discrimination. Such changes, however, might lead to a loss of privilege for those who benefit from present policies; therefore, there is strong motivation to find some concept that legitimizes inherited privilege while still placing the blame for poverty or lack of success on the poor.

The concept of intelligence neatly solves this problem: if people accept the idea that intelligence can explain how well people do, then the fiction that people's rank in society depends solely on their own innate ability can be maintained. Moreover, if it can be shown that intelligence is inherited, then we can explain why the children of successful people tend to be successful, and why certain groups, notably people of colour and immigrants of certain characteristics, are disproportionately poor.

The failure of the thesis that cranial capacity, and hence brain size, reveals intelligence did not end all attempts to link intelligence to success and to race and ethnic class membership. There has been, instead, a continuing effort on the part of some members of the scientific establishment to marshal evidence that intelligence is inherited and varies among racial groups. These efforts have included the work of Arthur Jensen in the 1960s and 1970s and, more recently, the publication in 1994 of *The Bell Curve* by Richard J. Herrnstein and Charles Murray. Missing from most of these accounts is any acknowledgment that intelligence itself is a social construct, an invented idea. We need, then, to look closely at our concept of intelligence. How did it evolve?

To begin, anthropologist Allan Hanson (1993) notes that the concept of intelligence contains several questionable assumptions. First, intelligence is assumed to be a single entity. Second, it is assumed to be measurable and unequally distributed in the population. Third, the amount people have is assumed to be relatively fixed throughout life. Fourth, the amount people have is assumed to largely explain their degree of success in life. Finally, it is assumed to be largely inherited.

Each of these assumptions is critical to the intelligence construct as most people think of it, and each has been the subject of enormous scientific attention and criticism. The first assumption requires that we accept the idea that if someone is intelligent in one way, they will be intelligent in other ways, rather than believing that some people can be intelligent in some ways but not in others. The second assumption implies that we can somehow measure innate intelligence, as opposed to achievement, and the third presumes we can show that whatever is measured does not vary throughout a person's life. The fourth is built on the idea that people who have more measurable intelligence are more likely to be successful, while the fifth assumption requires us to show that the children of people with high measurable intelligence also have high measurable intelligence.

In spite of the number of assumptions that lie behind the notion of intelligence, and in spite of the studies that illustrate how questionable each of these assumptions really is, most North Americans take the notion for granted. Yet it is an almost unique idea, one not shared by many other societies. Indigenous maritime navigators of the South Pacific, for example, learned to read wave patterns, wind direction, celestial constellations, and other signs and find their way thousands of miles from one island to another. Yet others in the same society who are unable to duplicate this feat did not view the navigators as somehow being smarter—they saw them as people who could navigate. The Japanese view what we call intelligence in much the same way as we view health: except in certain (and generally temporary) circumstances, we all have enough of it.

This book is not the place to summarize all those works that call the concept of intelligence into question. Nevertheless, we might learn something about the social construction of ideologies of class by looking briefly at the early history of the intelligence construct and by reviewing how reputable scientists proceeded to develop it. Three pioneers— Francis Galton, Karl Pearson, and Charles Spearman —supplied the basic ideas and experimental proofs for the classic concept of intelligence as a fixed "mental" entity that is differentially distributed in the population, is measurable, largely explains a person's educational and occupational success, and is inherited.

Francis Galton was one of the leading intellectual figures of the late 19th century. He was the founder of modern statistics as well as the founder of eugenics, or the attempt to identify the most desirable human traits, specify the individuals who possess them, and through selective reproduction, enhance the number of people possessing those desired characteristics. In his best-known work, *Hereditary Genius* (1869), he sought to demonstrate that the "genius" of selected eminent men was linked to the fact that they had eminent parents and, it followed, that their "genius" was largely inherited. In his sample of 997 eminent British men, he found that 31 percent had eminent fathers, 48 percent had eminent sons, and 41 percent had eminent brothers—far higher percentages than one would expect by chance. For Galton, this illustrated the power of heredity in the distribution of "genius." He was, of course, rightly criticized for ignoring the impact of environment. But he did something else that was more interesting, something that went largely unchallenged: he selected the eminent men from the British upper and upper-middle classes, ignoring the "captains of industry and finance," as well as any women. For Galton, eminence was eminence only within a select range of activities and occupations. A nephew of Charles Darwin and of upper-middle-class background, he was faithfully reproducing the judgments of his own status as to what constituted intelligence.

Much of Galton's later research was devoted to arguing that what he called "genius," "mediocrity," and "imbecility" were analogous in their statistical distribution within a society to certain physical characteristics. He developed a number of tests for cranial capacity and for sensory capacities—the ability to discriminate between colours or smells, for example. Around 1900, however, there was a move away from these kinds of measures because they weren't showing any correlations with one another and, more important, because they showed only a low correlation with teachers' estimates of the mental capability of their students. Regardless, by 1900 the classic

intelligence construct had been laid out, although its proof was somewhat wanting.

The next figure is Karl Pearson, one of the most fascinating figures of the late 19th and early 20th centuries. In 1901, Pearson published a study in the *Proceedings of the Royal Society of London* in which he concluded that "the mental characteristics in man are inherited in precisely the same manner as the physical. Our mental and moral nature is quite as much as our physical nature, the outcome of hereditary factors" (155).

It is instructive to look at how Pearson reached this conclusion. He took pairs of brothers and measured specific physical characteristics, such as stature, forearm length, hair colour, eye colour, and cephalic, or cranial, index. He found, not surprisingly, that there were high correlations among brothers for these traits, as well as a mean correlation of .5171. He then asked teachers, using a separate sample, to rank brother-pairs on seven "mental characteristics": intelligence, vivacity, conscientiousness, popularity, temper, self-consciousness, and shyness. Thus, under "conscientiousness" teachers were asked to rate each child as "keen" or "dull" and to choose among six subdivisions of intelligence. When the teachers' evaluations of brother-pairs were tabulated, Pearson found a strong correlation between brother ratings and a mean correlation of .5214, thereby proving the power of inheritance.

Much about this study is questionable, but of particular note is the role of teachers' judgments. Clearly, teachers were evaluating selected behaviour patterns and personal characteristics: patterns and characteristics that they judged to be evidence of various "mental characteristics." In other words, the teachers' judgments were highly subjective and, at best, questionable. But Pearson's work marked an important development in the construction of our concept of intelligence: he claimed to show that whatever intelligence was, it was obviously inherited at least as much as physical characteristics.

Let's now move forward a few years to the next important stage in the construction of the intelligence construct: Charles Spearman and "general intelligence."

Spearman's research, published in the *American Journal of Psychology* in 1904, was designed to prove that there were different degrees of correspondence between an individual's performance on different types of tests. Thus, one would expect a high correspondence between one's performance on geometrical tests and tests of spatial perception, and a low degree of correspondence between one's performance on, say, tests of musical ability and tests of weight discrimination.

If some degree of correlation existed between all the test results, it would point to some general factor, or g, that affected performance on all tests. Thus, tests that resulted in a high correlation (e.g., geometrical ability and spatial perception) would be heavily saturated with g, while tests with little correlation would not be. For example, to use an athletic analogy, if someone hits both a baseball and a golf ball a long way, we might assume that there exists some general factor for athletic ability accounting for both skills.

Spearman was suggesting that the g factor underlay all mental operations and that if it could be found, it would approximate true intelligence. His was a major claim, for if the existence of g could be proved, it would dismiss the idea—widely held at that time—that different people can be intelligent in different ways and that each person has a unique contribution to make. With g, people would be intellectually different in only one way, and people with lots of g would have more to contribute than people with only a little g.

To experimentally prove the existence of general intelligence, Spearman isolated four kinds of intelligence that, he claimed, when correlated would show a high degree of correspondence: "present efficiency," "native capacity," "general impression produced upon other people," and "common sense." "Present efficiency" referred to the "ordinary classification according to school order" in subjects such as Greek, Latin, and mathematics. "Native capacity" was arrived at by taking the difference between a child's rank in school and the child's age, while "general impression produced on other people" was obtained by asking the teacher of a class who

was the brightest pupil, the next brightest, and so on. "Common sense" was arrived at by asking the oldest child in a class to rank her school fellows on the basis of "sharpness and common sense out of school." As Spearman said, she seemed "to have no great difficulty in forming her judgments concerning the others, having indeed known them all her life." As a check on the reliability of judgments, he also asked the rector's wife to rank the children, although as Spearman notes regretfully, she did not know some of them. Spearman, not surprisingly, found that children who ranked high on one kind of intelligence tended to rank high on others, thereby validating the existence of g.

Obviously, the methodology of these classic studies was seriously flawed, relying as it did on subjective judgments as to who was intelligent and who was not—judgments that were bound to be biased by such factors as the social class of teachers and students. From Galton's first major work on hereditary genius through Spearman's work on general intelligence, members of the professional middle class were selecting as intelligent those people whose behaviour patterns and appearance most conformed to their own. Moreover, little effort was made to conceal the fact: subjective judgments of members of the professional class were the principal means for defining intelligence. Regardless, the intelligence construct as we know it was generally complete and was perceived by reputable scientists as having been validated experimentally: intelligence, represented by g, was a singular trait that was inherited and differentially distributed in the population.

Much more was to come, of course, in the social construction of intelligence. Most notable in this regard was the development of the Stanford-Binet IQ test and later the Scholastic Aptitude Test (SAT; recently renamed the Scholastic Assessment Test). Among the additional and more sophisticated experiments performed were some that claimed to support the conclusions of Galton, Pearson, Spearman, and other early researchers. But the most interesting feature was the continued part played by the social judgments of people—largely teachers, psychologists, and school administrators—in determining what did or did not constitute intelligence. As late as the 1960s, intelligence test results were still being cross-checked with teachers' judgments and students' ranks in class; if the test scores failed to correlate with the teachers' judgments, the tests were changed.

QUESTION 7.3: HOW IS GENDER A FORM OF SOCIAL HIERARCHY?

Constructing Male and Female

We often assume that gender, like race, is biological. But there is an academic distinction between the terms "sex" and "gender." *Sex* refers to biological, hormonal, and chromosomal differences between males and females; *gender*, by contrast, is cultural. In other words, gender is the cultural interpretation of sex. Cross-culturally, different standards apply to being male and female. As such, there is no cross-cultural, universal understanding of what is considered to be "appropriate" dress, demeanour, behaviours, occupations, or roles for men or women; rather, these understandings must be learned in their respective cultural contexts.

sex
Hormonal, chromosomal, or physical differences between males and females.

gender
Culturally constructed ideals of behaviour, dress, occupations, roles, and comportment for particular sexes.

third gender
A gender role given to someone who does not fit within strictly masculine or feminine gender roles in a society that recognizes the possibility of at least three genders.

Societies also vary in the number of gender categories they recognize. For example, many Native American societies recognize a **third gender**, such as that of the *two-spirit* among the Cheyenne and Lakota. The *two-spirit* is a biological male who does not fill a standard male role. Such individuals are not seen as men, nor are they defined as women. They occupy a third role, one that is culturally defined, accepted, and, in some cases, revered. Male children among the Lakota and Cheyenne thus can choose from two gender categories, rather than learning that gender roles are defined by physiology. Among the Lakota, male children learn that, if they desire, they can adopt the dress and work roles of women and have sex with men, although the *two-spirit* role does not necessarily involve sexual behaviour. The *two-spirits* do not play only women's roles, however; some are noted for their hunting skills and exploits in war. In North American societies, in contrast, individuals who do not assume the gender roles associated with their anatomy are most often defined as deviant, abnormal, or nonconformist, unless the reversal of gender roles is framed as play.

One way to learn about how a society constructs gender differences and relationships is to explore theatrical and ritual transvestism, as Michael Taft (1997) did on the Canadian Prairies when he studied mock weddings. The principal feature of a mock wedding is role reversal: men dress and act like women and sometimes women dress and behave like men. These mock figures are often as much caricatures as stereotypes, reflecting some feature of the identities of the actual wedding pair.

Taft's (1997) study focused on men who dressed as women in these rituals of reversal, which were filled with ludic, or playful, behaviour. He repeatedly asked men why they did this, and the most frequent answer he received was that they were just being "good sports." As good sports, men do not attempt to become women in their role in the mock wedding. In Taft's words, "they play clownish and distorted women. They exaggerate the female physique with over-large breasts and behinds. They mince and wiggle in mockery of femininity" (135).

In this photograph of a mock wedding ritual on the Canadian prairies, transvestism represents a form of gendered social commentary on notions of power, equality, and the position of women in this community.

Thus, these men are expressing their views of women to one another. Taft suggests that one reason men do this may have something to do with the economic conditions of farming on the Prairies. Although farmers or ranchers may *seem* to be independent, in reality they are dangerously dependent on government bureaucrats, subsidies, and the world market. In contrast, women have considerable power on farms and often do the same work as men, besides working part-time off the farm in order to pay the bills. By making fun of women, men may be reasserting their own importance. Whatever the men's motives, Taft (1997, 137) argues that "wherever it is found, theatrical transvestism acts as a sounding board for commentaries on gender relations."

Constructing Stratification by Gender

As discussed earlier, the biases that falsely linked race to biology and intelligence to class also led to the belief in the "natural" (as opposed to socially constructed) superiority of men over women. Many people believed that women's bodies defined both their social position and their function, which was to reproduce, in the same way that men's bodies dictated that they manage, control, and defend.

The view that the biology of females makes them lesser persons than males is embedded in North American cultures, sometimes in subtle ways. An example is the language used by professionals to describe women's bodily processes of menstruation and menopause. Anthropologist Emily Martin (1987) says that during the 19th century, Americans regarded the female body as if it were a factory whose job was to "labour" to produce children. Menopause was viewed negatively because it marked the end of productive usefulness, and menstruation was described as a sign of the failure of the implantation of a fertilized egg. Medical writers of the time, such as Walter Heape, a Cambridge zoologist and militant antisuffragist, described how in menstruation the entire epithelium (cellular tissue) is torn away, "leaving behind a ragged wreck of tissue, torn glands, ruptured vessels, jagged edges of stroma, and masses of blood corpuscles, which it would seem hardly possible to heal satisfactorily without the aid of surgical instruments" (Martin 1987, 35).

According to Martin, the same attitudes toward female reproductive functions that existed in the 19th century persist today, encoded in contemporary medical and biology textbooks. Menstruation is likewise described even today as a breakdown in the reproductive process. When an egg is not implanted, the process is described in negative terms as a disintegration or shedding. Here is one example Martin found:

> The fall in blood progesterone and estrogen "deprives" the "highly developed endometrial lining of its hormonal support," constriction of blood vessels leads to a "diminished" supply of oxygen and nutrients, and finally "disintegration starts, the entire lining begins to slough, and the menstrual flow begins." Blood vessels in the endometrium "hemorrhage" and "the menstrual flow consists of this blood mixed with endometrial debris." The "loss" of hormonal stimulation causes "necrosis" (death of tissue). (Martin 1987, 45)

SOCIAL HIERARCHIES

Another otherwise objective text states that "when fertilization fails to occur, the endometrium is shed, and a new cycle starts. This is why it used to be taught that 'menstruation is the uterus crying for lack of a baby'" (quoted in Martin 1987, 45).

In yet another textbook, menstruation is depicted as a sign of an idle factory, a failed production system, a system producing "scrap" or "waste." However, Martin notes that very different language is used in the same textbooks to describe male reproductive functions. For example, the textbook from which the above description of menstruation is taken describes the production of sperm as follows: "The mechanisms which guide the remarkable cellular transformation from spermatid to mature sperm remain uncertain. Perhaps the most amazing characteristic of spermatogenesis is its sheer magnitude: the normal human male may manufacture several hundred million sperm per day" (Martin 1987, 48).

This text, which describes menstruation as "failed production," fails to mention that only about one of every 100 billion sperm ever makes it far enough to fertilize an egg. Moreover, other bodily processes that are similar to menstruation are not spoken of in terms of breakdown and deterioration. Seminal fluid picks up shredded cellular material as it passes through the male ducts, and the stomach lining is shed periodically. Why are these processes not described in the same negative terms as menstruation? According to Martin, the reason is that both men and women have stomachs, but only women have uteruses. The stomach falls on the positive side, the uterus on the negative.

Rather than describing menstruation as failed production, Martin suggests that it might be more accurate to describe it as the successful avoidance of an egg implant. If a couple has done anything to avoid the implantation of an egg, is it still appropriate to talk of the reproductive cycle in terms of production?

Emily Martin's analysis reveals that in contemporary North American societies, the ideology of gender stratification remains embedded in our language and in our ideas about the bodily functions of males and females. Describing the bodily processes of women in negative terms makes women seem to be lesser human beings. Moreover, describing menstruation and menopause in negative terms leads women themselves to believe that their bodily functions are less clean and less worthy than those of men.

Gender Stratification and the Privileging of Hegemonic Masculinities

All societies have particular images and stereotypes of masculinity and femininity that are privileged as normative—that is, as societal ideals. These ideals of masculinity, for instance, are referred to as **hegemonic masculinity**. Industrialized societies, for example, often view traits such as athleticism, courage, rationality, and heterosexuality as markers of an ideal "manliness."

Hegemonic masculinities are often used to construct gendered hierarchies in societies. For instance, those individuals who fall outside hegemonic gendered ideals are often labelled as "less masculine" than others, which can lead to the proliferation of homophobia and the objectification of women. Canadian anthropologist David Murray (2002), for instance, has studied how performances of a hegemonic masculinity on the Caribbean island of Martinique are dependent on "proving" one's heterosexuality through the aggressive pursuit of women, cat calling, and flirting with the opposite sex. Men who fail to pursue women aggressively are often labelled *macumé,* a derogatory word in Martinique that is equivalent to "sissy." In a society marked by intense homophobia, all men, whatever their sexual orientation, go to great lengths to uphold the norms of hegemonic masculinity

hegemonic masculinity
Refers to ideals and norms of masculinity in a society, which are often privileged over others.

in public settings. To be labelled *macumé* is a social liability, and a man risks physical and verbal abuse if he does not conform to societal ideals of gender.

Hegemonic masculinities are also constructed, performed, and maintained within societies through sports, competitions, and rituals. Fraternities, for instance, are a means of constructing hegemonic masculinities; they are also a way to promote often dangerous gendered hierarchies within university settings, which lead to the objectification, abuse, and marginalization of women.

Peggy Reeves Sanday (2007 [1990]), in her study of college fraternity gang rape, provides a vivid portrait of how male identity is defined and reinforced in American society. Gang rape, or "pulling train," as it is called in fraternities, begins with the coercion of a vulnerable young woman who is seeking acceptance. The ritual incorporates the man into a group whose activities reinforce a male identity, defined largely by the degradation of female identity through sexual conquest and physical abuse. "Pulling train" is both an expression of male sexuality and a display of the brotherhood's power to control and dominate women. In other words, gang rape is but one instance of the abuse and domination that begin during the initiation and that are continued later in relations with women and new pledges.

When a woman is too weak or intoxicated to protest, a "train" of men have sex with her. Gang rape is not limited to college campuses; it is also associated with sports teams, street gangs, and other groups of men for whom the act often serves, according to Sanday, as a male bonding ritual.

Sanday and her associates interviewed fraternity members, women who were associated with them, and victims of rape, seeking to explain what it was about male identity that encouraged these actions. Three things seemed to stand out in her account.

First, there is a heavy emphasis in fraternities on male bonding and male-bonding behaviour, to the extent that a college man's self-esteem and social identity depend on gaining entry to a fraternity and being accepted by the brothers. Fraternities confer status; on most college campuses they are recognized as places "where the action is." They also provide reassurance, security, and a ready-made identity. Membership in a fraternity transforms outsiders into insiders.

Second, sex constitutes a major status and identity marker. Masculinity is defined and demonstrated by sexual conquest. In the fraternity in which the gang rape occurred, a major activity was persuading a woman to have sex. Men who had more success gained status, while those who often failed were in danger of being labelled "nerds" or, worse, "fags." Sex in this case is a public thing. Men in the fraternities that Sanday interviewed bragged publicly about their sexual conquests and arranged for brothers to witness them. Some fraternities posted weekly newsletters listing brothers' sexual conquests.

A third element in the identity of fraternity men concerns their attitudes toward women. Many of the fraternity members in Sanday's study implied that women were sex objects to be abused or debased. A woman's identity among fraternity men was determined largely by her sexual interactions with them. Women who were sexually unresponsive were "frigid," women who allowed advances only up to a point were "cockteasers," and women who had sex with many men were "sluts." Such labels indicate that the role of "girlfriend" is virtually the only role without negative connotations that a woman can play for fraternity men. The debasement of women is interwoven with the themes of male bonding and sexual conquest.

Part of the reason men bond in college, says Sanday, is to achieve the domination and power they think is owed to males. Sanday uses the term "phallocentrism," "the deployment of the penis as a concrete symbol of masculine social power and dominance" (2007 [1990], 40), to describe the use of sex and the debasement of women to demonstrate masculinity. Phallocentrism, as well as the themes of male bonding, sexual prowess, and the debasement of women, are all manifested in the act of pulling train. It is a form of bonding, it publicly legitimizes a male's heterosexuality, and it makes women an object of scorn and abuse.

Sanday is quick to emphasize that not all college men subscribe to the ideology of phallocentrism and that not all fraternity men measure their masculinity by sexual conquest. In the case that initiated her study, all the women who knew them described the six men charged with gang rape as "among the nicest guys in the fraternity." Individually, probably none of them would have committed the act they were charged with. In the context of the fraternity, however, gang rape was the credible outcome of a process of identity formation manifested in fraternity life in general and in the fraternity initiation ritual in particular.

Gender Stratification and the Feminization of Poverty

Throughout the world, gender and age are significantly related to whether a person lives in poverty. In *Women and Children Last* (1986), Ruth Sidel draws an analogy between the doomed ship *Titanic* and society in the United States at the end of the 1980s. Both, she says, were gleaming symbols of wealth that placed women and children at a disadvantage. When the *Titanic* went down, women and children were indeed saved first, but only those who were travelling in first- or second-class accommodations. Women and children in third class and steerage were not saved. Although only 8 percent of the women and 3 percent of the children in first and second class drowned on the night the *Titanic* sank, 45 percent of the women and 70 percent of the children in steerage died. As with the *Titanic*, Sidel says, certain women and children in the United States are not the first to be saved; instead, they are the first to fall into poverty.

Most of the world's poor are women and children. As Michael Todaro, an economist, explains: "[Women] are more likely to be poor and malnourished and less likely to receive medical services, clean water, sanitation, and other benefits" (2000, 172). Female-headed households make up the poorest segments of Third World populations. For instance, as of 2000, 40 percent of all households in Kenya and 20 percent in India had no male wage earners. The percentages have increased since then. Women's potential earnings are far below those of males. Women have less access to education and government employment programs, and are more likely to be employed in the informal sector, where neither wages nor working conditions are regulated. Even in households where there is a male wage earner, women may not have access to the household income. In countries where there is a strong male bias, such as India and China, household resources may be distributed unevenly. In India, it is estimated that "girls are four times more likely to suffer from acute malnutrition and boys are 40 times more likely to be taken to a hospital when ill" (Todaro 2000, 173–74). This imbalance not only results in more female infant deaths, but also contributes to an extremely high female child mortality rate.

When gender is combined with other factors that contribute to poverty, such as indigenous status, women face a combination of risks. Linda Gerber argues that in Canada, Métis, Inuit, and "Indian" women face "multiple jeopardy"—first as women, then as members of a "visible minority," and finally "as residents of uniquely dependent communities" (1990, 72). In the area of education, 7.7 percent of all Canadian females have not completed grade 9, but the percentages are much higher for Métis women (34.8 percent), Inuit women (62 percent), and "Indian" women (35.9 percent) (1990, 75). Moreover, Métis women have an average income 70 percent that of Métis men, Inuit women earn 76 percent of what Inuit men earn, and the average income of "Indian" women is 73 percent that of "Indian" men (1990, 79).

Body Image and Gender Hierarchies

One of the most important identity features for many North Americans is body shape. Although desired body shapes vary cross-culturally and across historical periods, in the West today a thin person is judged to be superior to a heavier person. When researchers asked children aged six to nine to examine three body silhouettes and to describe the kind of person represented by each body type, the children described the "thinner" figure as friendly, kind, happy, and polite, while they described the heavier figure as lazy, lying, and cheating. When ten- and eleven-year-olds were shown drawings of other children, they consistently ranked heavier figures lowest, even below drawings of children with missing limbs or a child in a wheelchair.

Weight is a handicap also in the education system, where teachers perceive heavy children as having more behavioural problems than others and as being less well liked by their classmates. Later in life, people who are overweight face hostile work environments and job discrimination. Workers judged unattractive by their peers—especially women—are consistently described in more negative terms.

The relationship between self-image and body shape is particularly relevant for female adolescents, as anthropologist Mimi Nichter (2000) discovered during a three-year study among high-school girls in Arizona. Adolescent girls are particularly vulnerable to body image issues because during adolescence girls will gain up to 11.5 kilograms of body fat and thus are likely to be more critical of their own bodies. Young girls, says Nichter, are embedded in a morality play in which thinness is good, fatness is bad, and dieting is the way to get in shape. Nichter found that most of the girls in her study were thinking about their bodies either "all of the time" (24 percent) or "a lot of the time" (31 percent) and that 90 percent of white girls in the study were dissatisfied with their weight.

The adolescent girls in Nichter's study formed their idea of the "perfect" body largely from television, films, magazines, and, of course, Barbie. The ideal woman was tall (170 centimetres) and had long hair (preferably blond), long legs, a flat stomach, a clear complexion, and "good" clothes.

Weight, however, was the key factor: being "thin" was believed to be the ticket to happiness and popularity. As with many adult women that Nichter knew, the girls seemed to see the world in terms of fat and thin.

The girls rarely talked about weight with classmates whom they judged to be "fat"; nevertheless, they made moral judgments about them, believing that if someone who was overweight really wanted to lose weight, she could. Not losing weight implied that the girl was unconcerned about her personal appearance or was lazy. The lack of respect for overweight girls, says Nichter, was a theme that emerged repeatedly in discussions with the students. One girl explained:

I have a friend that's overweight and I feel that she should—I mean, I don't have anything against her 'cause she's overweight—but I guess it makes me mad that she doesn't do anything about it. She could do something about it and she doesn't. It's like her responsibility … like last night I went over there and right when I walked in she had a bag of Doritos—she was just, I mean, it's just like she's constantly eating. She's addicted to food. She just can't stop. (Nichter 2000, 42)

EXERCISE 7.2

Men and Body Image

Men rarely talk about dieting, or at least not as much as women do, but concerns about body image are not restricted to women. How, then, do men address the gap between their body image and the cultural ideal represented in advertisements and the media? Do men talk about this issue, and, if so, how is it articulated?

SOCIAL HIERARCHIES

© Lev Dolgachov/Alamy

Anthropologist Mimi Nichter argues that in North America, women and girls are often subjected to, and subject themselves to, moral judgment based on their weight.

Language, Gender, and Racial Hierarchies

Societies provide a social landscape along with the symbols or codes through which a person's place on the landscape is conveyed to others. For individuals these symbols or codes serve as toolboxes from which to fashion an identity. Societies may vary in the extent to which people are allowed to negotiate their place on the landscape, but all allow people some leeway.

Language, as we mentioned, is one tool that people have to signal how they want to be placed in society. Voice pitch, for example, does tend to differ because men's vocal tracts are longer, thus giving men a deeper voice. But children, whose voice tracts do not yet differ in size, will unconsciously lower or raise their pitch to conform to gender expectations; that is why you can usually tell from the voice the gender of a child. As Penelope Eckert and Sally McConnell-Ginet point out in *Language and Gender* (2003), people use language to present themselves as a certain kind of person, to project an attitude or a style, along with gender. All parts of language can be used in this way. The phonology, that is, the sounds, of a language can convey gender. For example, the /s/ sound can be made by pressing the tip of the tongue against the teeth. When pressed against the teeth it is still recognized as /s/, but this creates a slight lisp associated among English speakers in the United States and Canada with femininity in women and gayness in men.

Grammar can signal gender. Thus in French, there are male and female forms of nouns; in English, the third-person singular *he* and *she* force us to differentiate gender. In Japanese there are sentence-final particles that add to or soften the force of an utterance, with so-called women's language characterized as more mild. Thus "I am going" can be said as a mild assertion (*iku wa*), as a neutral assertion (*iku*), or as an emphatic assertion (*iku ze / iku zo*), with the latter being characterized as more masculine.

Whether or not to speak can convey gender. Children, for example, are encouraged to speak or to remain silent. Among the Araucanians of Chile, men are encouraged to talk since it is a sign of masculine intelligence and leadership, while the ideal woman is submissive and silent in her husband's presence.

Conversational styles may also convey gender. Linguist Robin Lakoff (1975) was one of the first to draw attention to the way a woman's identity in society influences how she speaks. Women, said Lakoff, are constrained to minimize their expression of opinion with various linguistic devices such as tag questions ("This election mess is terrible, **isn't it**?"), rising intonations on declaratives ("When will dinner be ready? **Six o'clock**?"), the use of hedges ("That's **kinda** sad" or "It's **probably** dinnertime"), boosters or amplifications ("I'm **so** glad you're here"), indirection (e.g., saying "I've got a dentist's appointment then," to convey an inability or reluctance to meet at that time and asking the other to propose another time).

The general thrust of Lakoff's argument has to do with the relative powerlessness of women stemming from their relatively weak social position. Speaking "as a woman," suggests Lakoff, requires avoiding firm commitment or expressing strong opinions and, in general, being restricted to using a "powerless" language.

Language can also be used to construct others, or groups from which people want to separate themselves. Ward Churchill (1994) discusses the consequences of naming sports teams the "Braves," "Chiefs," "Redskins," "Seminoles," and "Savages," names that he suggests are deeply demeaning to Native Americans. Since apologists claim that this is just "fun," with no harm intended, Churchill suggests that we spread the fun around and use nicknames from other groups to name sports teams, such as the Kansas City "Kikes," the Hanover "Honkies," the Dayton "Dagos," the Wisconsin "Wetbacks," and so on. Churchill draws attention to the way we use language, often unknowingly, that stigmatizes the identities of others.

QUESTION 7.4: HOW ARE DIFFERENT FORMS OF SOCIAL HIERARCHY INTERWOVEN WITH EACH OTHER?

In the preceding section of this chapter, we unpacked a few of the most common forms of social stratification and discussed the ways in which they come to seem natural, inevitable, or commonsense ways of explaining and perpetuating inequality. We have discussed them as separate phenomena, but in practice, different forms of inequality are often experienced as overlapping or interwoven. For instance, as noted earlier, Canada's Aboriginal peoples experience disproportionately high levels of poverty, and Aboriginal women are faced with a "multiple jeopardy" because their gender makes them even more vulnerable to the structural forces of inequality. Furthermore, as we see in the examples below, race and class, or race and immigrant status, or race and gender, often overlap and sustain each other conceptually, as well.

Race, Class, and Social Hierarchies in Brazil

Despite the efforts of some scientists to find a biological basis for racial hierarchies, it should now be clear that race is culturally constructed, as is class. We can now turn our attention to an ethnographic example of how categories such as race and class are negotiated in Brazil. Anthropologist Alexander Edmonds (2010) has explored the ways in which race and class converge in Brazil to form social hierarchies. While conducting his doctoral dissertation fieldwork in Rio de Janeiro, Edmonds noticed that plastic surgery clinics proliferated in urban areas of Brazil. Furthermore, while access to plastic surgery had once been a marker of middle- or upper-class status (due to the high cost of such surgeries), the attainment of physical "beauty" was regarded as a necessary means of achieving social mobility. In Brazil, plastic surgery rates are among the highest in the world, and the government subsidizes plastic surgeries for the working classes. There are even plastic surgeons who practise "charity" surgeries on behalf of the urban poor. "Beauty" is thus a marker of class status and is increasingly viewed as a "right" that should be available for everyone.

SOCIAL HIERARCHIES

Plastic surgery, however, is also a means by which non-white Brazilians can seek to "whiten" their appearance by correcting what some of Edmonds's informants viewed as undesirable—a "Negroid" nose, for instance. In Brazilian society, race exists along a continuum, and white skin and stereotypically "white" facial features are associated with power, privilege, and prestige. Indeed, many of Edmonds's informants, especially young women, did improve their employment prospects, and ultimately their class status, by undergoing plastic surgery. In this context, plastic surgery represents a means by which some Brazilians can "whiten" their bodies and, by extension, improve their social standing in Brazilian society. Interestingly, Brazil has been mythologized as a multicultural nation, and while its citizens are encouraged to celebrate diversity, there exists enormous social pressure to emulate the powerful—that is, the white upper class—in Brazilian society. Racial identity is also understood to be malleable and linked to one's social class: according to a popular Brazilian adage, "money whitens." Ultimately, this ethnographic example highlights the fluid and interconnected nature of social hierarchies such as class and race, as well as the ways in which the conscious manipulation of features like "attractiveness" are viewed as a means of achieving a sense of individual fulfillment, well-being, and status.

Constructing a New Racism

In 2006, a soup kitchen in Paris discovered by chance that poor Muslims and Jews would not eat soup made with pork. Their response? They began making soup only with pork. The soup kitchen leader, Odile Bonnivard, declared that "European civilization and Christian culture is our choice," proclaiming the right to racial preference and initiating a campaign across France labelled "Ours Before the Others" (Goldberg 2009, 179–80).

The "identity soup" campaign, as it came to be called, is an example of **new racism**—based not on biological characteristics but on cultural differences that are assumed to be insurmountable. And counter to the claims by some that we have achieved a "raceless" society, it is just one bit of evidence that racism persists in one form or another. Quite simply, being "white," however "whiteness" is defined, still matters. As such, anthropologist Leith Mullings (2005, 684) says that racism is not a singular phenomenon, but rather, a "relational concept":

a set of practices, structures, beliefs, and representations that transform certain forms of perceived differences, generally regarded as indelible and unchangeable, into inequality. It works through modes of dispossession, which have included subordination, stigmatization, exploitation, exclusion, various forms of physical violence, and sometimes genocide. Racism is maintained and perpetrated through coercion and consent and is rationalized through paradigms of both biology and culture. It is, to varying degrees at specific temporal and special points, interwoven with other forms of inequality, particularly class, gender, sexuality, and nationality.

The fieldwork of Alexander Edmonds, described above, thus demonstrates the way that racism, gender, and class are interwoven in Brazil, but this issue is equally salient in Canada, if in different ways. Despite our policy of multiculturalism, recent immigrants are one group whose collective experiences often exemplify the ways in which new racism is interwoven with other forms of equality. However, one's country of origin and ethnic background may result in very different experiences of these forms of inequality, as we discuss below in reference to recent experiences of Pakistani immigrants to Canada.

> **new racism**
> A form of "soft" racism that posits racial differences as cultural, rather than biological, but which still views such differences as immutable or insurmountable.

Pakistani Immigrant Women and the Construction of the "Sanitized Body"

Anthropologist Lalaie Ameeriar (2012) has conducted fieldwork in Karachi, Pakistan, and in Toronto with women who migrated to Canada for work. In Toronto, her work focused particularly on the kinds of spaces where multiculturalism is negotiated: government offices, settlement services agencies, mosques, cultural festivals, immigration consulting offices, and women's homes; she conducted interviews not only with recent Pakistani immigrants, but also with government workers, translators, mullahs (Islamic clerics or leaders), and non-profit workers. Her work was, at least in part, an effort to understand and contextualize the marginalization and poverty experienced within Toronto's Pakistani community. Despite the fact that many come to Canada as highly skilled professionals, many Pakistani immigrants experience their move to Canada in terms of decline: Pakistani women have an unemployment rate of over 20 percent; Statistics Canada puts the poverty rate for the Pakistani community at 40 percent; and many in the community "become deskilled, working in what are known as 'survival jobs,' such as cashiering, and living in pockets of poverty in marginal parts of the city" (Ameeriar 2012, 511).

Based on her fieldwork, Ameeriar found that there are two contradictory strains of multicultural practice in Canada, both of which she frames in terms of embodiment: there exist simultaneously a denial of the "difference" of immigrant bodies, and a recognition of that very difference. For Pakistani immigrants, this phenomenon was experienced through, on the one hand, the celebration of "multiness" in South Asian cultural festivals and public celebrations; on the other, Pakistani women experienced the "imposition of the dominant culture through government-funded settlement services that institute new ideals of bodily comportment … by teaching them how to dress and act" (509–510).

Ameeriar proposes the concept of "the sanitized sensorium" to understand the forms of embodiment required for inclusion in the multicultural public sphere, including smell and appearance. Her research suggests that, when it comes to the integration of foreign labour in the workplace, multiculturalism is less about getting employers not to discriminate and much more about making oneself, as an immigrant, into someone who will not be discriminated against. For instance, women in a government-funded workshop about finding employment were told, "Don't show up smelling like foods that are foreign to us," "make sure your clothes are clean," "don't wear the shalwar cameeze," and "don't wear headscarves" (509). The painful irony is that while, foreign food smells, clothes, and practices are deemed repugnant or inappropriate when too closely associated with immigrant bodies, when disembodied—at cultural festivals, restaurants, and stores—the same smells are fragrant, the clothes deemed beautifully exotic, and the practices considered entertaining. Pakistani women, many of whom do most of the cooking for their families at home, and who are routinely exhorted by government agencies to "dress plainly," find themselves particularly vulnerable to these contradictions when seeking employment. Their often impressive education and qualifications are not enough to overcome this. In this way, the body of the Other is sanitized, and the "Canadian" body is rendered neutral (that is, non-immigrant and non-racialized). At the same time, the smell of food becomes both a private "problem" for Pakistani immigrant women (one with real, negative socioeconomic consequences) and a "public, commodified, accessible form of pleasure for white Canadian consumption" (510).

EXERCISE 7.3

In Canada, we tend to pride ourselves on being an accepting, multicultural nation. However, there are many examples of embedded or institutionalized racism in our society. Select a recent Canadian newspaper or magazine article that offers an example of embedded racism. By "recent," we mean published within the past two years. Provide a brief overview of the article, and outline how institutionalized racism is at work.

QUESTION 7.5: CAN A NON-STRATIFIED COMMUNITY EXIST WITHIN A LARGE SOCIETY?

Many people who are convinced of the harmful effects of social stratification believe nevertheless that in a modern, industrial society, the system is inevitable. It may be possible for the Inuit or the Ju/'hoansi to have a relatively egalitarian society, for example, but it is not possible in a modern, industrial state. Yet for thousands of years, there have been attempts by groups in stratified societies to create classless, egalitarian, utopian social settings. Christianity began as a utopian dream of universal equality, and the idea of a real-life utopia emerged with the idea that man, under God, has the power to create an earthly paradise. Among the earliest expressions of this idea was Christian communalism, which led to the founding of Catholic monastic orders: isolated, virtually self-sufficient communities in which the work was collective and egalitarian. In the 19th century, industrialists such as Robert Owen endeavoured to build utopian factory communities, and Karl Marx's goal was to build a national-utopian society. All of these efforts to construct utopian societies are evidence of the long history of the search for an egalitarian social order.

Anthropologist Charles Erasmus (1977) examined hundreds of utopian communities in an effort to discover why most failed, but some succeeded. He concluded that the main problem for these communities is trying to motivate community members to work and contribute to the common good without the promise of individual material rewards, status, or prestige. Of the successful utopian communities in North America, the most notable are those of the Hutterites, a Christian Protestant sect that originated in Moravia in the 16th century. Why did the Hutterites succeed while so many others failed? Is it possible to use communities such as theirs as models for modern egalitarian communities?

The Hutterites and the Colony of Heaven

"If there will ever be a perfect culture it may not be exactly like the Hutterites—but it will be similar." These words of a member of a Hutterite colony express the feeling that the group has succeeded in building utopian communities. The Hutterites originated during the Protestant Reformation. In 1528 they began to establish colonies throughout what are now Germany, Austria, and Russia. Their pacifism and refusal to perform military service brought them into conflict with European governments, and, in 1872, to avoid conscription, they immigrated to the United States and established colonies in South Dakota. During the First World War, a confrontation over military conscription with state and federal authorities in the United States resulted in the imprisonment of Hutterite men in Alcatraz, where some of them died from abusive treatment. As a consequence, many colonies moved to Canada and settled in Alberta and Saskatchewan. Although a significant number of Hutterites returned to the United States after 1920, many remained in western Canada. By the early 1970s there were more than 37,000 Hutterites in the United States and more than 21,000 in Canada. Peter Stephenson, a Canadian anthropologist, has conducted long-term fieldwork among Hutterite communities in western Canada.

Cooperation is valued in Hutterite society, where community members worship, work, and eat as a group. Here, women are shown preparing a meal for the entire community.

The goal of Hutterites is to create a "colony of heaven." Drawing their inspiration from the Old and New Testaments of the Christian Bible, the Hutterites believe in communal living and the proper observance of religious practice. They reject competition, violence, and war and believe that property is to be used, not possessed. They respect the need for government but do not believe they should involve themselves in it or hold public office. A Hutterite colony is governed by an elected board that includes the religious leaders and the community teacher, so authority is group centred. It is a family-based, agricultural community in which everyone is expected to contribute to the work and to share equally in the bounty. Unlike the Amish, whose beliefs they in essence share, the Hutterites accept and use modern technology; they are acknowledged to be among the most successful agriculturists in North America. Hutterite colonies in Canada are often million-dollar farm enterprises, and because no labour costs are involved in their farming expenses, the colonies are able to maintain a competitive edge on other farmers in Canada.

It is important to keep in mind that Hutterites are not totally egalitarian. Their society is ranked by age and gender; members do not participate in decision making until they are baptised and married. Baptism is a very important event in a Hutterite community because it marks a person's entry into adulthood. Until a member is baptised, that person is not thought to be "morally accountable for his or her actions and thoughts" (Stephenson 1991, 127). Although women are considered intellectually and physically inferior to men, Hutterites reject the unequal distribution of wealth as well as competition among members for status, prestige, or personal possessions. Hutterites minimize competition by renouncing private adornment and ostentatious displays of wealth and by practising collective consumption. There is little difference in dress, and adornment is usually frowned on. All the housing is plain and utilitarian. And, as in most Christian communes, the Hutterites are careful to indoctrinate their children against competition within the colony. Children are taught to avoid seeking honours or placing themselves above others. They are taught never to envy others.

One way Hutterites build commitment to the group is through frequent face-to-face interaction. Members eat together in a communal dining hall, work together, and meet frequently to discuss the affairs of the community. Almost every evening the entire community gathers for a church service. Although the Hutterites have no formal means of punishing those who violate group rules, they do practise a form of ostracism called *den Frieden nehmen*, "taking away the individual's peace of mind." An ostracized man, for example, is not allowed to talk to other members, including his own wife. He may also be assigned a special room in which to sleep apart and may be required to eat alone.

Stephenson points out that social movements have difficulty maintaining long-range goals, especially as wealth accumulates. The Hutterites address this problem by dividing the communities, or branching, every 15 years. During a 15-year period, each community saves a portion of its earnings to purchase additional land, build houses and barns, and accumulate necessary machines and livestock to start a new colony. When the new physical facilities are complete, members of the community draw lots to determine which families will relocate. Branching provides each Hutterite community with a tangible goal. Wealthier colonies that delay branching are often disrupted by internal quarrels and become examples of the danger of failing to branch on schedule. Branching also has a built-in renewal factor; new communities reproduce the founding enthusiasm and ideals. If there is competition, it is between colonies, rather than individuals.

In sum, the Hutterites, by a collective effort, have created within the larger societies of Canada and the United States communities without poverty, without economic classes, and with little or no crime, where each person, without the promise of material reward, contributes to the common good. There are, however, some negatives: the Hutterites are a Christian

Bible–based religious community that teaches male supremacy and severely limits individual freedoms. Nonetheless, it is worth asking whether cooperative communities, such as Hutterites, can serve as a model for the poor in the larger society; that is, does the establishment of closed, collective communities offer a solution to the endemic poverty of those at the bottom level of modern society, and does the success of Hutterites suggest that it is within our means to build societies without poverty?

EXERCISE 7.4

Imagine for a moment that you have just been hired by NASA (National Aeronautics and Space Administration) to plan the development of the first human extraterrestrial settlement. NASA wants you to use your knowledge of other societies to build an ideal community, avoiding the problems of modern society. How would you go about the task? For example, what communities or societies that you know about might you choose as models for an extraterrestrial settlement? Which core values would you build into your community? How would people be rewarded for the work they performed? How would you maintain order and settle conflicts? What kind of education system would you propose? Finally, what are the most serious problems in modern society that you would want to avoid?

QUESTION 7.6: HOW CAN ANTHROPOLOGY BE APPLIED TO ALLEVIATE THE EFFECTS OF INEQUALITY?

It is all too easy, and perhaps even understandable, to resign oneself to hopelessness or helplessness when it comes to permanently alleviating poverty and oppression caused by social stratification. Inequality, as we discussed earlier, is striking and is growing worse both within wealthy countries and between the rich and the poor countries of the world. Worse yet, inequality produces differential access to life's necessities—food, water, shelter, healthcare, and protection from torture and cruel punishment and polluted environments. The question is, of course, what can be done to alleviate these problems, and what role might anthropology play in addressing them?

There are various ways that a background in anthropology is relevant for dealing with problems stemming from inequality. Anthropology prepares people for careers in, for example, delivering health services, administering treatment programs, counselling dysfunctional families, and finding the connections between old age and depression. We have already examined in previous sections anthropological work in the areas of economic development, HIV/AIDS prevention, and counselling for adolescent girls. But perhaps some of the most significant contributions that can be made by people with a background in anthropology are in the design and implementation of measures to protect people from human rights abuses.

Anthropology and Human Rights

The idea of individual rights comes to us from the 17th- and 18th-century Enlightenment, as codified most notably by Thomas Jefferson in the U.S. *Declaration of Independence*. That idea, however, is clearly biased by the notion of the egocentric view of society (discussed in Chapter 6). However, some of the rights outlined in the *Universal Declaration of Human Rights*,[2] adopted on 10 December 1948 by the General Assembly of the United Nations, could be extended across cultures. These might include the right to be free of the threat of torture or cruel, inhuman, or degrading treatment or punishment,

---

[2] You can access the *Universal Declaration of Human Rights* at http://www. un.org/Overview/rights.html.

Spirituality, Religion, and Shamanism

IN THIS CHAPTER
YOU WILL LEARN TO

- Articulate how religion is related to other parts of a cultural system.

- Distinguish a cross-cultural variety of supernatural beings and spiritual forces.

- Compare different types of rituals and their functions in society.

- Describe how religions legitimize spiritual leadership.

- Recognize why places become sacred sites and turn into pilgrimage destinations.

- Explain beliefs in evil magic, or witchcraft, linking this to fear and social control.

- Interpret why shamanic healing is thought to be effective.

- Analyze the connection between cultural upheaval and new religious movements.

Religions play an important role in determining cultural identity in many societies across the globe, sometimes overruling other major identity markers such as kinship, social class, and ethnicity or nationality. From an anthropological point of view, spirituality and religion are part of a cultural system's *superstructure*, earlier defined as the collective body of ideas, beliefs, and values by which members of a culture make sense of the world and their place in it. In contrast to theology or other disciplines, anthropology examines the entirety of shared concepts concerning the ultimate shape and substance of reality in terms of a people's **worldview**.

Notably, just 16 percent of the world's population is categorized as nonreligious (**Figure 13.1**). A small minority in that category is atheist, a broad label covering a range of worldviews, including individually held spiritual beliefs that do not fit any formally institutionalized religion.

As touched on in earlier chapters, and here discussed in greater detail, the superstructure of cultural systems is intricately connected with the infrastructure and social structure. Guided by our barrel model, we therefore expect adaptations in the superstructure when there are technological, economic, social, and/or political changes. Based on that principle, worldwide transformations in the ideological landscape are to be anticipated as an integral component of globalization. Reviewing world history for the past few thousand years, scholars recognize radical transformations in religious and spiritual beliefs and rituals everywhere. Taking the long view, we discover that, like political states discussed in the previous chapter, most religions we know today are, in fact, not that old. And even those that appear to be old are quite different from when they began.

In this chapter we offer a cross-cultural review and comparative historical perspective on a wide range of spiritual traditions and religions. We explain how societies have developed worldviews concerning the non-ordinary, mysterious, transcendental, supernatural, or metaphysical—cultural superstructures with particular repertoires of spiritual beliefs, ritual practices, and religious institutions, often considered sacred or holy.

worldview The collective body of ideas that members of a culture generally share concerning the ultimate shape and substance of their reality.

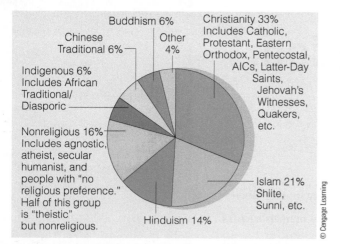

Figure 13.1 Major Religions of the World This chart shows the world's major religions with percentages of their adherents. The total adds up to more than 100 percent due to rounding. Two have enormous followings: Christianity, with almost 2.2 billion adherents (half of whom are Roman Catholic), and Islam, with about 1.7 billion (an overwhelming majority of whom are Sunnis). Within both religions are numerous major and minor divisions, splits, and sects.

Sources: adherents.com; Pew Research Center, 2011.

Roles of Spirituality and Religion

Among people in all societies, particular spiritual or religious beliefs and practices fulfill individual and collective psychological and emotional needs. They reduce anxiety by providing an orderly view of the universe and answers to existential questions, including those concerning suffering and death. They provide a path by which people transcend the burdens of mortal existence and attain, if only momentarily, hope and relief.

Spiritual or religious beliefs and practices also serve numerous cultural purposes. For instance, a religion held in common by a group of people reinforces community values and provides moral guidelines for personal conduct. It also offers narratives and rituals used to confirm a social hierarchy and sanction political power; conversely, it may allow for narratives *countering* the legitimacy of powerholders, even providing justifications and rituals to resist and challenge them. Last but not least, people often turn to religion or spirituality in the hope of reaching a specific goal, such as restoring health, securing a harvest, ending violence, or being rescued from danger (Figure 13.2).

Figure 13.2 Bugi Sailors Praying, Indonesia The Bugi of Sulawesi (Celebes) are famous for their oceangoing schooners. For generations, these Indonesian seafarers have plied the waters between Malaysia and Australia, transporting spices and other freight. Life at sea is risky—sudden storms, piracy, and other mishaps—and sailors pray for safety. This prayerful Bugi gathering in Jakarta on Java Island took place on a holiday ending Ramadan, the Islamic month of fasting. During that time Muslims refrain from eating, drinking liquids, smoking, and sexual activities, from sunrise to sunset. This taboo serves to purify thought and build restraint for Allah's sake.

Anthropologists recognize that not everyone believes in a supernatural force or entity, but they also agree that there is no known culture that does not provide some set of ideas about existence beyond ordinary and empirically verifiable reality, or—for lack of a better word—ideas concerning the supernatural or metaphysical. Because such ideas serve cultural purposes and fulfill emotional and psychological needs, it makes sense that spirituality and religion developed tens of thousands of years ago and spread across the globe.

In the wake of major technological inventions and new discoveries since the 1600s, European intellectuals predicted that magic, myth, and religion would be replaced by empirical research, proven facts, and scientific theories. They expected that as science progressed, beliefs and rituals based on what they argued to be ignorance and superstition would gradually disappear. Some even forecasted the end of religion altogether. But to date, and despite tremendous scientific achievements, that has not occurred. In many places, the opposite trend seems to prevail, in particular where radical technological, social, and economic transformations destabilize the long-established cultural order, challenge deeply embedded worldviews, and leave people feeling insecure and threatened. Confronted by sweeping changes over which people have little or no control, many turn to religion and spirituality.

Anthropological Approach to Spirituality and Religion

Worldwide, people are inspired and guided by strongly held ideas about the supernatural, putting into practice what they deeply believe to be true or right. It is not the responsibility of anthropologists to pass judgment on the metaphysical truth of any particular faith system, but it is their challenge to show how each embodies a number of revealing facts about humanity and the particular cultural superstructure, or worldview, within which these religious or spiritual beliefs are ideologically embedded.

Based on a cross-cultural and comparative historical perspective on worldviews, we define **religion** as an organized system of ideas about the spiritual sphere or the supernatural, along with associated ceremonial practices by which people try to interpret and/or influence aspects of the universe otherwise beyond their access or control. Similar to religion, **spirituality** is concerned with the sacred, as distinguished from ordinary reality, but it is often individual rather than collective and

does not require a formal institution. Both indicate that many aspects of the human experience are thought to be beyond natural or scientific explanation.

Because no culture, including those of modern industrial and postindustrial societies, has achieved complete certainty in controlling existing or future conditions and circumstances of human life, spirituality and/or religion continue to play a role in all known cultures. However, considerable variability exists globally (**Figure 13.3**).

At one end of the anthropological spectrum are food-foraging peoples, whose technological ability to control their natural environment is limited. Broadly speaking, they hold that nature is pregnant with the spiritual. Embedded and manifested in all aspects of their culture, spirituality permeates their daily activities—from food hunting or gathering to making fires, building homes, and conversations about life before or after death. It also mirrors and confirms the egalitarian nature of social relations in their societies, in that individuals do not plead with high-ranking deities for aid the way members of stratified societies more typically do. Their holistic worldview is often referred to as *naturalistic*, an imprecise but workable term.

At the other end of our spectrum are state societies with commercial or industrial economies, sophisticated technologies, and social stratification based on a complex division of labor. There, high-ranking social groups typically seek to control and manage the construction of a society's worldview as an ideological means of legitimizing and reinforcing their vested interests in its hierarchical structure. Usually featuring a ranked order of supernatural beings—for instance, God and (in some religions) the angels, saints, or other holy figures—it simultaneously reflects and reinforces the stratified system in which it is embedded. In such societies, religion tends to be less integrated into everyday activities, and its practice is usually confined to specific times, occasions, and locations.

Religions provide a powerful ideology justifying inequality in a state society, but may also inspire subordinated peoples to envision an alternative social order freeing them from exploitation, repression, and humiliation. Thus, religiously motivated social movements have challenged political establishments.

---

religion An organized system of ideas about the spiritual sphere or the supernatural, along with associated ceremonial practices by which people try to interpret and/or influence aspects of the universe otherwise beyond their control.

spirituality Concern with the sacred, as distinguished from material matters. In contrast to religion, spirituality is often individual rather than collective and does not require a distinctive format or traditional organization.

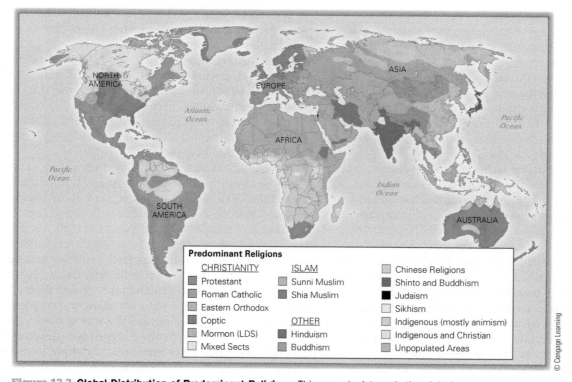

Figure 13.3 Global Distribution of Predominant Religions This map depicts only the global distribution of major religions, indicating where they predominate. In some areas, the mixture of different religions is such that no single faith is shared by most of that region's inhabitants. Not detailed enough to show pockets with significant numbers of a particular faith, it also omits many religions that are dispersed or eclipsed by others—including several worldwide ones such as Ahmadiyya (a Muslim sect, with 10 million adherents); Jehovah's Witnesses (a Christian sect with 7 million adherents); and Bahá'í (with 6 million adherents, emphasizing the spiritual unity of all mankind and recognizing divine messengers from various religions).

Myth and the Mapping of a Sacred Worldview

Because much remains beyond human capacity to actually observe and explain based on obvious or empirical evidence alone, people have creatively worked out narratives explaining the fundamentals of human existence—where we and everything in our world came from, why we are here, and where we are going. Describing a worldview, these narratives are referred to as **myths** (*mythos*, Greek for "word," "speech") and play a fundamental role in religious and spiritual beliefs. Mapping a people's *cosmology*—their understanding of the universe, its form and working—myths are believed to be true, even sacred, by those subscribing to the particular worldview engendering such narratives.

Typically, a myth features supernatural forces or beings engaged in extraordinary or miraculous performances. It may offer a morality play, providing an ethical code for its audience and guidelines for human behavior. For example, the Puranas (a body of religious texts, including cosmological myths, considered sacred by Buddhists and Hindus) are rich in such material. So are the Bible, Koran, and Torah, each held sacred in distinct but historically related religions originating in Southwest Asia. We will discuss myths further within the context of art in the next chapter, but here it is important to underscore that these stories, whether orally transmitted or in writing, have been passed on from generation to generation and inform believers with a sacred map of the cosmos or universe and their place in it.

Supernatural Beings and Spiritual Forces

A hallmark of religion is belief in spiritual forces and supernatural beings. Attempting to control by religious means what cannot be controlled in other ways, humans turn to prayer, sacrifice, and other religious or spiritual rituals. Their actions presuppose the existence of spiritual forces that can

---

myth A sacred narrative that explains the fundamentals of human existence—where we and everything in our world came from, why we are here, and where we are going.

Figure 13.4 Judeo-Christian God Giving Life to Adam The patriarchal nature of traditional Euramerican society is depicted on the ceiling of the Sistine Chapel in Rome, Italy. The image of a supreme male diety creating the first man, named Adam ("human being"), is culturally articulated and ideologically justified by its Judeo-Christian theology. Afterward, according to this biblical story, the first woman, named Eve, is formed from Adam's rib.

be tapped into, or supernatural beings interested in human affairs and available for aid. In many cultures, these supernatural forces or spiritual beings are associated with unique geographic locations valued as sacred sites—extraordinary rocks, lakes, wells, waterfalls, mountains, and so forth.

Supernatural beings can be divided into three categories: deities (gods and goddesses), ancestral spirits, and other sorts of spirit beings. Although the variety of deities and spirits recognized by the world's cultures is tremendous, it is possible to make certain generalizations about them.

Gods and Goddesses

Not all religions *anthropomorphize* the divine, but many do. Symbolically constructing a divine order that mirrors a society's gender structure, many religions recognize male and female deities. Gods and goddesses, or divinities, are the great and more remote supernatural beings. Generally speaking, cultures that subordinate women to men attribute masculine gender to the more powerful gods or supreme deity. For instance, in traditional Christian religions believers speak of God as a father who had a divine son born from a human mother but do not entertain thoughts of God as a mother or as a divine daughter (Figure 13.4). Such male-privileging religions developed in many societies traditionally based on the herding of animals or intensive agriculture, frequent warfare, and politics controlled by men.

Goddesses, by contrast, are likely to be prominent in societies where women play a significant role in the economy and enjoy relative equality with men. Such societies are most often those that depend on crop cultivation traditionally carried out solely or mostly by women. Typically, these may feature fertility and earth goddesses.

Some religions recognize deities represented as male–female combinations. For example, one of the Greek gods, also recognized in the Roman empire, was Hermaphroditus, the beautiful two-sexed son of Hermes (alias Mercury) and Venus (alias Aphrodite). A similar third-gender divinity is recognized by Hindus worshiping Ardhanarishvara ("the Lord who is half woman").

If a religion recognizes only one supremely powerful divinity as creator and master of the universe, we speak of **monotheism**. If it acknowledges more than one divinity, each governing a particular domain, we label it **polytheism**. Gods and goddesses of ancient Greece illustrate the latter: Zeus ruled the sky, Poseidon the sea, and Hades the underworld and the dead. In addition to these three brothers, Greek mythology features a host of other deities, both male and female, each similarly concerned with specific aspects of life and the universe. Athena and Nike, for instance, were goddesses of war and victory, respectively. A **pantheon**, or the collection of gods and goddesses such as those of the Greeks, is common in many religions, today most famously in Hinduism.

Because states typically have grown through conquest, often their pantheons have expanded, with local deities of conquered peoples being incorporated into the official state pantheon. A frequent feature of pantheons is the presence of a supreme deity, who may be all but totally ignored by humans. Aztecs of the Mexican highlands, for instance, recognized a supreme duo to whom they paid little attention. Assuming this divine pair was unlikely to be interested in ordinary humans, they devoted themselves to lesser deities thought to be more directly concerned with human affairs.

Ancestral Spirits

Beliefs in ancestral spirits support the concept that human beings consist of intertwined components: body/matter (physical) and mind/soul (spiritual). This dualistic concept carries with it the possibility of a spirit being freed from the body—through dream, trance, or death—and even having a separate existence. Frequently, where a belief in

---

monotheism The belief in only one supremely powerful divinity as creator and master of the universe.

polytheism The belief in multiple gods and/or goddesses, as contrasted with monotheism—the belief in one god or goddess.

pantheon All the gods and goddesses of a people.

ancestral spirits exists, these nonphysical beings are seen as retaining an active interest and membership in society.

Beliefs in ancestral spirits are found in many parts of the world, especially among people having unilineal descent systems with their associated ancestor orientation. In several African cultures, the concept is highly elaborate, and people believe ancestral spirits behave much like humans. They are able to feel hot, cold, and pain and may even die a second death by drowning or burning. Because spirits sometimes participate in family and lineage events, seats will be provided for them, even though they are invisible. If spirits are annoyed, they may send sickness or death. Eventually, they are reborn as new members of their lineage, so adults need to observe infants closely to determine just who has been reborn.

Ancestor spirits also play an important role in the patrilineal society of traditional China. Giving birth to sons is historically regarded as an obligation to the ancestors because boys inherit their father's ancestral duties. For the gift of life, a boy is forever indebted to his parents, owing them obedience, deference, and a comfortable old age. Even after their death, he has to provide for them in the spirit world, placing food, money, and incense on ancestral altars on the anniversaries of their births and deaths.

Other Types of Supernatural Beings and Spiritual Forces

Animism

One widespread concept concerning supernatural beings is **animism**, a belief that nature is enlivened or energized by distinct personalized spirit beings separable from physical bodies or the material substance they inhabit. Spirits such as souls and ghosts are thought to dwell in humans, animals, and plants, as well as human-made artifacts and natural features such as stones, mountains, and wells; for animists, the world is filled with particular spirits.

These spirit beings are a highly diverse lot. Less remote than gods and goddesses, they may be benevolent, malevolent, or just plain neutral. Involved in people's daily affairs, they also may be awesome, terrifying, lovable, or mischievous. Because they may be pleased or irritated by human actions, people are obliged to be concerned about them.

Animism is typical of those who see themselves as being a part of nature rather than superior to it (Figure 13.5). This includes most food foragers and food gardeners, among others. Deities, if they are believed to exist at all in such societies, may be seen as having created the world and perhaps making it fit to live in; but in animism, spirits are the ones to beseech when ill, the ones to help or hinder the shaman, and the ones whom the ordinary hunter may meet when off in the wilderness.

Animatism

Although supernatural power is often thought of as being vested in spirit beings, it does not have to be. Such is the case with **animatism**—the belief that nature is enlivened or energized by an impersonal force or supernatural energy, which may make itself manifest in any special place, thing, or living creature. This basic concept, which probably developed well before the first transition from food foraging to food production 10,000 years ago, is still present in many societies around the

Figure 13.5 Inuit Food Ritual Inuit of Arctic Canada refer to spirit beings as *anirniit* (singular *anirniq*, meaning "breath") and still obey certain taboos and perform rituals when killing game animals and dividing the meat. This is to avoid offending the animal's spirit (which remains alive and may take revenge on the hunter). Today, most Inuit are Christians, and their concept of *anirniq* is akin to "soul." But traditional food rituals continue. In this photo, Inuit at Baffin Island pray before a shared Easter feast of fish and seal meat.

world today. For example, in China it appears in the form of a concept known as *qi* (or *ch'i*), which may be translated as "vital energy." Inuit people in Arctic Canada think of this force in terms of a "cosmic breath-soul" they call *sila*. In northeastern America, Algonquian-speaking indigenous peoples refer to impersonal spirit power as *manitou*.

One of the best-studied examples of animatism can be found in the Pacific where Oceanic peoples inhabiting hundreds of islands share a concept they refer to as *mana*. Not unlike the idea of a cosmic energy passing into and through everything, affecting living and nonliving matter alike, *mana* is probably best defined as "supernaturally conferred potency" (Keesing, 1992, p. 236)—similar to "the force" in the *Star Wars* films. Traditional Maori, Tahitians, Tongans, and other Oceanic peoples typically attribute success (identified by actual achievements such as triumph in combat, bountiful harvest, abundant fish or game, and so on) to *mana*—and see it as proof of *mana*. In short, this metaphysical concept rests on pragmatic evidence.

Animism (a belief in distinct spirit beings) and animatism (which lacks particular substance or individual form) are not mutually exclusive and are often found in the same culture. This is the case among the Inuit pictured in Figure 13.5, who believe in spirit beings known as *anirniit* as well as in the impersonal spirit power they call *sila* (Merkur, 1983).

In many religious traditions, certain geographic places are thought to be spiritually significant or are held sacred for various reasons, including ideas here discussed in terms of animism and animatism. Typically, such sites are rivers, lakes, waterfalls, islands, forests, caves, and—especially—mountains. We revisit the topic of sacred sites later in the chapter.

Religious Specialists

Most cultures include individuals who guide others in their spiritual search and ritual practices. Thought to be inspired, enlightened, or even holy, they command respect for their skills in contacting and influencing spiritual beings and manipulating or connecting to supernatural forces. Often, they display unique personality traits that make them particularly well suited to perform these tasks for which they have undergone special training.

Priests and Priestesses

In societies with resources to support a full-time religious specialist, a **priest or priestess** will be authorized to perform sacred rituals and mediate between fellow humans and supernatural powers, divine spirits, or deities. In many societies, they are familiar figures known by official titles such as *lama, kahuna, imam, priest, minister, rabbi, swami,* or *copa pitào*. How they dress, what they eat, where they live, and numerous other indicators may distinguish them from others in society and symbolically indicate their special status.

Reserving exclusive rights to exercise spiritual power, groups of priests and/or priestesses bond together in an effort to monopolize the means of sacred practice. This includes controlling holy sites of worship, supervising prescribed rituals, and maintaining possession of regalia, relics, statues, images, texts, and other representations of holiness. In so doing, they also create, promote, and maintain the ideological sources needed to symbolically construct the religious authority from which they derive their legitimacy.

When deities are identified in masculine terms, it is not surprising that the most important religious leadership positions are reserved for men. Such is the case in Judaism, Islam, as well as the Roman Catholic Church, the latter of which has always been headed by a male pope and his all-male council, the College of Cardinals.

Female religious specialists are likely to be found only in societies in which women are acknowledged to significantly contribute to the economy, and gods and goddesses are both recognized (Lehman, 2002). Also, all around the world women fully devoted to a religious life have formed their own gender-segregated institutions such as all-female convents headed by an abbess. Such nunneries not only exist in countries with longstanding Christian traditions, but were also founded in the Himalayas and many other Buddhist regions in southern and eastern Asia, including Taiwan, as described by American anthropologist Hillary Crane in the Biocultural Connection on the next page.

Spiritual Lineages: Legitimizing Religious Leadership

As with political institutions discussed in the previous chapter, religious organizations are maintained by rules that define ideological boundaries, establish membership criteria, and regulate continuity of legitimate leadership in the faith community. And, like other institutions, religions have always been challenged by changes. Even in a highly stable cultural system, every generation must deal with natural transitions in the life cycle, including death

---

animism The belief that nature is enlivened or energized by distinct personalized spirit beings separable from bodies.

animatism The belief that nature is enlivened or energized by an impersonal spiritual force or supernatural energy, which may make itself manifest in any special place, thing, or living creature.

priest or priestess A full-time religious specialist formally recognized for his or her role in guiding the religious practices of others and for contacting and influencing supernatural powers.

BIOCULTURAL CONNECTION

Change Your Karma and Change Your Sex?

By Hillary Crane

As Mahayana Buddhists, Taiwanese Chan (Zen) monastics believe that all humans are able to reach enlightenment and be released from reincarnation. But they believe it is easier for some because of the situation into which they are born—for example, if one is born in a country where Buddhism is practiced, in a family that teaches proper behavior, or with exceptional mental or physical gifts.

Chan monastics view contrasting human circumstances as the result of the karma accrued in previous lives. They believe certain behavior—such as diligently practicing Buddhism—improves karma and the chances of attaining spiritual goals in this lifetime or coming back

in a better birth. Other behavior—such as killing a living being, eating meat, desiring or becoming attached to things or people—accrues bad karma.

One way karma manifests itself is in one's sex. Taiwanese Buddhists believe that being born female makes it harder to attain spiritual goals. This idea comes, in part, from the inferior status of women in Taiwan and the belief that their "complicated bodies" and monthly menstruation cycles can distract them. Moreover, they believe, women are more enmeshed in their families than men, and their emotional ties keep them focused on worldly rather than spiritual tasks.

Taiwanese Buddhists who decide to become monks and nuns must break from their families to enter a monastery. Because women are thought to be more attached to their families than are men, leaving home is seen as a particularly big step for nuns and a sign that they are more like men than most women. In fact, a nun's character is considered masculine, unlike the frightened, indecisive, and emotional traits usually associated with women in Taiwan. When they leave home nuns even stop referring to themselves as women and call one another *shixiong* ("dharma brother"). They use this linguistic change to signal that they identify themselves as men and to remind one another to behave like men, particularly like the monks at the temple.

Monastics also reduce their attachments to worldly things like music and food. Nuns usually emphasize forsaking food and eat as little as possible. Their appearance, already quite masculine because they shave their heads and wear loose, gray clothing, becomes even more so when they lose weight—particularly in their hips, breasts, and thighs. Also, after becoming monastics, they often experience a slowing or stopping of their menses. Although these physical changes can be attributed to change in diet and lifestyle, the nuns point to them as signs they are becoming men, making progress toward their spiritual goals, and improving their karma.

BIOCULTURAL QUESTION
The Zen Buddhist ideal of enlightenment, realized when the soul is released from reincarnation, prescribes an extreme ascetic lifestyle for nuns that makes them physically incapable of biological reproduction. Do you think that their infertility allows these female monastics to emotionally adapt to a way of life that denies them motherhood?

Written expressly for this text, 2008. For a more detailed treatment of this topic, see Crane, H. (2001). Men in spirit: The masculinization of Taiwanese Buddhist nuns. Ph.D dissertation, Brown University.

---

of religious leaders. In many religions, spiritual leadership is thought to be vested in divine authority, representing or even embodying the divine itself. How do religions secure legitimate successors and avoid disruption and confusion?

spiritual lineage A principle of leadership in which divine authority is passed down from a spiritual founding figure, such as a prophet or saint, to a chain of successors.

Several major religions follow a principle of leadership in which divine authority is passed down from a spiritual founding figure, such as a prophet or saint, to a chain of successors who derive legitimacy as religious leaders from their status in such a lineage. Here identified as **spiritual lineage**, this principle has been worked out in numerous cross-cultural variations over the course of thousands of years. It not only applies to leadership of entire religions but to segmental divisions of religions, such as sects and orders.

Whereas kings in traditional political dynasties derive legitimacy from their ancestral blood lineage, religious leaders obtain it from their spiritual line of descent as specified in each particular religious tradition. The longer these lineages have existed, the greater their opportunities for building up a fund of symbolic capital—ideas and rituals, including sacred gestures, dances, songs, and texts. This fund also includes regalia, paintings, statues, and sacred architecture such as shrines, tombs, and temples, along with the land on which they stand. Thus, some religious leaders and their followers have accumulated a considerable amount of material wealth utilized in the exercise of religious authority, in addition to the immaterial holdings of traditional knowledge and sacred rituals.

Here, to illustrate the cross-cultural range of spiritual lineages, we distinguish four major forms. First, in some religions, spiritual leaders or high-ranking priests claim divine authority based on recognized biological descent from a common ancestor believed to have been a prophet, saint, or otherwise sacred, holy, or even divine being. Such is the case with *kohanim*, high-ranking Israelite priests, claiming patrilineal descent from the legendary high priest Aaron believed to have lived about 3,500 years ago.

In other religions, leaders personally groom, train, and appoint a spiritual heir, a successor tasked with guarding and continuing the spiritual legacy of the order or sect as established by its founder. For example, a sect of Muslim mystics known as Sufi is widely dispersed across Asia and North Africa and historically divided into many dozens of orders, or brotherhoods. Each brotherhood is headed by a master teacher, known by an honorific title such as *sheikh*. The sheikh derives his spiritual authority from his position in a *silsila* (Arabic, meaning "chain"), named after a founding saint who originally laid down a particular method of prayer and ritual practiced by followers seeking oneness with God (Abun-Nasr, 2007; Anjum, 2006).

A third form of legitimizing the authority of a religious leader is by election. In such cases, a group of leading elders comes together in a ritual gathering at a traditionally designated location and chooses one of their own to succeed the deceased leader. One of the best-known examples in world history is the election of a pope by a group of cardinals— "princes" of the Roman Catholic Church who proclaim the new pope to be the divinely ordained spiritual heir of St. Peter, Vicar of Christ. Believed by 1.2 billion Christians to hold the sacred key to heaven, the pope is traditionally addressed as "Holy Father." The current Pope Benedict XVI is the 265th holder of this nearly 2,000-year-old religious office.

A fourth and final example of spiritual lineage is found in Tibetan Buddhism, divided into four major orders or schools. Each has its own monasteries, monks of various ranks from novice to lama, and a wealth of ancient texts, ritual practices, meditations, and other sacred knowledge passed on largely by oral tradition. Highest in rank among the monks are reincarnated saints. These are individuals who, fully emanating the divine Buddha spirit, achieved enlightenment during their lifetime; led by compassion, they chose to give up *nirvana* ("eternal bliss") after death to return to life on earth. To fulfill this role, such a saintly person must be recognized. Toward this end, a select group of high-ranking lamas guided by omens seeks out a newborn boy believed to be a *tulku* ("emanated incarnation") of a recently deceased saintly lama in their spiritual lineage. Once they find the little boy, they ritually induct and enthrone him and begin grooming him for his designated spiritual leadership position in the Buddhist order (Figure 13.6).

Of about 500 *tulku* lineages in Tibetan Buddhism, the most famous is the Dalai Lama ("teacher who is spiritually as deep as the ocean"). This illustrious lineage traces its origins to a high-ranking monk named Gendun Drup (1391–1474), thought to have embodied the Buddha spirit of compassion. A few years after the death of the thirteenth Dalai Lama in 1933, high-ranking monks from his order identified a 2-year-old boy in a small farming village as his reincarnated "wisdom mind." Renaming him Tenzin Gyatso, they later enthroned the little *tulku* as His Holiness, the fourteenth Dalai Lama— the highest-ranking political and spiritual position among Tibetan Buddhists for centuries.

Shamans

Societies without religious professionals have existed far longer than those that have them. Although lacking full-time specialists, they have always included individuals considered capable of connecting with supernatural beings and forces—individuals such as shamans. That capacity, partially based on learned techniques, is also based on personality and particular emotional experiences that could be described as "mystical." Supplied with spiritual knowledge in the form of a vision or some other extraordinary revelation, they are believed to be supernaturally empowered to heal the sick, change the weather, control the movements of animals, and foretell the future. As they perfect these and related skills, they may combine the role of a diviner and a healer, becoming a shaman.

Originally, the word *shaman* referred to medical-religious specialists, or spiritual guides, among the Tungus and other Siberian pastoral nomads with animist beliefs. By means of various techniques such as fasting, drumming, chanting, or dancing, as well as hallucinogenic mushrooms (*fly agaric*), these shamans enter into a trance. In this waking dream state, they experience visions of an alternate reality inhabited by spirit beings such as guardian animal spirits who may assist with healing. Similar spiritual practices exist in many indigenous cultures outside Siberia, especially in the Americas. For that reason, the term *shaman* is frequently applied to a variety of part-time spiritual leaders, diviners, and traditional healers active in many other parts of the world (Kehoe, 2000).

105

VISUAL COUNTERPOINT

Figure 13.6 Buddhist Lama Dilgo Khyentsé Rinpoche and His Reincarnation Dilgo Khyentsé Yangsi Rinpoche There are many spiritual lineages in Tibetan Buddhism not as well known as that of the Dalai Lama. The monk on the left is a reincarnation of a Buddhist master identified as the first Khyentsé ("Compassionate Wisdom"). In 1832 at age 12, the first Khyentsé was recognized as the combined incarnation of an 8th-century Tibetan religious king and a profoundly learned Buddhist master. Renamed Jamyang Khyentsé Wangpo and receiving intensive training, he was ordained throne-holder of a major Tibetan monastery and became a living saint. Dying in 1892, he reincarnated in 1910 as a little boy—a *tulku* renamed Dilgo Khyentsé Rinpoche (*Rinpoche*, a title given to *tulkus*, means "Precious One"). Before Dilgo Khyentsé passed away at the Shechen Monastery in Nepal at age 81, he gave subtle indications concerning how and where his "wisdom mind" would be reincarnated. After his death, another high-ranking lama in his order, who had been his close friend and disciple, had visions and dreams. Guided by these instructions, a search party identified a boy born in Nepal in the summer of 1993 as his reincarnation. The boy (*right*) was renamed Dilgo Khyentsé Yangsi in 1996. With his legitimate status in this *tulku* lineage confirmed by the Dalai Lama, the young monk was enthroned at his predecessor's monastery the following year.

Anthropologist Michael Harner (see Anthropologist of Note feature), a modern-day shamanic practitioner famous for his participant observation among Shuar (or Jivaro) Indian shamans in the Amazon rainforest, defined a **shaman** as someone who at will enters an altered state of consciousness "to contact and utilize an ordinarily hidden reality in order to acquire knowledge, power, and to help other persons. The shaman has at least one, and usually more, 'spirits' in his or her personal service" (Harner, 1980, p. 20).

shaman A person who at will enters an altered state of consciousness to contact and utilize an ordinarily hidden reality in order to acquire knowledge, power, and to help others.

Shamanic Experience

Someone may become a shaman by passing through stages of learning and practical experience, often involving psychological and emotional ordeals brought about by isolation, fasting, physical torture, sensory deprivation, and/or *hallucination* (Latin, for "mental wandering"). Hallucinations may occur when one is in a trance state; they can come about spontaneously, but they can also be induced by drumming or consuming mind-altering drugs such as psychoactive vines or mushrooms.

Because shamanism is rooted in altered states of consciousness and the human nervous system universally produces these trance states, individuals experience

ANTHROPOLOGIST OF NOTE

Michael J. Harner (b. 1929)

A world-renowned expert on shamanism, American anthropologist **Michael Harner** studied at the University of California, Berkeley. Starting out in archaeology and collaborating with Alfred Kroeber on Mohave pottery research, he later switched to ethnography. Intrigued by the Jívaro, legendary for shrinking human heads, he ventured into eastern Ecuador's tropical forest in 1956, at age 27. For nearly a year, he lived among these Amazonian Indians, now better known as Shuar. They still subsisted on food gardens and by hunting and gathering; they fiercely guarded their freedom and launched raids on enemy tribes.

Holding an animistic worldview, the Shuar distinguish between what Harner has identified as ordinary and non-ordinary realities. They believe that supernatural forces govern daily life and that spirit beings can be perceived and engaged only by shamans capable of entering non-ordinary reality. They access this reality by drinking *natema*, a bitter brew made from a jungle vine known as *ayahuasca* ("vine of the soul"). As they told Harner, drinking this hallucinogenic potion, shamans enter an altered state of consciousness in which they perceive and engage what they believe are the "true" forces governing sickness and health, life and death.

Harner returned to the Upper Amazon in 1960 for more ethnographic fieldwork, this time among the Conibo in eastern Peru. Seeking greater insight on *ayahuasca's* psychological impact on the native cosmology, he drank the magic brew. Passing through the door of perception into the shamanic view of reality, he found himself in a world beyond his "wildest dreams": a supernatural landscape inhabited by spirit beings. Singing incredibly beautiful music, they began to carry his soul away and he felt he was dying. Coming out of this experience, and later ones with Conibo shamans, Harner realized that anthropologists had seriously underestimated the powerful influence hallucinogenic drugs had on Amazonian Indian ideologies and practices.

In 1963, Harner earned his doctorate at UC Berkeley, and the next year went back to Shuar country for additional shamanic experience. In 1966, having taught at UC Berkeley and served as associate director of the Lowie Museum of Anthropology, he became a visiting professor at Yale and Columbia Universities. In 1969, he did fieldwork among a neighboring Jivaroan-speaking tribe, the Achuara, and the following year joined the graduate faculty of the New School for Social Research in New York City. Over the next few years he published his monograph, *The Jívaro: People of the Sacred Waterfalls*, an edited volume titled *Hallucinogens and Shamanism*, and numerous academic articles.

Continuing cross-cultural research on shamanism, Harner became interested in drumming as an alternative means of achieving what he now identifies as SSC (shamanic state of consciousness). Learning and using this method of monotonous percussive sound ("sonic driving"), he began offering training workshops and in 1979 founded the Center for Shamanic Studies. A year later, he published *The Way of the Shaman*, a groundbreaking book now translated into a dozen languages.

Collaborating with his wife, clinical psychologist Sandra Harner, he established the Foundation for Shamanic Studies, a nonprofit charitable and educational organization dedicated to the preservation, study, and transmission of shamanic knowledge. Its Urgent Assistance program supports the survival of shamanic healing knowledge among such indigenous peoples as the Canadian Inuit, Scandinavian Sámi, and Tuvans of central Asia and Siberia.

Since resigning from his university professorship in 1987, this anthropologist has been fully devoted to shamanic studies and healing practice, training others, including physicians, psychotherapists, and other health care professionals. The Foundation's faculty assists him in this work.

In his most recent book, *Cave and Cosmos: Shamanic Encounters with Spirits and Heavens* (2013), Harner recounts and compares experiences of shamanic "ascension" and offers instructions on his core-shamanism techniques.

Michael Harner—anthropologist, shaman, and founder of the Foundation for Shamanic Studies in Mill Valley, California.

Figure 13.7 Traditional Shaman in Mongolia This female shaman in Mongolia, bordering Siberia, uses a drum crafted from the wood of a tree struck by lightning and covered with leather made from a female red deer. It is believed that when the shaman goes into a trance, her drum transforms into a magical steed that carries her into the dark sky of her ancestors.

similarly structured visual, auditory, somatic (touch), olfactory (smell), and gustatory (taste) hallucinations. The widespread occurrence of shamanism and the remarkable similarities among shamanic traditions everywhere are consequences of this universal neurological inheritance. But the meanings ascribed to sensations experienced in altered states and made of their content are culturally determined; hence, despite their overall similarities, indigenous traditions typically vary in particular details (Figure 13.7).

Shamans can be contrasted with priests and priestesses in that the latter serve dieties of the society. As agents of divine beings, priests and priestesses order believers what to think and do, whereas shamans may challenge or negotiate with the spirits. In return for services rendered, shamans may collect a fee—money, fresh meat, or some other valuable. In some cases, shamans are rewarded by the prestige that comes as a result of a healing or some other extraordinary feat.

Shamanic Healing

Shamans are essentially spiritual go-betweens who acts on behalf of some human client, often to bring about healing or to foretell a future event. Typically, they enter a trance state, experience the sensation of traveling to the alternate world, and see and interact with spirit beings. Shamans try to impose their will upon these spirits, an inherently dangerous contest, considering the superhuman powers that spirits are thought to possess.

An example of this can be seen in the trance dances of the Ju/'hoansi Bushmen of Africa's Kalahari Desert. Traditional Ju/'hoansi belief holds that illness and misfortune are caused by invisible arrows shot by spirits.

The arrows can be removed by healers, those who possess the powerful healing force called *n/um* (the Ju/'hoansi equivalent of *mana*). Some healers can activate *n/um* by solo singing or instrument playing, but more often this is accomplished through the medicinal curing ceremony or trance dance (Figure 13.8).

Acting on behalf of a client or patient, a shaman may put on a dramatic performance; such an artful

Figure 13.8 Ju/'hoansi Shaman Healer and Helper in Trance Dance Ju/'hoansi shamans may find their way into a trance by dancing around a fire to the pulsating sound of melodies sung by women. Eventually, sometimes after several hours, "the music, the strenuous dancing, the smoke, the heat of the fire, and the healers' intense concentration cause their *n/um* to heat up. When it comes to a boil, trance is achieved. At that moment, the *n/um* becomes available as a powerful healing force to serve the entire community. In trance, a healer lays hands on and ritually cures everyone sitting around the fire" (Shostak, 2000, pp. 259–260).

demonstration of spiritual power assures members of the community that prevailing upon supernatural powers and spirits otherwise beyond human control can bring about invulnerability from attack, success at love, or the return of health.

The precise effects of the shamanic treatment are not known, but its psychological and emotional impact is thought to contribute to the patient's recovery. For healing to occur, the shaman needs to be convinced of the effectiveness of his or her spiritual powers and techniques. Likewise, the patient must see the shaman as a genuine healing master using appropriate techniques. Finally, to close the triangle's "magic field," the community within which the shaman operates on the patient must view the healing ceremony and its practitioner as potentially effective and beneficial. From an anthropological perspective, shamanic healings can be understood by means of a three-cornered model: the *shamanic complex* (Figure 13.9). This triangle is created by the interrelationship of the shaman, the patient, and the community to which both belong.

Shamanic healing ceremonies involve social-psychological dynamics also present in Western medical treatments. Consider, for example, the *placebo effect*—the beneficial result a patient experiences after a particular treatment, due to the person's expectations concerning the treatment rather than from the treatment itself. Notably, some people involved in modern medicine work collaboratively with practitioners of traditional belief systems toward the healing of various illnesses (Harner & Harner, 2000; Offiong, 1999).

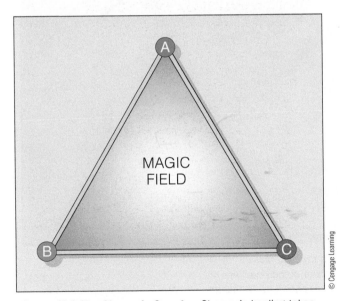

Figure 13.9 The Shamanic Complex Shamanic healing takes place within a "magic field" created when the shaman (A) and patient (B), as well as their community (C), are all convinced that the shaman is a genuine healing master using appropriate techniques that are effective and beneficial. Similar psychological processes are involved in Western medical treatments.

Ritual Performances

Rituals are culturally prescribed symbolic acts or procedures designed to guide members of a community in an orderly way through personal and collective transitions. Relieving anxiety and tensions in crises, rituals provide symbolic means of reinforcing a group's social bonds. Not all of them concern the sacred (consider, for example, college graduation ceremonies in North America). But those that do are ideologically linked to beliefs in the supernatural, playing a crucial role as spirituality or religion in action.

Anthropologists have classified several different types of ritual. These include rituals of purification, rites of passage, rites of intensification, and magical rituals, including witchcraft.

Rites of Purification: Taboo and Cleansing Ceremonies

In many religious and spiritual traditions, rituals have been developed to symbolically restore one's place in the cosmic order, removing "dirt," washing "impurity," and making "clean" in body, mind, and soul. Anthropologists specializing in comparative religion have been intrigued by the cross-cultural variation in cultural categories classifying certain animals, plants, objects, or acts as unclean or dirty and others as dangerous.

In every society, people follow certain culturally prescribed rules about what is dirty or filthy, or whichever term symbolically represents pollution—rules that say what they cannot eat, drink, touch, talk, or even think about. For instance, many millions of Hindus eat pork but avoid beef because they regard the cow as a sacred animal. On the other hand, many millions of Muslims consume beef but avoid pork because in Islam swine is considered unclean. In the words of British anthropologist Mary Douglas, "Dirt offends against order. Eliminating it is not a negative movement, but a positive effort to organise the environment" (1966, pp. 2–3).

Culturally prescribed avoidances involving ritual prohibitions are known as **taboo**, a term derived from the Polynesian word *tabu* (or *tapu*). Among Pacific Islanders it refers to something that has supernatural power and is to be avoided. It can apply to an object (such as food), a person (such as a high-ranking noble), or a place (a shrine or temple). Especially applied to blood and anything associated with sickness and death, taboos are

---

ritual A culturally prescribed symbolic act or procedure designed to guide members of a community in an orderly way through personal and collective transitions.

taboo Culturally prescribed avoidances involving ritual prohibitions, which, if not observed, lead to supernatural punishment.

taken very seriously. When a taboo is violated, believers expect supernatural punishment will follow. This penalty may come in magical form as misfortune—an unlucky accident, resulting in loss, sickness, or death. It is also possible that the taboo breaker will be punished by designated members in the community and may be ordered to undergo a purification ritual and make a sacrifice. Sometimes, the ultimate sacrifice is demanded, and the offender is executed.

For complex historical reasons of their own, some societies stress taboos much more than others. For instance, as discussed in the previous chapter, the traditional hierarchy in the Hindu caste society is religiously reinforced by strict rules against ritual pollution that govern the lives of members of the different *varnas*.

Whether someone has violated a taboo, or is otherwise no longer clean, many cultures have developed **rites of purification** to establish or restore purity. These may involve one person, but many are group or community ceremonial affairs. As symbolic acts, purification rituals are filled with spiritual or religious meaning. They impact participants emotionally and psychologically (restoring a sense of inner peace and cosmic harmony), as well as socially, such as by establishing or restoring harmony within their family, community, or some other group.

A cross-cultural comparison of these spiritual or religious ceremonies shows that the four elements of water, air, fire, and/or earth have been used in a wide range of rituals for thousands of years all across the globe. For instance, cleansing by water is very common in many forms of baptism, hot steam is used in sweat lodges, burning fragrant organic matter (such as plant leaves or resins) is used in smoking and smudging ceremonies. The human body and mind may also be subjected to rituals of internal purification by means of prayer, meditation, chanting, fasting, or dancing (Figure 13.10).

Figure 13.10 A Sufi *Sema* (Prayer Dance) in Aleppo, Syria Sufism, a mystical Muslim movement that emerged a thousand years ago, emphasizes the surrender of individual ego and attachment to worldly things in order to be receptive to God's grace. Known as "whirling dervishes," these Sufi dancers are part of the Mevlevi brotherhood, a spiritual lineage founded by the Persian Sufi master (*mawlana*) Jalal ad-Din ar-Rumi in the 13th century. According to Mevlevi tradition, during the *sema* the soul is freed from earthly ties and is able to jubilantly commune with the divine. (*Dervish* literally means "doorway" and is thought to be an entrance from the material world to the spiritual.) The felt hat represents personal ego's tombstone, and the wide skirt symbolizes its shroud.

Rites of Passage

Rites of passage are rituals marking important ceremonial moments when members of a society move from one distinctive social stage in life to another, such as birth, marriage, and death. When crossing the boundary (*limen*) between such stages, people briefly cease to be part of the stage left behind and have not yet become integrated into the next. Like travelers passing through a border area between two countries not controlled by either of them, they are neither here nor there. Guiding people through such uncertain transit zones, rituals associated with changing social status unfold in three phases: *separation* (pre-liminary), *transition* (liminary), and *incorporation* (post-liminary).

Phase one is the ceremonial removal of the individual from everyday society, phase two a period of ritual isolation, and phase three the formal return and readmission back into society in his or her new status (Van Gennep, 1960). Because certain transitions in the human life cycle are crucially important to the individual as well as to the social order of the community, these rituals may involve a religious specialist, such as a priest or priestess.

This sequence of phases occurs in a great array of rites of passage all around the world—from wedding ceremonies marking the transition from single to married status to ceremonies identifying the transference of religious leadership in a spiritual lineage to a designated heir to ceremonies initiating new members into a distinctive group. An example of the latter, described in an earlier chapter, is when young Maasai men in East Africa's grasslands move into the Warrior age grade; they are removed from their families and ritually initiated by circumcision, returning weeks later as *moranes*, armed warriors with a distinctive hairstyle and dress.

Likewise, when Mende girls in West Africa's savannahs begin menstruating, they are ritually prepared for womanhood. Separated from family, they spend weeks in seclusion. Discarding their childhood clothes, they learn the moral and practical responsibilities of motherhood from senior women. Believing circumcision enhances a girl's reproductive potential, these elders are tasked with removing each girl's clitoris (considered a female version of a penis). A good deal of singing, dancing, storytelling, and food accompany the ordeal and the training, which produces a strong sense of sisterhood. The girls emerge from their initiation as women in knowledgeable control of their sexuality, eligible for marriage and childbearing.

Rites of Intensification

Rites of intensification are rituals that take place during a crisis in the life of the group and serve to bind individuals together. Whatever the precise nature of the crisis—a drought that threatens crops, the sudden appearance of an enemy war party, the onset of an epidemic—mass ceremonies are performed to ease the sense of danger.

© Luca Tettoni/Corbis

Figure 13.11 Hindu Cremation Ceremony in Bali, Indonesia Balinese people deal with death by turning what could be a painful emotional experience of grief and loss into a joyous celebration of life's progressive continuity through rebirth in a future existence. As a social reminder of Hindu caste differences, the family of a deceased relative uses this ceremony to display wealth and social rank. Funeral pyres built for members of a noble or royal family on the island are duly impressive.

This unites people in a common effort so that fear and confusion yield to collective action and a degree of optimism. The balance in the relations of all concerned is restored to normal, and the community's values are celebrated and affirmed.

An individual's death might be regarded as the ultimate crisis or point of separation in that person's life, but it is, as well, a point of separation for the entire group, particularly if the group is small. A member of the community has been removed, so its composition has been seriously altered. The survivors, therefore, must readjust and restore balance. They also need to reconcile themselves to the loss of someone to whom they were emotionally tied. As such, a funerary ceremony is an example of an intensification ritual that permits the surviving family and community to express in nondisruptive ways their emotional upset over the death while providing for social readjustment (**Figure 13.11**).

rite of purification A symbolic act carried out by an individual or a group to establish or restore purity when someone has violated a taboo or is otherwise unclean.

rite of passage A ritual that marks an important ceremonial moment when members of a society move from one distinctive social stage in life to another, such as birth, marriage, and death. It features three phases: separation, transition, and incorporation.

rite of intensification A ritual that takes place during a crisis in the life of the group and serves to bind individuals together.

Rites of intensification do not have to be limited to times of overt crisis. In regions where human activities change in accordance with seasonal climatic shifts, these rites take the form of annual ceremonies. They are particularly common among horticultural and agricultural peoples. Ritually articulating traditional ideas about the role of the supernatural in the cyclical return of rain, the light and warmth of the sun, and other factors of nature vital to healthy and bountiful crops, these ceremonies are staged to correspond with the crucially important planting and harvesting seasons. A similar cultural linkage between the annual subsistence cycle and the ceremonial calendar with its rites of intensification can be found in societies based on seasonal fishing and herding or hunting of migratory animals.

Magical Rituals

People in many cultures believe that supernatural powers can be compelled to act in certain ways for good or evil purposes by recourse to specified formulas. In short, they believe in **magic** and carry out magical rituals to ensure positive ends such as good crops, fertility of livestock, replenishment of hunted game, prevention of accidents, healing of illness, protection against injury, promise of victory, and the defeat of enemies, real or imagined. In traditional societies many of these rituals rely on *fetishes*—objects believed to possess magical powers (**Figure 13.12**).

Magical rituals are also popular in wealthy industrialized societies. Individuals commonly seek "good luck" when the outcome is in doubt or beyond one's influence—from lighting a votive candle for someone going through a hard time, to wearing lucky boxers on a hot date, to the curious gesturing baseball pitchers perform on the mound.

Anthropologists distinguish between two fundamental principles of magic. The first principle—that like produces like—is identified as **imitative magic** or *sympathetic magic*. In Myanmar (Burma) in Southeast Asia, for example, a rejected lover might engage a sorcerer to make an image of his would-be love. If this image were tossed into water, to the accompaniment of certain charms, it was expected that the girl would go mad and suffer a fate similar to that of her image.

The second principle is that of **contagious magic**—the idea that things or persons once in contact can influence each other after the contact is broken. The most

Figure 13.12 Congolese Fetish This 100-year-old carving from the Democratic Republic of Congo is a *nkondi*, with supernatural power coming in part from magic herbs hidden inside by a diviner. Such fetishes are traditionally used to identify wrongdoers, including thieves and witches responsible for mishaps, diseases, or death. A *nkondi* is activated by provocations (such as hammering nails into it) or invocations urging magic punishment of the suspects.

common example of contagious magic is the permanent relationship between an individual and any part of his or her body, such as hair, fingernails, or teeth. For instance, the Basutos of Lesotho in southern Africa were careful to conceal their extracted teeth to make sure they did not fall into the hands of certain mythical beings who could harm the owners of the teeth by working magic on them. Related to this is the custom in Western societies of treasuring things that have been touched by special people. Such items range from a saint's relics to possessions of other admired or idolized individuals, from rock stars to sports heroes to spiritual gurus.

magic Specific formulas and actions used to compel supernatural powers to act in certain ways for good or evil purposes.
imitative magic Magic based on the principle that like produces like; sometimes called *sympathetic magic*.
contagious magic Magic based on the principle that things or persons once in contact can influence each other after the contact is broken.

© Ann Bingley Gallops, Open Spaces Feng Shui

Figure 13.13 Assessing Ch'i Energy Feng shui master R. D. Chin determines the *ch'i* of a new office space in a Manhattan skyscraper, one side of which faces the city's central *ch'i* point—the Empire State Building. The consultant is planning the space, with the location of stairways and the CEO's office to be determined.

Divination: Omens and Oracles

Designed to access or influence supernatural powers, magical rituals have also been developed to prepare for the uncertain future—for the unseen and for the not yet present. Fears of pending dangers—for example, storms, attacks, betrayals, diseases, and death—call for precautionary measures, such as what to avoid and where to go. How does one find and interpret the signs, or *omens*, foretelling the future? The answer, as developed in many cultures, is through **divination**, a magical ritual designed to discover what is unknowable by ordinary means, in particular signs predicting fate or destiny.

Various ancient methods of divination exist, including *geomancy* (from Greek, *geo* for "earth" and *manteia* for "divination"), a technique traditionally considered sacred and practiced by shamans, prophets, fortunetellers, or other oracles in communication with supernatural forces. Skilled to interpret omens, a diviner practicing geomancy may toss a handful of sand or pebbles, for example, and then analyze its random patterns, searching for information hidden to ordinary people. Other divination methods include decoding flame or smoke patterns in a fire (*pyromancy*), wind and cloud formation in the air (*aeromancy*), or colors, ripples, and whirls in water (*hydromancy*).

Whereas Mongolian and Chinese shamans traditionally use an animal shoulder blade (*scapulamancy*) for divination purposes, Aymara *yachajs* ("possessors of knowledge") in the Andean highlands may probe sacred coca leaves or the convoluted pile of intestines of a slaughtered guinea pig for omens. Much better known, of course, is the divination technique involving palm reading (*chiromancy*), perhaps most famously practiced by female Gypsy fortunetellers. So-called mediums are popular, too, also in the United States, where many people believe them to be capable of contacting spirits of deceased relatives ready

to pass on messages from beyond by means of an ancient ritual method known as *necromancy*.

Believed to possess knowledge hidden from ordinary people, diviners are feared in many cultures. However, they are also in high demand among those who believe in diviners' capacity to predict the future, and those believers may seek consultation before undertaking something important or risky. An example of this is *feng shui*, an ancient Chinese divination technique. Literally translated as "wind-water," its traditional Chinese characters signify "tao of heaven and earth." In the past few decades, this method has grown in popularity in North America as well, in particular in California, where homebuilders and buyers frequently hire feng shui consultants to help them design or redesign homes and offices to conform to the principle of *qi* or *ch'i* ("vital energy") (**Figure 13.13**).

In some religious traditions, including Christianity, fortunetelling and other divination rituals have long been viewed with suspicion, and in many places these practices have been prohibited. Especially when performed by individuals functioning in other religious or spiritual traditions believed to be false or worse, divination is condemned as evil magic, sorcery, or witchcraft.

Witchcraft: Anxiety and Fears of Evil Magic

Magical rituals intended to cause misfortune or inflict harm are often referred to as sorcery, or **witchcraft**, believed to be practiced by individuals embodying evil

divination A magical procedure or spiritual ritual designed to discern what is not knowable by ordinary means, such as foretelling the future by interpreting omens.
witchcraft Magical rituals intended to cause misfortune or inflict harm.

spirit power or those collaborating with malevolent supernatural beings. In contrast to magic-working experts inclined to do good, these individuals inspire awe, or even fear. Historically, such dangerous magic-working individuals are known in English under a variety of names such as *wizard, sorcerer,* or simply *witch*—imprecise terms often used interchangeably. This is also true for other languages using a variety of terms like *brujo* (Spanish), *uwisin* (Shuar), *umthakathi* (Zulu), *mchawi* (Swahili), and *wu* (Chinese).

Fear of witches is especially prevalent during periods of uncertainty and transition. When mysterious illnesses, devastating droughts, accidental deaths, economic uncertainties, and other upheavals disturb the cultural order, confusion may result in a surge of suspicion and a focus on disliked, unsociable, isolated individuals. Especially in patrilineal or patrilocal communities, the accused is often an older woman, typically single or widowed and without children. For instance, about 80 percent of the estimated 50,000 "witches" tried, tortured, and killed in Europe in the 16th and 17th centuries were female. Among matrilineal and matrilocal groups, however, people tend to think of witches as male.

Not all people suspected of mysterious malevolence are prosecuted, let alone executed, but witchcraft accusations clearly function as a social control mechanism, horribly reinforcing the moral code. Fear of being accused of being a witch encourages individuals to suppress as best they can those personality traits that are looked upon with disapproval. A belief in witchcraft thus serves as a broad control on what is believed to be antisocial behavior (Behringer, 2004).

Navajo Skin-Walkers

Beliefs in evil magic are widespread and take many forms. One interesting example comes from the Navajo, Native Americans historically surviving as sheepherders and small-scale irrigation farmers in the vast deserts of Arizona and New Mexico. The Navajo have a substantial repertoire of sacred rituals for healing victims of sorcery, all related to accusations of evil magic.

Among Navajos, who live in a residence group organized around a head woman, traditional belief holds that a person suffering from severe anxiety disorder, repetitive nightmares, or delusions is a victim of sorcery. The idea is that a ghost or some other evil spirit, traveling under cover of darkness, is responsible. And

according to the Navajo, the suspect is a powerful sorcerer, almost always a man, probably someone who has killed a relative and committed incest.

These dangerous Navajo sorcerers, resembling the werewolf of European folklore and the *nagual* in rural Mexico, are believed to be able to change themselves into animal form. Referred to as a *'ánt'įįhnii* ("skin-walker"), such a sorcerer stealthily goes to a secluded spot, such as a cave at night. There, he transforms into a coyote or wolf. Disguised in animal form, he emerges and runs fast toward his victim, bringing on *'ánt'į* ("the curse"). Having completed his accursed mission, the skin-walker swiftly returns to his hideaway, transforms again into human form, and slips back into his home before dawn (Kluckhohn, 1944; Selinger, 2007).

Sacred Sites: Saints, Shrines, and Miracles

Sacred sites are typically positioned in a transitional, or *liminary*, zone between the natural and supernatural, the secular and spiritual, earth and heaven. Reaching high into the sky, mountaintops are often considered to be magical places, shrouded in mystery. For instance, the Japanese view the snowcapped perfect volcanic cone of Mount Fuji ("Ever-Lasting Life") as a sacred place. Ancient Greeks considered Mount Olympus to be the mythological abode of Zeus, the king of all their gods. Likewise, Kikuyu view Mount Kenya as the earthly dwelling place of their creator god Ngai.

Some sites become sacred because they are places where ordinary human beings experienced something extraordinary—heard a divine voice or saw a guardian spirit, patron saint, or archangel. Often a site is declared sacred because believers associate it with a miracle-working mystic, saint, prophet, or other holy person. The tombs of such individuals often turn into shrines (*scrinium*, Latin for "round box" or "container," holding relics). For example, stories of miraculous events and special powers emanating from Muslim tombs are common wherever Sufism, a far-reaching mystical branch of Islam, is popular (Gladney, 2004).

Based on the principle of contagious magic, any material substance physically linked to a miraculous event or individual may itself become revered as holy or sacred. This may include bones, fingernails, hair, or any other body part believed to have belonged to a saint, or something the person wore, possessed, or simply touched. All these things may be treasured as holy relics and safeguarded in a shrine, inspiring the faithful.

Burial sites of saints often gain such importance that people feel inspired to construct a very large shrine for the saint's entombment; termed a *mausoleum*, some of these are large enough for the interment of lesser saints and pious individuals desiring proximity to the sacred saint after death. However large or small, shrines are religious focal points for prayer, meditation, and sacrifice.

Figure 13.14 Pilgrims at Mount Kailash in Tibet Rising 6,700 meters (over 22,000 feet), this mountain has been sacred for many generations to Buddhists and Hindus, as well as Jains and followers of Bön (Tibet's indigenous religion). Every year a few thousand pilgrims make the tortuous 52-kilometer (32-mile) trek around it, some of them by crawling the entire distance.

Pilgrimages: Devotion in Motion

Every year, many millions of devotees of many religions— including Buddhism, Christianity, Hinduism, Islam, and their many branches—walk, climb, or even crawl to a sacred or holy site. Whether it is a saint's tomb, a mountain, lake, river, waterfall, or some other particular place believed to be metaphysically significant, *pilgrims* (from Latin *peregrinus*, meaning "wanderer") travel there seeking enlightenment, proving their devotion, and/or hoping to experience a miracle.

On their sacred journey, pilgrims participate in a religious drama, performing ritually prescribed acts such as prayers, chants, or prostrations. A devotion in motion, the **pilgrimage** demands personal sacrifices from the travelers. Enjoying little comfort, they may suffer from thirst and hunger, heat and cold, pain and fear while on the road, sometimes for many days or even months. Pilgrims often travel through unfamiliar territories where they may run into problems, including robbery, kidnapping, starvation, and even death. To identify their status as spiritually inspired travelers, some wear special clothes, shave their heads, carry amulets, chant prayers, or perform other prescribed rituals along the way.

One of the most challenging pilgrimages is the climb up the slopes of a mountain range in the Himalayas where Mount Kailash rises 6,700 meters (over 22,000

feet). Located in western Tibet, this black, snowcapped mountain stands out boldly in a dramatic landscape sacred to Hindus and Buddhists, as well as Jains and Bönpos (**Figure 13.14**). The latter, who practice an ancient Tibetan shamanic religion, refer to this hallowed mountain as Tisé ("Water Peak") because it is the source of four sacred rivers. For Hindus, it is the holy abode of Lord Shiva, the destroyer of ignorance and illusion and the divine source of yoga. Jains view Kailash as the sacred place where their divine cultural hero Rishabha ("Bull")—an incarnation of Lord Vishnu—first achieved full enlightenment. Finally, Tibetan Buddhists revere it as Gangs Rinpoche ("Snow Lord") and believe it to be the abode of Khorlo Demchok ("Circle of Bliss")—a wrathful deity who uses his power to destroy the three major obstacles to enlightenment: anger, greed, and ignorance.

For all four of these religious traditions, climbing to the summit of this holy mountain is taboo. So, pilgrims demonstrate their devotion by means of a ritual encirclement, or circumambulation—clockwise by Buddhists and Hindus, and in reverse by Jains and Bönpos. The rugged, 52-kilometer (32-mile) trek is seen

pilgrimage A devotion in motion. Traveling, often on foot, to a sacred or holy site to reach for enlightenment, prove devotion, and/or experience a miracle.

as a sacred ritual that removes sins and brings good fortune. Each year thousands follow the ancient tradition of encircling the mountain on foot. The most devout pilgrims turn their circumambulation into a sacrificial ordeal: Prostrating their bodies full length, they extend their hands forward and make a mark on the ground with their fingers; then they rise, pray, crawl ahead on hands and knees to the mark, and then repeat the process again and again.

One of the world's largest pilgrimages is the *hajj*— a performance of piety now made by 1.8 million Muslims traveling to Mecca in Saudi Arabia each year from all across the globe. The largest contingent of hajjis—about 300,000 a year—comes from Indonesia. One of the five pillars of Islam, the hajj brings all of these pilgrims together for collective prayers and other sacred rituals at the Kaaba in Mecca, their religion's holiest site.

Christianity, originating in what was an eastern province of the Roman empire about 2,000 years ago, has created a sacred landscape dotted with dozens of major pilgrimage sites in Southwest Asia and Europe. As in other ancient religions, these sites are symbolically associated with miracles and legendary holy men and women. For example, for nearly a millennium Christian pilgrims from all over Europe have made the long and difficult journey to Santiago de Compostela. Tens of thousands travel to this Spanish seaport each year— most by foot, some by bicycle, and a few on horseback like their medieval counterparts. About 180,000 pilgrims walk the final 100 kilometers to the old cathedral with the shrine containing the sacred remains of the apostle Saint James venerated as Santiago (Santo-Iago) since the Middle Ages and recognized as the official patron saint of Spain. Many more Roman Catholics make pilgrimages to shrines devoted to Saint Mary, as described following.

Female Saints: Divine Protection for the Weak

Many religions consider the divine order primarily or exclusively as masculine, as noted earlier. Ideologically reproducing the hierarchical social order dominated by men, this arrangement reflects the worldview of traditional cultures that revere male deities, prophets, and saints in officially sponsored cults and devotions. But religions are not monolithic, and some provide flexible spiritual space for alternatives, such as Christian cults devoted to female saints such as Mary, the virgin mother of Jesus Christ, the son of God.

More powerful than the pope in Rome, Mary has been loved and adored as a holy mother residing in heaven. Worldwide, Roman Catholic multitudes look up to her for divine protection. Like other Christian saints, she is thought to perform miracles and to be capable of physically manifesting herself at places and times of her choosing. Through the centuries, many believers claim to have witnessed such holy moments, some officially reporting the miracle. Typically, these believers are young members of the underclass—herders, peasants, or fishermen, for example. Beyond stories about the female saint manifesting herself to such low-status rural folk, the discovery of sacred relics (such as a drowned or buried statue representing Mary) may also generate excitement and hope in difficult times.

Stories and relics religiously associated with miracles performed by saints such as the Virgin Mary quickly attract popular attention and turn into myths. Inspired or led by individuals claiming divine authority based on immediate revelation, devotees typically build a shrine to commemorate the encounter or to safeguard the sacred relic. Developing outside the power structure of established religious institutions, these local devotions may turn into popular cults. Difficult if not impossible to stop, these cults may spawn mass movements, leading church authorities to consider whether to formally approve of the cult and take control of the Marian (Saint Mary) devotion. Sanctioned by the church or not, these shrines attract pilgrims in search of divine forgiveness, protection, healing, and compassionate love.

Among the best known Marian pilgrimage sites are the ones in Lourdes (France) and Fatima (Portugal), along with the Mexican shrine dedicated to the brown-skinned Virgin of Guadalupe detailed in the next section.

Black Madonnas and Brown-Skinned Virgin Mothers

As folk-based popular religious movements, Saint Mary cults not only developed across Europe, but also in Latin America, the Philippines, and other parts of the world historically colonized and dominated by Roman Catholics originating from Europe. The religious ideas and rituals of Catholicism changed many indigenous cultures—and were also changed by them. Of particular interest in this shifting religious landscape are Black Madonnas: brown or dark-colored clay or wooden statues, or painted images, representing the virgin mother. One of the many Black Madonna statues is enshrined in Aparecida, Brazil, where a popular cult emerged in her honor in the mid-18th century and now attracts over 10 million pilgrims annually.

Another popular devotion involving brown-skinned Saint Mary concerns the Virgin of Guadalupe, highlighted in this chapter's opening photo. As mentioned there, this Mexican cult originated in 1531, a decade after the Aztec Indian empire had been conquered by a Spanish army. That year, a recently converted young

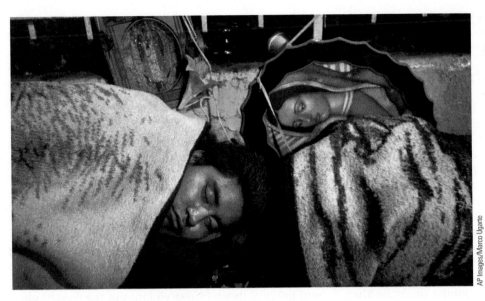

Figure 13.15 Virgin of Guadalupe Pilgrim, Mexico City On December 9, 1531, Saint Mary appeared to Mexican Indian Juan Diego, a recent Christian convert, as he passed by Tepeyac Hill in what is now Mexico City. At the site of this encounter, the Basilica of Our Lady of Guadalupe was built with a shrine containing sacred evidence of this miraculous apparition. Pictured here is a weary pilgrim, sleeping alongside images of the virgin outside the basilica.

AP Images/Marco Ugarte

Aztec Christian named Juan Diego proclaimed a remarkable encounter with a holy woman who appeared to him in a blaze of light. Speaking his native Nahuatl tongue, she identified herself as the virgin mother and asked that a shrine be built in her honor. After their miraculous meeting, he discovered her image mysteriously imprinted on the inside of his simple white-hemp *tilma* ("cloak"). Seen as divine proof of Mary's manifestation, this sacred relic was soon enshrined in the chapel built in her honor at the foot of the hill where she appeared—now part of Mexico City.

A few decades later, a powerful Spanish bishop imposing religious order in the Mexican colony became aware of the emerging brown-virgin cult and saw it as an ideological means of unifying and controlling a racially divided population. Eventually, in 1780 church authorities officially declared her patron saint of Mexico, even promoting her to the title of Empress of the Americas in 1945. In 2002, nearly 500 years after Juan Diego's mystical encounter started this Marian devotion, Pope John Paul II canonized him before a crowd of 12 million. Diego became the first Native American to be declared a Roman Catholic saint. Today, most of the 6 million pilgrims who visit the Virgin of Guadalupe's shrine each year to see the sacred *tilma* relic discovered by Diego are mestizo or indigenous Mexicans (**Figure 13.15**).

Desecration: Ruining Sacred Sites

Although popular shrines are destinations for believers from near and far, they are also potential targets of **desecration**. By means of such ideologically inspired

violation of a sacred site, enemies aim to inflict harm, if only symbolically, on people judged to have impure, false, or evil beliefs and ritual practices. Desecrations have occurred across the globe for thousands of years, as evidenced in archaeological sites and recorded in oral traditions or historical documents.

For example, during the Protestant Reformation in the 16th and 17th centuries, Christian Protestant iconoclasts campaigning against idolatry in the Netherlands and England destroyed untold numbers of ancient Roman Catholic statues and other treasures kept in sacred shrines. More recently, in Afghanistan, Taliban religious authorities shattered two huge 1,500-year-old statues they considered to be idols. Carved into the side of a sandstone cliff in the high mountain valley of Bamiyan, one of them, representing a celestial wisdom Buddha ("the enlightened one") stood 55 meters (180 feet) high; the other, representing Siddhartha Gautama, the founder of Buddhism himself, rose to 37 meters (121 feet). In 2001, the Taliban obliterated both monuments with artillery and dynamite.

Destruction in the name of religion is not unique to Christian or Muslim puritans, as militant Hindus and others also engage in similar desecrations. All of this pales in comparison with China's Cultural Revolution in the 1960s, when masses of activists, swept up in state-sponsored antireligious fervor, went on a rampage destroying religious monuments, sculptures, carvings, and paintings, as well as a large number of age-old sacred shrines.

desecration Ideologically inspired violation of a sacred site intended to inflict harm, if only symbolically, on people judged to have impure, false, or even evil beliefs and ritual practices.

Cultural Dynamics in the Superstructure: Religious and Spiritual Change

New technologies, improved means of transportation, internationalization of production and labor markets, and worldwide movements of ideas and practices all contribute to challenging and even destabilizing long-established cultural systems and associated worldviews. Reacting to these challenges and radical upheavals, people often turn to the supernatural to allay the anxiety of a world going awry.

The need to find deeper meaning in life and to make sense of an increasingly complex, uncharted, confusing, and sometimes frightening existence drives humans to continue their explorations—religious and spiritual, as well as scientific. Some people bundle or devise their own spiritual beliefs and rituals. Others form or join new spiritual movements.

Reactionary religious movements are also on the rise in culturally destabilized societies. Typically, these call for a radical return to traditional foundations prescribed in sacred texts and narrowly interpreted by conservative spiritual leaders. Examples include Islamic fundamentalism in countries such as Afghanistan, Egypt, and Iran; Jewish fundamentalism in Israel and the United States; and Hindu fundamentalism in India. Christian fundamentalism is represented in the dramatic growth of evangelical denominations in the United States, Latin America, and sub-Saharan Africa.

Revitalization Movements

No anthropological consideration of religion is complete without some mention of **revitalization movements**—movements for radical cultural reform in response to widespread social disruption and collective feelings of great stress and despair.

As deliberate efforts to construct a more satisfying culture, revitalization movements aim to reform not just the religious sphere of activity but may also impact an entire cultural system. Many such movements developed in indigenous societies where European colonial exploitation caused enormous upheaval. They also occurred in 16th-century Europe—as evidenced in the emergence of Puritans, Mennonites, and other Protestant groups when traditional societies faced radical transformations triggered by early capitalism and other

forces. Likewise, revitalization movements emerged in response to the industrial revolution triggering similar radical transformations in agrarian societies in the 19th century, not only in Europe but also in the northeastern United States, where Mormonism, Jehovah's Witnesses, Seventh-Day Adventists, and others began as Christian revitalization movements.

Revitalization movements can be found in many religions. One of the best known among Muslims is Ahmadiyya, founded in South Asia during British colonial rule in the late 19th century when Christian missionaries were actively proselytizing in predominantly Hindu, Muslim, or Sikh communities. Known as Ahmadis, followers of this Muslim sect number about 10 million across the globe. They believe that Allah (God) sent Mirza Ghulam Ahmad (1835–1908) as a prophet, a divinely ordained reformer (*mujjaddid*) like Muhammad. As the long-awaited Messiah, he embodied the second coming of the Christ, sent to bring about, by peaceful means, the final triumph of Islam as the only true religion for humanity, end all religious strife, and restore divinely guided morality, justice, and peace.

Recent U.S. revitalization movements also include the revival or introduction of traditional American Indian ceremonies such as the sweat lodge now common on many tribal reservations in North America, as well as the spectacular Sun Dance ceremony held each summer at various reservations in the Great Plains. Similar cultural revivals of "spiritual neo-traditions" are on the rise in many parts of the world, including Europe (Prins, 1994). Tens of thousands of people in Great Britain, attracted to a naturalistic worldview, now practice forms of "ecospiritualism" (Prins, 1996, p. 206), which often involves a revival of the ancient pre-Christian Celtic tradition of Druidry (Figure 13.16).

A similar nature-centered revival of pre-Christian beliefs and rituals is under way in Germanic-speaking parts of northern Europe, such as among Asatru in Scandinavia. Seeking a sacred relationship with nature, they worship the earth, elements of the sky, and forces such as thunder, as well as spirits they believe arise from sacred places like mountains and rivers. Similar tradition-based ecospiritual movements are developing throughout the industrialized world, including the United States.

Syncretic Religions

In Africa, during and following the period of foreign colonization and missionization, indigenous groups resisted or creatively revised Christian teachings and formed culturally appropriate religious movements. During the past century, thousands of indigenous Christian churches have been founded in Africa. These churches are often born of alternative theological interpretations and new divinely inspired revelations. They also originate from disapproval

---

revitalization movements Social movements for radical cultural reform in response to widespread social disruption and collective feelings of great stress and despair.

Figure 13.16 **Stonehenge, Wiltshire County, England** In 2010, the neo-tradition of Druidry was officially recognized as a religion in Great Britain. Stonehenge, a 4,500-year-old Neolithic site, is one of its sacred centers. With 10,000 followers, modern Druidry is rooted in the pre-Christian tradition of the Celtic peoples indigenous to the British Isles.

by foreign missionaries concerning the preservation of traditional beliefs and rituals culturally associated with animism, ancestor worship, and spirit possession, as well as kinship and marriage.

Today, the African continent is as religiously and spiritually diverse as ever. Although at least 40 percent of the population is Christian, and more than another 40 percent is Muslim, myriad African indigenous religions persist and are often merged with Christianity or Islam.

Syncretic Religions Across the Atlantic: Vodou in Haiti

In almost four centuries of trans-Atlantic slave trading, African captives stolen from hundreds of towns and villages from Mauretania south to Angola and beyond were shipped without material belongings to labor on cotton, sugar, coffee, and tobacco plantations from Virginia to Brazil. Ripped from family and community, individual slaves clung to some of their ancestral beliefs and knowledge of rituals.

Sharing a life of forced labor, slaves from different ethnic, linguistic, and religious backgrounds formed small communities, pooled remembered religious ideas and rituals, and creatively forged a spiritual repertoire of their own. Founded on a mix of Yoruba and other African beliefs and practices, their emerging religions also incorporated Christian features, including terminology from the languages of slave-owning colonists. In some cases,

elements from a region's indigenous American cultures were also included.

Such creative blending of indigenous and foreign beliefs and practices into new cultural forms illustrates what anthropologists define as **syncretism**. Especially after slavery was abolished in the course of the 1800s, these syncretic spiritual repertoires developed into Afro-Caribbean religions such as Vodou in Haiti and Santería in Cuba, which resemble Candomblé in Brazil. All of these religions are spreading as adherents freely migrate across borders (Fernández Olmos & Paravisini-Gebert, 2003).

Vodou emerged in Haiti in the early 1800s after this small tropical country in the Caribbean Sea won its independence from France in a decade-long slave revolt. The name means "divine spirit" in the language of the Fon, a large ethnic group in Benin and southwestern Nigeria. Providing an escape from the indignities of poverty and hopelessness, Vodou was developed by ex-slaves speaking French-based Creole. Now mostly poor black peasants, they are nominal Roman Catholics who, like their African ancestors across the Atlantic, believe in spirit possession.

Vodou rituals center on the worship of what Haitians refer to as *loas*—also known by Creole terms such as *anges* ("angels"), *saints* ("saints"), or simply as *mystères* ("mysteries"). This tradition is essentially based on a belief in

syncretism The creative blending of indigenous and foreign beliefs and practices into new cultural forms.

Figure 13.17 Haitian Women in a Vodou Bathing Ritual In mid-July every year, thousands of Haitian pilgrims journey to a sacred waterfall in the mountains north of Port-au-Prince, Haiti, in reverence to a Black Madonna known as Our Lady of Carmel. This Marian devotion is ritually associated with a major *loa*, or Vodou spirit, named Erzulie Dantor, who mysteriously appeared on a palm tree at this waterfall about 150 years ago. Since then, an important devotional activity is bathing in this sacred water, a deeply spiritual experience in which Vodou practitioners like these women enter a trance filled with divine grace.

a reciprocal relationship between the spirits of the living and those of the dead, representing multiple expressions of the divine. Spirits of deceased ancestors and other relatives can be summoned by means of drumming in a temple. Dancing to the beat, worshipers enter into trance. This is when a person's spirit temporarily vacates the human body, replaced by a *loa* from the spirit world who takes possession—the moment of divine grace (Figure 13.17).

Religious Pluralism and Secularization

Although Christianity in Europe is losing ground as a result of Islam's rise, a much more substantial decline is due to **secularization.** In this process of cultural change, a population tends toward a nonreligious worldview, ignoring or rejecting institutionalized spiritual beliefs and rituals. Over the last few decades, growing numbers of western Europeans have declared themselves to be without religion.

Secularization is especially noteworthy in a prosperous capitalist country like Germany, which has been for many

centuries predominantly Lutheran and Roman Catholic. Today, almost 40 percent of Germans identify themselves as nonreligious, compared to a mere 4 percent forty years ago. In contrast, religion is becoming *more* important in many parts of eastern Europe where atheism was communist state ideology for several generations in the 20th century.

Secularization also takes place in other wealthy industrialized countries. In the United States, for example, 20 percent of all adults are religiously unaffiliated—and the figure jumps to about 35 percent among adults under 30. Their ranks include more than 13 million self-described atheists and agnostics—nearly 6 percent of the U.S. public (Pew Research Center, 2012). As in other large countries, there are regional contrasts, with the secularization trend among New Englanders far outpacing several areas in the southeastern United States, where 80 to 85 percent claim that religion plays an important role in their lives.

With over 2,000 distinctive faiths, the U.S. religious landscape is highly diversified, and the country has given birth to many new religions, a few of which have gone global. Moreover, in the past few decades, Asian immigrant groups have greatly added to the religious diversification in North America as well as in Europe. In response, even global finance business is adapting to the changing ideological landscape, as illustrated in this Original Study on Shariah-compliant banking.

secularization A process of cultural change in which a population tends toward a nonreligious worldview, ignoring or rejecting institutionalized spiritual beliefs and rituals.

Sacred Law in Global Capitalism BY BILL MAURER

I will never forget my introduction to Islamic banking. It happened at a 1998 conference when I happened into a darkened room where the founder of an Islamic investment firm was showing a clip from the old Hollywood classic movie, *It's a Wonderful Life*. On the screen, George Bailey, played by Jimmy Stewart, faces an anxious crowd of Bedford Falls citizens, who have rushed into his Building and Loan, passbooks in hand, desperate to get their money. There is about to be a run on the bank.

One of the townspeople says he wants his money, *now*. George protests, "But you're thinking of this place all wrong—as if I had the money back in a safe. The money's not *here*. Why, your money's in Joe's house that's right next to yours, and in the Kennedy house, and Mrs. Macklin's house, and in a hundred others. You're lending them the money to build and then they're gonna pay it back to you as best they can. . . . Now, we can get through this thing all right. We've got to stick together, though. We've got to have faith in each other." The people cry, "I've got doctor's bills to pay!" "Can't feed my kids on faith!"

Then Mary, George's newlywed bride, shouts from behind the counter, "I've got two thousand dollars!" and holds up a wad of bills. It is the money for their honeymoon. George chimes in, "This'll tide us over until the bank reopens tomorrow." He proceeds to disburse money based on people's stated needs ("Could I have $17.50?" one woman asks meekly) and guaranteed only by his trust in them.

Seconds before six o'clock, the last client leaves. George has just two dollars left. He, Mary, his Uncle Billy, and two cousins count down the seconds and then lock the doors. They have managed to stay in business for one more day. They place the two remaining dollars in a tray, and George offers a toast: "To Mama Dollar and to Papa Dollar, and if you want this old Building and Loan to stay in business you better have a family real quick." "I wish they were rabbits," says Cousin Tilly.

At this point in the film, the conference host paused the video and said, "This is the first *lariba* movie." A murmur went through the crowd. No one quite knew what he meant. Most of the audience was Muslim; this was a Christmas movie. What was our host trying to say?

I now know that *lariba* is Arabic for "no increase." The Koran invokes the term *riba* (increase) twenty times, and the term is often translated as interest or usury (excessive interest). Islamic banking and finance aim to avoid *riba* through profit-and-loss sharing, leasing, or other forms of equity- or asset-based financing.

We are all aware of the recent global financial crisis, which led to the collapse of major corporations, the nationalization of big banks and car companies, massive unemployment, and unnerving insecurity for many people in the United States and around the world. One of the leading causes of the crisis was the marketing of debt to people who probably could not repay, and the packaging of those debts into complicated financial instruments that were supposed to curb risk but instead increased it.

What, you might ask, does anthropology have to contribute to the study of the financial markets, money, and the wider economy? Quite a lot, actually. Among other things, anthropologists have repeatedly demonstrated that economic decisions thought to be purely rational and self-interested are actually deeply embedded in social relationships, cultural values, and religious beliefs.

Take securitized debt instruments, for example—loans like mortgages, chopped up and rebundled together into salable commodities. When they started to go sour, many commentators blamed the instruments' complexity and called for a return to an economy based on real things instead of abstract tradable debt. However, we know from our research across the globe that peoples in different cultures do not always differentiate the real from the abstract in the same way. A person's reputation might be deemed more solid and real than a piece of gold. And a piece of gold has real value only because people agree to it as a convention.

After that 1998 conference, I began my study of global Islamic banking, including the efforts of American Muslims to create a new kind of "Islamic" mortgage that enables devout Muslims to buy a home in accordance with Islam's prohibition of interest. Instead of financing a home purchase with interest-bearing debt, Islamic alternatives rely on either leasing contracts (a sort of rent-to-own arrangement where the bank owns the house and the purchaser buys out the bank's share over time) or a partnership arrangement (like a joint business venture). Rather than having debt and interest at the center of the mortgage, as in a conventional loan, the house itself and its fair market rental value are at the center. The purchaser buys out the bank's share over time. At the center is the asset—the real thing—not the debt.

Of course, there is no reason why a joint partnership to own a piece of property is any more "real" or less "abstract" than bundling together debt. It depends on one's point of view, and one's precommitments to certain values—prohibiting interest and sharing risk, for example, or distributing risk onto others. In Islamic finance, the former is seen as "Shariah compliant," or in accord with Islamic law; and the latter, as unjust because it offloads one's own share of risk onto others.

Until the early 1990s, millions of Muslims throughout the world had few investment opportunities due to the ethics derived from Shariah law. Since then, hundreds of Islamic financial institutions have emerged in over fifty countries. Big American and European banks, including Citibank, have also entered the Islamic banking business in order to tap into the rising oil wealth. Today, Shariah-compliant banks manage well over $750 billion globally. Here we see three Muslim women in Kuala Lumpur, Malaysia.

At the same time, Islamic mortgages often require relatively large down payments; this excludes poorer people from achieving the American dream of homeownership. So, we need to ask ourselves whether the virtues of adherence to the precepts of one's religion outweigh broader social goals of financial inclusion.

Global Islamic banking today owes much to the immigration of Middle Eastern and South Asian students and professionals to the United States and western Europe since the 1970s, and the consolidation of large U.S.–Muslim organizations. The oil boom in the Middle East during the 1970s, which sparked renewed interest in Islamic banking in many Muslim-majority countries, also encouraged the development of a loosely knit interconnected network of Muslim international businessmen, who, working for oil and chemical companies as well as financial firms, gained experience in Western regulatory and business environments.

Islamic home financing expanded greatly after the 2001 terrorist attack on New York's World Trade Center and the Pentagon; these attacks sent shockwaves through the capitalist world system dominated by Wall Street. First of all, Americans in general, Muslims included, took their money out of the stock market after the attack and started investing in real estate, buoyed by low interest rates and feeding the speculative real estate bubble. Second, Islamic mutual funds had been able to maintain their "Islamicity" in part by contributing a portion of their profits to charity in order to religiously "cleanse" the funds; however, as charities came under governmental suspicion for terrorist money laundering, many Muslims withdrew their investments from these funds. Third, home financing, American Muslims told me, is the cornerstone of the "American dream," and they were eager to demonstrate their commitment to that dream.

People involved in Islamic banking and finance are continually engaged in an effort to define precisely what their field is. Is *riba* simply Arabic for "interest," or does *riba* refer only to "excessive interest" or usury? Does the prohibition say something about justice, or does it moralize about proper market relationships? Like any aspect of culture—economy included—Islamic banking is always a field of debate. And more debate, not less, may help us all to find just, peaceful, and profitable ways out of the various catastrophes we continually make for ourselves, as we create the abstractions and realities that mutually determine our lives together.

Written expressly for this text, 2010.

In this cross-cultural survey of religion and spirituality, we explored and contrasted numerous worldviews with their symbolic constructs of the universe and our place in it. Made and remade in the course of history, all of these ideological systems reflect human wonderings and ponderings—about life and death, health and illness, past and future, real time and dream time, the known and unknown. Dynamic and inherently complex as the superstructure of a cultural system, a worldview provides imaginative answers, even as it creates mysteries of its own. Whatever its symbolic substance or form, it plays a powerful role in social bonding and control, forging ideological ties that bind and divide.

Religions, as explained and illustrated in this chapter, are not just about spiritual beliefs and rituals, however important these may be. They are also fundamental in the symbolic construction of social identities—the ways in which billions of people see themselves—and motivate people to act or not act in prescribed ways. Performing religion or spirituality, individually or collectively, people not only express what they feel and think but also *who* they are. By tradition or choice, this provides them with another identity marker, beyond features such as gender, speech, kinship, place, or status. Given the cultural variations and historical changes, different markers are stressed or recognized as socially significant.

The cultural upheavals triggered by globalization have made the anthropological study of religion not only fascinating but crucial in our efforts to better understand our species in all its creative and destructive cultural capacity.

CHAPTER CHECKLIST

What are religion and spirituality, and what role do they play in a cultural system?

● Religion is an organized system of ideas about the spiritual sphere or the supernatural, and it is a key part of every culture's worldview. Religion consists of beliefs and practices by which people try to interpret and/or influence aspects of the universe otherwise beyond their control.

● Like religion, spirituality is concerned with sacred matters, but it is often individual rather than collective and does not require a distinctive format or traditional organization.

● Among food-foraging peoples, religion is intertwined in everyday life. As societies become more complex, religion may be restricted to particular occasions.

● Spiritual and religious beliefs and practices fulfill numerous psychological and emotional needs, such as reducing anxiety by providing an orderly view of the universe and answering existential questions, including those concerning suffering and death.

● Myths are narratives that explain the fundamentals of human existence—where we and everything in our world came from, why we are here, and where we are going.

● A traditional religion reinforces group norms and provides moral sanctions for individual conduct. Its narratives and rituals confirm the existing social order, but it may also provide vehicles for challenging that order. People often turn to religion or spirituality in the hope of reaching a specific goal such as restoring health.

What types of supernatural beings and forces are included in the worldview of humans?

● Religion is characterized by a belief in supernatural beings and forces, which can be appealed to for aid through prayer, sacrifice, and other rituals. Supernatural beings may be grouped into three categories: major deities (gods and goddesses), ancestral spirits, and other sorts of spirit beings.

● Gods and goddesses are great but remote beings that control the universe. Whether people recognize gods, goddesses, or both has to do with how men and women relate to each other in everyday life.

● Monotheism holds that there is one supreme divinity; polytheism acknowledges more than one deity.

● Belief in ancestral spirits is based on the dualistic idea that human beings consist of a body and a soul, or vital spirit. Freed from the body at death, the spirit continues to participate in human affairs. This belief is characteristic of descent-based groups with their associated ancestor orientation.

● Animism, the belief that nature is animated (enlivened) by distinct personalized spirit beings separable from bodies, is common among peoples who see themselves as part of nature rather than superior to it.

● Animatism, sometimes found alongside animism, is a belief that nature is energized by an impersonal spiritual force—as in the Chinese concept of *ch'i*.

What are the different types of religious specialists?

● Priests and priestesses are full-time religious specialists authorized to perform sacred rituals and mediate with supernatural powers on behalf of others.

● Priests and priestesses typically hold their position by way of spiritual lineage in which divine authority is passed down from a spiritual founder to a chain of successors.

● There are four major forms of spiritual lineage: biological descent, training and appointment by religious leaders, election, and recognition of a reincarnated saint.

● Shamans are individuals skilled at entering an altered state of consciousness to contact and utilize an ordinarily hidden reality in order to acquire knowledge and supernatural power to help other people. Their special powers have come to them through some personal experience.

What are religious rituals and rites, and what purposes do they serve?

● A religious ritual is a culturally symbolic act or procedure designed to guide members of a community in an orderly way through personal and collective transitions. It is religion in action—the means through which people relate to the supernatural.

● Rites of purification are rituals performed to establish or restore purity when someone has violated a taboo or is otherwise unclean.

● Rites of passage are rituals marking an important stage in an individual's life cycle, such as birth, marriage, and death. They feature three phases: separation, transition, and incorporation.

● Rites of intensification are rituals that ease anxiety and bind people together when they face a collective crisis or change.

What are magic, divination, and witchcraft?

● People in many cultures believe in magic: the idea that supernatural powers can be compelled to act in certain ways for good or evil purposes through specified formulas.

● Many societies have magical rituals to ensure good fortune. Magic is considered to be both imitative (like produces like) and contagious.

● Divination is a magical procedure or spiritual ritual designed to find out what is not knowable by ordinary means, particularly through signs foretelling fate or destiny. Examples include geomancy and chiromancy (palmistry).

● Witchcraft—magical rituals intended to cause misfortune or inflict harm and often referred to as sorcery—is believed to be practiced by people who embody evil spirit power or collaborate with malevolent supernatural beings.

● Belief in witchcraft is widespread, takes many forms, and is especially common during periods of uncertainty.

What are sacred sites and pilgrimages?

● Sacred sites come in many forms. Some are places where ordinary people experienced something extraordinary. Others are associated with a holy person, including shrines or burial sites. Exceptional natural places, especially mountaintops, are often considered magical or sacred.

● A pilgrimage is a devotion in motion—a journey, often on foot, to a sacred site by individuals reaching for enlightenment, proving devotion, and/or hoping to experience a miracle. Among the largest pilgrimages is the hajj made by 1.8 million Muslims traveling to Mecca in Saudi Arabia each year from all around the world.

● Many pilgrimages center on cults of the Virgin Mary. These include Black Madonnas—dark-colored clay or wooden statues or painted images representing the virgin mother. One of them, the Virgin of Guadalupe in Mexico City, draws 6 million pilgrims annually.

● Sacred sites are potential targets of desecration—ideological violation of a sacred site aimed at harming, if only symbolically, people judged to have impure, false, or evil beliefs and ritual practices.

What are revitalization movements, and how are they connected to social upheaval?

● Revitalization movements, which can happen in any culture, arise when people seek radical cultural reform in response to widespread social disruption and collective feelings of anxiety and despair.

● Revitalization movements are not restricted to indigenous peoples historically dominated by colonial powers. They include the 19th-century rise of Mormonism in the United States and ecospiritualism in many Western nations, such as the rise of Druidry in England.

● The revival of traditional American Indian ceremonies such as the sweat lodge and Sun Dance ceremony are other revitalization examples.

● Syncretism, the creative blending of indigenous and foreign beliefs and practices into new cultural forms, can be found worldwide. This includes the practice of Vodou among former slaves in Haiti, which features elements of Roman Catholicism and traditional African beliefs such as spirit possession.

What is secularization?

● Secularization is a process of cultural change in which a population tends toward a nonreligious worldview, ignoring or rejecting institutionalized spiritual beliefs and rituals.

● Fairly common in wealthy countries, secularization has become especially prevalent in western Europe.

QUESTIONS FOR REFLECTION

1. There is more to culture than making survival possible, as humans also search for meaning in the universe and their place in it. Many put their faith in spirit forces, supernatural beings, or deities, seeking existential answers and praying for protection and support. Christian pilgrims in Mexico put their faith in a holy mother figure in heaven. Does your worldview provide you with the same or a similar spiritual support in times of hardship or suffering?

2. People in every culture experience anxiety, fear, and social tension, and many attribute accidents, illnesses, or other misfortunes to evil magic practiced by malevolent individuals such as witches or sorcerers. Do you believe people really possess such supernatural powers to inflict harm?

3. Do the basic dynamics of the shamanic complex also apply to preachers or priests in modern churches and medical doctors working in modern hospitals? Can you think of some similarities among the shaman, preacher, and medical doctor in terms of their respective fields of operation?

4. Graduation is a rite of passage, also known as commencement or convocation, when a high-ranking university official presents students who have completed their studies an academic degree. Can you identify the three phases in this ceremony?

5. Revitalization movements occur in reaction to the upheavals caused by rapid colonization and modernization. Do you think that the rise of religious fundamentalism among Christians, Muslims, Jews, and Hindus is a response to such upheavals as well?

ONLINE STUDY RESOURCES

CourseMate

Access chapter-specific learning tools, including learning objectives, practice quizzes, videos, flash cards, glossaries, and more in your Anthropology CourseMate.

Log into **www.cengagebrain.com** to access the resources your instructor has assigned and to purchase materials.

Body Ritual among the Nacirema

HORACE MINER
University of Michigan

THE anthropologist has become so familiar with the diversity of ways in which different peoples behave in similar situations that he is not apt to be surprised by even the most exotic customs. In fact, if all of the logically possible combinations of behavior have not been found somewhere in the world, he is apt to suspect that they must be present in some yet undescribed tribe. This point has, in fact, been expressed with respect to clan organization by Murdock (1949: 71). In this light, the magical beliefs and practices of the Nacirema present such unusual aspects that it seems desirable to describe them as an example of the extremes to which human behavior can go.

Professor Linton first brought the ritual of the Nacirema to the attention of anthropologists twenty years ago (1936:326), but the culture of this people is still very poorly understood. They are a North American group living in the territory between the Canadian Cree, the Yaqui and Tarahumare of Mexico, and the Carib and Arawak of the Antilles. Little is known of their origin, although tradition states that they came from the east. According to Nacirema mythology, their nation was originated by a culture hero, Notgnihsaw, who is otherwise known for two great feats of strength-the throwing of a piece of wampum across the river Pa-To-Mac and the chopping down of a cherry tree in which the Spirit of Truth resided.

Nacirema culture is characterized by a highly developed market economy which has evolved in a rich natural habitat. While much of the people's time is devoted to economic pursuits, a large part of the fruits of these labors and a considerable portion of the day are spent in ritual activity. The focus of this activity is the human body, the appearance and health of which loom as a dominant concern in the ethos of the people. While such a concern is certainly not unusual, its ceremonial aspects and associated philosophy are unique.

Body Ritual Among the Nacirema by Horace Miner from *American Anthropologist*, June 1956, pages 503-507, American Anthropological Association.

The fundamental belief underlying the whole system appears to be that the human body is ugly and that its natural tendency is to debility and disease. Incarcerated in such a body, man's only hope is to avert these characteristics through the use of the powerful influences of ritual and ceremony. Every household has one or more shrines devoted to this purpose. The more powerful individuals in the society have several shrines in their houses and, in fact, the opulence of a house is often referred to in terms of the number of such ritual centers it possesses. Most houses are of wattle and daub construction, but the shrine rooms of the more wealthy are walled with stone. Poorer families imitate the rich by applying pottery plaques to their shrine walls.

While each family has at least one such shrine, the rituals associated with it are not family ceremonies but are private and secret. The rites are normally only discussed with children, and then only during the period when they are being initiated into these mysteries. I was able, however, to establish sufficient rapport with the natives to examine these shrines and to have the rituals described to me.

The focal point of the shrine is a box or chest which is built into the wall. In this chest are kept the many charms and magical potions without which no native believes he could live. These preparations are secured from a variety of specialized practitioners. The most powerful of these are the medicine men, whose assistance must be rewarded with substantial gifts. However, the medicine men do not provide the curative potions for their clients, but decide what the ingredients should be and then write them down in an ancient and secret language. This writing is understood only by the medicine men and by the herbalists who, for another gift, provide the required charm.

The charm is not disposed of after it has served its purpose, but is placed in the charm-box of the household shrine. As these magical materials are specific for certain ills, and the real or imagined maladies of the people are many, the charm-box is usually full to overflowing. The magical packets are so numerous that people forget what their purposes were and fear to use them again. While the natives are very vague on this point, we can only assume that the idea in retaining all the old magical materials is that their presence in the charm-box, before which the body rituals are conducted, will in some way protect the worshipper.

Beneath the charm-box is a small font. Each day every member of the family, in succession, enters the shrine room, bows his head before the charm-box, mingles different sorts of holy water in the font, and proceeds with a brief rite of ablution. The holy waters are secured from the Water Temple of the community, where the priests conduct elaborate ceremonies to make the liquid ritually pure.

In the hierarchy of magical practitioners, and below the medicine men in prestige, are specialists whose designation is best translated "holy-mouth-men." The Nacirema have an almost pathological horror of and fascination with the mouth, the condition of which is believed to have a supernatural influence on all social relationships. Were it not for the rituals of the mouth, they believe that their teeth would fall out, their gums bleed, their jaws shrink, their friends desert them, and their lovers reject them. They also believe that a strong relationship exists between oral and moral characteristics. For example, there is a ritual ablution of the mouth for children which is supposed to improve their moral fiber.

The daily body ritual performed by everyone includes a mouth-rite. Despite the fact that these people are so punctilious about care of the mouth, this rite involves a practice which strikes the uninitiated stranger as revolting. It was reported to me that the ritual consists of inserting a small bundle of hog hairs into the mouth, along with certain magical powders, and then moving the bundle in a highly formalized series of gestures.

In addition to the private mouth-rite, the people seek out a holy-mouth-man once or twice a year. These practitioners have an impressive set of paraphernalia, consisting of a variety of augers, awls, probes, and prods. The use of these objects in the exorcism of the evils of the mouth involves almost unbelievable ritual torture of the client. The holy-mouth-man opens the client's mouth and, using the above mentioned tools, enlarges any holes which decay may have created in the teeth. Magical materials are put into these holes. If there are no naturally occurring holes in the teeth, large sections of one or more teeth are gouged out so that the supernatural substance can be applied. In the client's view, the purpose of these ministrations is to arrest decay and to draw friends. The extremely sacred and traditional character of the rite is evident in the fact that the natives return to the holy-mouth-men year after year, despite the fact that their teeth continue to decay.

It is to be hoped that, when a thorough study of the Nacirema is made, there will be careful inquiry into the personality structure of these people. One has but to watch the gleam in the eye of a holy-mouth-man, as he jabs an awl into an exposed nerve, to suspect that a certain amount of sadism is involved. If this can be established, a very interesting pattern emerges, for most of the population shows definite masochistic tendencies. It was to these that Professor Linton referred in discussing a distinctive part of the daily body ritual which is performed only by men. This part of the rite involves scraping and lacerating the surface of the face with a sharp instrument. Special women's rites are performed only four times during each lunar month, but what they lack in frequency is made up in barbarity. As part of this ceremony, women bake their heads in small ovens for about an hour. The theoretically interesting point is that what seems to be a preponderantly masochistic people have developed sadistic specialists.

The medicine men have an imposing temple, or *lati pso,* in every community of any size. The more elaborate ceremonies required to treat very sick patients can only be performed at this temple. These ceremonies involve not only the thaumaturge but a permanent group of vestal maidens who move sedately about the temple chambers in distinctive costume and headdress.

The *lati pso* ceremonies are so harsh that it is phenomenal that a fair proportion of the really sick natives who enter the temple ever recover. Small children whose indoctrination is still incomplete have been known to resist attempts to take them to the temple because "that is where you *go* to die." Despite this fact, sick adults are not only willing but eager to undergo the protracted ritual purification, if they can afford to do so. No matter how ill the supplicant or how grave the emergency, the guardians of many temples will not admit a client if he cannot give a rich gift to the custodian. Even after one has gained admission and survived the ceremonies, the guardians will not permit the neophyte to leave until he makes still another gift.

The supplicant entering the temple is first stripped of all his or her clothes. In everyday life the Nacirema avoids exposure of his body and its natural functions. Bathing and excretory acts are performed only in the secrecy of the household shrine, where they are ritualized as part of the body-rites. Psychological shock results from the fact that body secrecy is suddenly lost upon entry into the *lati pso*. A man, whose own wife has never seen him in an excretory act, suddenly finds himself naked and assisted by a vestal maiden while he performs his natural functions into a sacred vessel. This sort of ceremonial treatment is necessitated by the fact that the excreta are used by a diviner to ascertain the course and nature of the client's sickness. Female clients, on the other hand, find their naked bodies are subjected to the scrutiny, manipulation and prodding of the medicine men.

Few supplicants in the temple are well enough to do anything but lie on their hard beds. The daily ceremonies, like the rites of the holy-mouth-men, involve discomfort and torture. With ritual precision, the vestals awaken their miserable charges each dawn and roll them about on their beds of pain while performing ablutions, in the formal movements of which the maidens are highly trained. At other times they insert magic wands in the supplicant's mouth or force him to eat substances which are supposed to be healing. From time to time the medicine men come to their clients and jab magically treated needles into their flesh. The fact that these temple ceremonies may not cure, and may even kill the neophyte, in no way decreases the people's faith in the medicine men.

There remains one other kind of practitioner, known as a "listener." This witch-doctor has the power to exorcise the devils that lodge in the heads of people who have been bewitched. The Nacirema believe that parents bewitch their own children. Mothers are particularly suspected of putting a curse on children while teaching them the secret body rituals. The counter-magic of the witch-doctor is unusual in its lack of ritual. The patient simply tells the "listener" all his troubles and fears, beginning with the earliest difficulties he can remember. The memory displayed by the Nacirema in these exorcism sessions is truly remarkable. It is not uncommon for the patient to bemoan the rejection he felt upon being weaned as a babe, and a few individuals even see their troubles going back to the traumatic effects of their own birth.

In conclusion, mention must be made of certain practices which have their base in native esthetics but which depend upon the pervasive aversion to the natural body and its functions. There are ritual fasts to make fat people thin and ceremonial feasts to make thin people fat. Still other rites are used to make women's breasts larger if they are small, and smaller if they are large. General dissatisfaction with breast shape is symbolized in the fact that the ideal form is virtually outside the range of human variation. A few women afflicted with almost inhuman hypermammary development are so idolized that they make a handsome living by simply going from village to village and permitting the natives to stare at them for a fee.

Reference has already been made to the fact that excretory functions are ritualized, routinized, and relegated to secrecy. Natural reproductive functions are similarly distorted. Intercourse is taboo as a topic and scheduled as an act. Efforts are made to avoid pregnancy by the use of magical materials or by limiting intercourse to certain phases of the moon. Conception is actually very infrequent. When pregnant, women dress so as to hide their condition. Parturition takes place in secret, without friends or relatives to assist, and the majority of women do not nurse their infants.

Our review of the ritual life of the Nacirema has certainly shown them to be a magic-ridden people. It is hard to understand how they have managed to exist so long under the burdens which they have imposed upon themselves. But even such exotic customs as these take on real meaning when they are viewed with the insight provided by Malinowski when he wrote (1948:70):

> Looking from far and above, from our high places of safety in the developed civilization, it is easy to see all the crudity and irrelevance of magic. But without its power and guidance early man could not have mastered his practical difficulties as he has done, nor could man have advanced to the higher stages of civilization.

REFERENCES CITED

LINTON RALPH
      1936 The Study of Man. New York, D. Appleton-Century Co.

MALINOWSKI BRONISLAW
      1948 Magic, Science, and Religion. Glencoe, The Free Press.

MURDOCK GEORGE
      1949 Social Structure. New York, The Macmillan Co.

CHAPTER 6

RESOLVING CONFLICT

© Bilderbuch/Design Pics/Thinkstock

Canadian memorials to fallen soldiers, such as the Canadian National War Memorial, often evoke the sentiment "Lest We Forget." In the second half of the 20th century, Canada saw itself as a peacekeeper nation, striving to prevent or diminish violent conflict. However, as Richler notes in the chapter epigraph on the next page, Canada more recently became a "warrior nation," especially since it assumed a combat role in Afghanistan. How do Canadians make sense of our ambivalent relationship with war?

Often it is illuminating to see how history puts on different disguises even as the underlying habits of a place are fundamentally unaltered. This is to say either that Canada today is a "warrior nation"—that the peacekeeping version of Canada was a fifty-year aberration and a public that believes otherwise genuinely has ignored Canada's long military history—or that the Canada with an innate disposition toward "soft power," "making a difference" and the sort of peacekeeping work that is now so disparaged is the underlying constant and the "warrior nation" is the fiction.

Noah Richler, What We Talk About When We Talk About War (2012)

Problem 9

How do societies give meaning to and justify various forms of conflict resolution, both peaceful and violent?

INTRODUCTION

Justifying Violence and Imagining Peace

We often tend to think of violence and peace as conditions of existence that are universally understood, transparent, and commonsense: that violence is an innate human tendency and that peace is simply the absence of violence. It may be more useful, as anthropologists, to focus on peace-making and violence as two sides of the coin of conflict resolution. As with all human behaviours and experience, violence and peace are processes to which we collectively assign meaning within particular contexts. For instance, as Noah Richler points out in the epigraph to this chapter, when Canada sends its soldiers into conflict zones, their role can be understood and has been understood as peacekeeping or as war-making, depending on the dominant narratives of national identity at the time.

Throughout this text, we have taken a problem-based approach to understanding humanity, and many of the problems we have explored may give rise to conflicts, perhaps over resources, over identity, over inequality or injustice, and these conflicts demand some sort of resolution. In some cases, conflict results in collective violence: think, for instance, of the Cherokee Removal discussed in Chapter 3 or Sanday's analysis of fraternity gang rape in Chapter 7. In other cases, more peaceful forms of conflict resolution are favoured, as among the

Ju/'hoansi or the Hutterites, or in Wovoka's Ghost Dance revitalization movement, discussed in Chapter 4. In order to understand why humans choose one form of conflict resolution or another, it is necessary to think about how humans make sense of and justify violence and peace.

Violence, "a category in between peaceful disputing, and major planned warfare and fighting" (Strathern and Stewart 2002, 1), may seem to be an intrinsic feature of human societies. It is, in fact, difficult to find societies that do not sanction violence for one reason or another. But why is collective violence nearly universally sanctioned? Some suggest that human beings have an innate instinct toward aggression and that the roots of war and collective violence lie somewhere in the biological mechanisms that animals and humans have in common. Violent conflict is regarded, in this view, as a part of human nature. Others reject this explanation as simplistic; collective violence, they say, is, above all, a cultural construction whose roots lie in the human mind, not in the genes.

Moreover, some anthropologists argue that there is compelling ethnographic and historical evidence that "humans have a solid capacity for getting along with each other peacefully, preventing physical aggression, limiting the scope and spread of violence, and restoring peace following aggression" (Fry 2007, 21). We tend to overlook and underappreciate this capacity precisely because violence is exceptional and aberrant. It commands our scrutiny, attention, and concern. Put another way, "the view that [violence and] warfare is inevitable because it is an immutable part of human nature is also a cultural convention masquerading as fact" (Sahlins 2008, quoted in Lohmann 2014, 255). The ethnographic realities of conflict resolution suggest that "neither fully peaceful nor fully violent outcomes are actually the norm" (Strathern and Stewart 2011, ix); as anthropologists, we must endeavour to understand the factors that lead to or favour one form of conflict resolution over the other in different circumstances.

The fact that human beings construct systems of meaning to justify violent conflict and to distance themselves from its consequences suggests that it has little to do with a natural aggressive impulse. Acts of collective violence are rationalized as purposeful, noble, or inevitable, not as evidence of wanton cruelty. The problem is to discover how societies construct meanings for violent conflict that mask its consequences and that convince people it is right and proper.

It is equally important to understand what peace is and how it is created and maintained. As anthropologist Brian Ferguson (2008, 46–47) has argued, "peace is more than the absence of war." Rather, peace is an active social process, one that must be first imagined and then acted upon. Lohmann (2014) defines peace, therefore, as

> *A group activity, carried on by members of one community toward members of another community, in which the primary purpose is to maintain mutual benefit by successfully deploying means for enhancing political relations and preventing violence, by either directing contacts with goodwill or avoiding one another with an attitude of peace. (259)*

Just as violence must be justified, peace must be imagined and maintained; both are deeply social and political processes.

To make sense of these issues, the first question to be addressed is how societies create a bias in favour of collective violence. In other words, what kinds of meanings are constructed to encourage people to commit violence against others? Then, if there are societies without collective violence, how do they create a bias against it? How do they create peace? If violent conflict is not natural and inevitable but culturally constructed, it may be possible to learn from societies in which there is little if any violence. This focus raises the following question: are there significant social, economic, or political differences between violent and peaceful societies? Beyond that, what is the relationship between violence and the nation-state? Since collective violence is sanctioned in North American societies, it is instructive to ask how we have created a bias toward violent conflict and constructed meanings that allow us to contemplate, plan for, and pursue the destruction of millions of people in other nations. We will go on to explore the potential pitfalls and possible insights to be gained by conducting participant observation of, and during, violent conflicts. Finally, as a conclusion to the chapter and to the text as a whole, we will think about the roles that anthropologists can play in promoting peaceful forms of conflict resolution to the kinds of problems we have discussed throughout this book.

QUESTIONS

9.1 How do societies create a bias in favour of collective violence?

9.2 How do societies create a bias in favour of peaceful conflict resolution?

9.3 What are the economic, political, and social differences between peaceful and violent societies?

9.4 What is the relationship between violence and the nation-state?

9.5 How is it possible to justify the creation of weapons of mass destruction?

9.6 How do anthropologists do fieldwork in the midst of violent conflict?

QUESTION 9.1: HOW DO SOCIETIES CREATE A BIAS IN FAVOUR OF COLLECTIVE VIOLENCE?

Horses, Rank, and Warfare Among the Kiowa

One way societies create a bias toward collective violence is by rewarding it. Among the Native Americans of the western plains, for example, raiding other groups for horses was a means by which a man gained status. Horses symbolized wealth, and in many groups a man's importance was measured by the number of horses he owned and gave to others as gifts.

Horses are not indigenous to North America; they were brought to the continent by the Spaniards in the 1500s. Native American groups such as the Kiowa captured some horses and acquired others in trade with the Spaniards. The Kiowa also obtained horses by attacking other Native American groups with horse-raiding parties of as many as 30 men. The objective of these raids was to secure as many of the enemy's horses as possible and, as well, to demonstrate bravery. Among the Kiowa, rank was determined in two ways: by the number of horses a man possessed and by the honours accruing to him in warfare.

Kiowa society was divided into four ranks, or grades. In the top rank were *ongop*, men who were generous, who held considerable wealth, and, most important, who had distinguished themselves in war. In the second rank were *ondeigupa*, men who had property (especially horses), who were generous, but who had not yet distinguished themselves in war. The lower ranks of Kiowa society were occupied by *keen* or *dupom*, people who were poor, propertyless, or helpless.

To rise in status, a young Kiowa male needed to acquire a horse. Often, he began his climb through the ranks of Kiowa society by borrowing a horse from a kinsperson to go on a raid, hoping to repay the loan with another horse he had captured. With a horse of his own, he could participate in more raids, gradually obtaining enough horses to rise to the rank of *ondeigupa*, or, as the Kiowa put it, "rise out of the bush of *keen*." Several years of raiding might bring him 20 or 30 horses, at which point people would begin speaking of him with respect.

To rise to the top rank of *ongop*, however, also required the accumulation of honours won in war. The Kiowa had a very elaborate system of battle honours divided into three groups of brave deeds, with group I being the most honoured (see Table 9.1). Counting first coup, for example, involved

TABLE 9.1   KIOWA RANKING AND HONOURS

GROUP I	GROUP II	GROUP III
Counting first coup	Killing an enemy	Dismounting, turning horse loose, and fighting on foot
Charging an enemy while the party is in retreat, thus covering the retreat	Counting second coup	Counting third and fourth coup
Rescuing a comrade while the party is retreating before the enemy	Receiving a wound in hand-to-hand combat	Serving as raid leader
Charging the leading man of the enemy alone before the parties have met	Success in stealing horses	Efficiency in war camp life

Information from Bernard Mishkin, Rank and Warfare Among the Plains Indians (Seattle: University of Washington Press, 1940)

charging the enemy alone and striking one of them with a stick. The number of feathers a man wore in his headdress was a measure of his heroic exploits.

Anthropologist Bernard Mishkin (1940) estimates that about 10 percent of the men would rise to the top rank of Kiowa society by obtaining a significant number of horses and accumulating sufficient battle honours. In this way, the Kiowa rewarded aggressive behaviour and bravery in battle.

Good Hosts Among the Yanomamö

Another way societies create a bias in favour of collective violence is by making it a necessary means for protecting valuable resources. As we discussed in Chapter 2, a classic (but contentious) example is the Yanomamö of Venezuela. The Yanomamö live in villages of 40 to 250 people and practise slash-and-burn (swidden) agriculture, living primarily on the crops they grow in their gardens.

Warfare between villages is endemic among the Yanomamö. Anthropologist Napoleon Chagnon, who conducted fieldwork with them from the mid-1960s until the latter half of the 1990s, reports that one village of 200 people was attacked 25 times and that ten people were killed during a 15-month period, representing a loss of 5 percent of the village population. He estimates that 20 to 25 percent of all male deaths are the result of warfare.

For the Yanomamö, women and children are valuable resources. The men believe that to protect themselves and their resources, they must be fierce, and raiding another village is one way for them to demonstrate their ferocity. Raids may be conducted to avenge the death of a village member at the hands of an enemy village or as the result of an act of sorcery by an enemy. Raids may also be made to capture women or children. Violence can take the form of inviting members of another village to a feast and—usually with the aid of allies from another village—killing the guests and abducting their women. Raiding by other villages forces them to move fairly frequently, and sometimes they take refuge from their enemies in the villages of their allies. This practice is risky, however, because host villages generally expect sexual access to the wives of their guests or expect unmarried female guests to marry men of their village. These expectations often lead to open hostilities between hosts and guests.

Caracas
VENEZUELA

Yanomamo territory

PACIFIC OCEAN

Amazon River

BRAZIL

Brasilia

people were created from the blood of the moon, which had been shot with an arrow by beings who believed that their children's souls were being devoured by the moon. The first Yanomamö born of the blood of the moon were exceptionally fierce and waged constant war on one another.

The Yanomamö also socialize male children to be aggressive and hostile. Boys are teased to strike tormentors and to bully girls. At one gathering of two villages attended by Chagnon, men were to satisfy their grievances against each other with a chest-pounding duel. Prior to the duel the men gathered all the boys between the ages of 8 and 15 and forced them to fight one another. At first, says Chagnon, the boys were reluctant and tried to run away, but their parents dragged them back and insisted that they hit each other. At the first blows the boys cried, but as the fight progressed, fear became rage, and they ended up pounding each other while they screamed and rolled in the dirt, to the cheers and admiration of their fathers.

Constructing Religious Justifications for Violence

Another way to justify violence is by framing it as a cosmic struggle between good and evil. Most modern religions contain sacred texts describing violent confrontations between the forces of good and the forces of evil. The Book of Revelation, with its description of the forces of Satan and the ultimate battle between good and evil, provides one of the most powerful (and most violent) metaphors of war and redemption in Western literature. As Elaine Pagels (1995) notes, the characterization of one's enemies as "Satanic" and of oneself as God's people has long been a formula for justifying hatred and mass slaughter.

So, it should not be surprising that people use religious rhetoric to justify violent acts, but more than that is often at work. When devout adherents to Christianity, Judaism, Sikhism, Buddhism, or Islam commit violent acts in the name of God or some spiritual mission, they are often responding

Expressions of ferocity may be directed among village members, as well. For example, men often vent anger and demonstrate their ferocity by beating their wives. A man who accuses another of cowardice or of making excessive demands for goods or women may challenge his opponent to a chest-pounding duel in which they take turns hitting each other in the chest as hard as they can. The duel generally ends when one of the contestants is too injured to continue. Fights with clubs are another form of settling disputes between men, although these generally result in free-for-alls, which can be deadly.

In this environment, where each man strives to acquire women from others, it is necessary to adopt an antagonistic stance toward others. This stance, in turn, encourages the development of what the Yanomamö call *waiteri* (ferocity). The *waiteri* complex, as Chagnon calls it, is evidenced in ways other than direct conflict. The Yanomamö express it in their origin myth, which tells how the original

RESOLVING CONFLICT

to social, political, or economic grievances, as well. Osama bin Laden sought the establishment of an Islamic caliphate, or form of government, but he was also protesting the Israeli occupation of Palestinian territories, the stationing of U.S. troops in Saudi Arabia, and the American support for oppressive governments in the Middle East. Of course, violence is not the only response to cosmic conflict and social grievances that the devout of any religion might be expected to make. Indeed, many adherents vehemently protest against such violence and advocate for peace in the name of their respective religions. For example, the Hutterites, as discussed in Chapter 7, reject violence and war as part of their interpretation and practice of Christianity.

Nonetheless, all religions have their violent militants. On 20 March 1995, five members of the Aum Shinrikyo movement, all of whom had scientific training, walked into the Tokyo subway and, with sharpened umbrellas, punctured plastic bags filled with deadly sarin gas, killing 12 people and poisoning more than 5,500. The group's members explained to Mark Juergensmeyer (2003) that Aum Shinrikyo represented for them a critique of Japanese religion and the "hierarchical" Japanese social system. The movement was founded by Shoko Asahara based on the idea that there would occur a world catastrophe—a Third World War or "Armageddon"—in which the forces of good and evil would confront each other and members of Aum Shinrikyo would survive.

Asahara justified his acts by reference to Tibetan Buddhism and the concept of *phoa*. Instead of focusing on the effect that killing has on the killer's moral purity, this doctrine focuses on the one who is killed and on the merit that comes after death. According to Asahara, if a person is a scoundrel or is part of an evil social system, he or she is accumulating negative karmic debt. Killing such people represents a mercy killing that allows their souls to move to a higher plane than if they continued to exist in sin.

Juergensmeyer (2003) asks under what conditions people are likely to use religious justifications

Aftermath of sarin attack on Tokyo subway in 1995.

for violence. He suggests that by locating a struggle on a cosmic scale, aggressors elevate its importance beyond local concerns and, instead, invoke legendary battles between good and evil. Osama bin Laden justified violence by projecting the struggle as one between the forces of Islam and those trying to destroy it. The rhetoric of wars of good versus evil is even part of the U.S. political mainstream, with terms such as "axis of evil."

There is real power, suggests Juergensmeyer, in elevating a political conflict to a cosmic war. To live in a state of war, he writes,

is to live in a world in which individuals know who they are, why they have suffered, by whose hand they have been humiliated, and at what expense they have persevered. The concept of war provides cosmology, history, and eschatology and offers the reins of political control. Perhaps most important, it holds out the hope of victory and the means to achieve it. In the images of cosmic war this victorious triumph is a grand moment of social and personal transformation, transcending all worldly limitations. One does not easily abandon such expectations. To be without such images of war is almost to be without hope itself. (2003, 158)

EXERCISE 9.1

Examples of group-sanctioned conflict are readily available in reports in newspapers and on the Internet. To examine the justifications for such conflict, follow a daily newspaper or news website for a couple of days and document the instances you find of group-sanctioned violence and the reasons attributed for it. What options, if any, are discussed or proposed for peaceful resolutions to such conflicts?

QUESTION 9.2: HOW DO SOCIETIES CREATE A BIAS IN FAVOUR OF PEACEFUL CONFLICT RESOLUTION?

Anthropologist Thomas Gregor (1990) suggests that since war is so widespread in human societies, the task of the social scientist is not so much to explain war as to explain peace. Peaceful societies, he says, are difficult to find. By peaceful, he means a society that is not involved in internal collective violence and in which there is little interpersonal violence. A peaceful society has no special roles for warriors and places a positive value on nonaggressive behaviour

and the peaceful resolution of conflict. Societies that have been characterized as relatively peaceful include the Ju/'hoansi, the Semai of Malaysia, and the Xinguano of the Amazon.

Characteristics of Peaceful Societies

Peaceful societies avoid conflicts over material resources through a strong emphasis on sharing and cooperation. It is understood that everyone in the group has a legitimate claim to what the group possesses. Among the Ju/'hoansi, the person whose arrow kills an animal is considered to be the owner of the game, but he is obligated to distribute it. The Ju/'hoansi will share arrows with the understanding that if they kill an animal with an arrow given to them by someone else, they will give the owner the game to distribute. This practice also works to spread out the responsibility for meat sharing and the glory (and perhaps the hostility) that accompanies meat distribution.

The Semai of Malaysia are known for their nonaggressiveness and avoidance of physical conflict. The approximately 15,000 Semai live in hamlets of fewer than 100 people each. Understanding Semai nonviolence, says anthropologist Clayton Robarchek (1990), requires understanding the Semai notion of *pehunan*, a state of being in which a person is unsatisfied in regard to some need or want, such as food or sex. The Semai believe that to refuse a request and deny a person a need intensifies the danger to both the individual and the group; for that reason, the group is obligated to help. The idea of *pehunan* encompasses a depiction of the community as nurturant caregivers. Instead of understanding that each person is obligated to meet his or her own needs, the Semai believe that all members of the community are obliged to help and give nurturance to others. Thus, Semai values stress affiliation, mutual aid, and the belief that violence is not a viable option for settling disputes.

Another way that people in peaceful societies create a bias against violence is by condemning

RESOLVING CONFLICT

those who boast or who make claims that can be interpreted as a challenge to others. Among the Ju/'hoansi, for example, no one is praised for gathering food or making a kill, and people go out of their way to minimize their accomplishments. Those who make boastful claims are ridiculed. Anthropologist Richard Lee (1969) painfully learned this lesson himself when, to show his appreciation to the Ju/'hoansi for the help they had given him, he brought a fine ox to be slaughtered and distributed at a Christmas feast. The Ju/'hoansi, much to Lee's chagrin, ridiculed the ox, claiming it was thin and unappetizing. Lee later realized that they were acting toward him as they would have to one of their own. They were letting him know that he wasn't as important as the gift and the killing of the ox made him think he was.

Thomas Gregor (1990) says that villagers in the Xingu basin of the Amazon maintain harmony by purposely sanctioning village monopolies in the production of certain goods such as shell belts, stone axes, salt, cotton, fish spears, and ceramic pots. In this way, each village has something that other villages need. The villages therefore maintain good relations, since to alienate another village might deprive one's own village members of a desired good. Moreover, trade is positively valued in itself. When villagers are asked why they don't make the goods they need themselves, they reply that doing so might anger those who do make them. Or they may claim that they do not have the knowledge to produce the items. (When temporarily cut off from a supply, though, they seem to learn how to make or acquire them very quickly.) Gregor says it is unlikely that any village could not produce the goods desired: marriage between groups is common so each village contains people with the skills of other villages.

The Xinguanos place a strong negative value on aggression and on things that symbolize aggression. Killing is wrong because it produces blood; even animal blood is considered defiling. Most game animals are considered inedible, and even fish must be well cooked so that there is no blood. The Xinguanos also hold strong negative stereotypes of aggressive groups. They consider non-Xingu Indians to be "wild Indians" who are violent, beating their children, raping their women, and shooting arrows at white men's planes. The wild Indian has almost the status of an animal and represents everything a Xinguano does not want to be. When Xingu villages have been the object of aggression by others, they have defended themselves, but successful warriors take no trophies and are given no special honour. In fact, they have to take special medicine to cleanse themselves of the defilement of the blood of those killed.

Peaceful societies also minimize violence and conflict through ceremony. The Ju/'hoansi believe that everyone has "medicine" or power. In the same way that nearby Bantu tribes have witchcraft and sorcery, and Europeans have pills and syringes, the Ju/'hoansi have *n/um*, a substance they say lies in the pit of the stomach. *N/um* has the capacity to keep people healthy and to help cure people who are sick. Most important, *n/um* can be transferred from someone who is acting as a healer to others through the medium of the trance dance, their most common ceremony. The idea of the dance is for a person to "heat up" his or her *n/um* by dancing; as the person dances, the *n/um* in the stomach is

This Xinguano will ensure that his catch is well cooked, so that there will be no blood.

vaporized and travels up the spinal cord into the brain, which causes the dancer to go into a trance. The dancer then goes from person to person laying on hands and transferring power to those who are touched, thereby enabling them to ward off sickness and death. Anyone can be a healer among the Ju/'hoansi; in a lifetime, each person is likely to serve as a healer at least once.

The trance dance has meanings that go beyond the power to heal, however. Some Ju/'hoansi are thought to have special powers that allow them to see the ghosts of dead ancestors who hover around the fires, to see distant scenes, to see through things, and, in special cases, to change themselves into lions and stalk the veldt in search of human prey. Trance dances are most frequent when large numbers of people come together (from about once a month in small groups, up to four times a week in large camps) and during certain occasions such as the arrival of visitors to a camp, the presence of meat, or sickness. The congregation of large numbers of people, the presence of meat, and the arrival of new people are all occasions that, in one way or another, create the potential for interpersonal conflict. The fact that trance dances are more frequent during such times seems to indicate that they may serve to heal social conflict as well as individual maladies. By bringing people together in the ceremony, by the sharing of n/um and the ritual recognition of common threats, the trance dance unites people and symbolizes the relationship between group harmony and individual well-being.

In sum, peaceful societies create a bias against violence by sharing, by valuing nonaggressive behaviour, by building relations of dependence between individuals and groups, and by engaging in collective behaviours that promote harmony. They are not, of course, always successful, and even among some societies characterized as peaceful, there is violence. Lee (1984, 148) collected accounts of 22 homicides among Ju/'hoansi groups during a 35-year period from 1920 to 1955, for example, but found little, if any sanctioned group violence.

QUESTION 9.3: WHAT ARE THE ECONOMIC, POLITICAL, AND SOCIAL DIFFERENCES BETWEEN PEACEFUL AND VIOLENT SOCIETIES?

Thomas Hobbes, a 17th-century philosopher, proposed that human beings in their natural state, without government or laws, are driven by greed and the quest for gain. Without some common power to keep them in awe, Hobbes said, they live in a state of war, with every person against every other person. In his book *Leviathan*, Hobbes famously describes his vision of life before civilization as "solitary, poore, nasty, brutish, and short" (Hobbes 1881 [1651], 94–96).

Hobbes saw human beings as having a natural inclination to be violent, an inclination that can be controlled only by some form of centralized authority. However, as anthropologists have discovered, societies with little formal government, such as the Ju/'hoansi and the Semai, are among the most peaceful in the world. Furthermore, these peaceful societies are small in scale and people make their living primarily by hunting and gathering or by swidden agriculture. Most are relatively isolated and lack formal mechanisms for resolving conflict once it begins. There are no courts, no police, no jails, and no formally sanctioned threats of violence, even against wrongdoers. Since there is little that people in these societies can do once violence begins, they go to great lengths to avoid it.

Had Hobbes (1881) known the Yanomamö, however, he might have found that his vision of a stateless society, "where every man is enemy to every man," was verified. Their social and economic life closely resembles that of the Semai, and they live in virtually the same environment and are neighbours of the peaceful Xinguano. But Yanomamö society creates attitudes favouring collective violence in order to protect its women and children. In this

RESOLVING CONFLICT

case, the lack of any centralized control or formal mechanisms for putting an end to conflict results in unrestrained violence rather than the avoidance of conflict.

The Need to Protect Resources

In societies without any form of centralized control and a bias toward collective violence, such as that of the Yanomamö, individuals must protect their own resources through force. Because the Yanomamö, for example, do not effectively control intravillage conflict, men of their own as well as other villages are constantly seeking to seduce one another's wives. Consequently, the men, individually or in groups, must build a reputation for fierceness in order to protect themselves and their families. Failure to control conflict and the need for men to build a reputation for aggressiveness in order to protect their resources combine to produce a society that places a positive value on violent behaviour.

The conditions that give rise to violent conflict among the Yanomamö are not unlike those that promote violence in street gangs in the United States. When he worked in the 1960s with the Vice Lords, a Chicago street gang (or "club," as they preferred to call themselves), Lincoln Keiser (1968) concluded that boys joined gangs because alone they could not protect themselves from shakedowns or safeguard their interests in girls. Where the Yanomamö encouraged *waiteri*—fierceness—the Vice Lords valued heart—a willingness to follow any suggestion regardless of personal risk. Where a Yanomamö demonstrated fierceness through chest-pounding duels, axe fights, and raids against enemy villages, members of street gangs in Chicago confirmed their heart in gang fights. Street gangs even formed alliances against other gangs, as do Yanomamö villages with each other. The similarities in the dynamics and values of violent conflict among Yanomamö and among street gangs in Canada and the United States illustrate how under certain conditions, individuals form groups to protect themselves against other groups. To discourage attacks from others in the absence of protection from other agencies, these groups cultivate a reputation for violence.

The gang violence that Keiser observed in Chicago during the late 1960s has escalated since, and weapons more typical of armed soldiers in the military are now being used. Alex Kotlowitz, in *There Are No Children Here* (1991), reported how the Vice Lords, one of three gang factions in Chicago in the early 1990s, made use of an arsenal that included Uzis and grenades. The purpose was the same, although the stakes were higher. Drugs have become the major source of contention among Chicago gangs (the head of one Vice Lord faction grossed $50,000 to $100,000 a week). When drug wars erupt over territory, the violence reflects the increased stakes and more massive firepower. A couple of years ago, four members of the Vice Lords came upon a rival gang member in the lobby of a housing project and shot him five times with an Uzi, two sawed-off shotguns, and a .25-calibre automatic handgun to establish their dominance in the neighbourhood.

The social and political conditions that characterize the societies of the Vice Lords and the Yanomamö are such that in each of them, individuals must mobilize and use force to protect or acquire desired resources. In neither case is there

Innocent bystanders may be killed in the midst of gang warfare waged due to a lack of other ways to protect valued resources or to settle disputes. Here, spokespeople for Toronto youth groups plead for help from municipal politicians to combat unchecked gang violence.

any effective centralized authority to guarantee the safety of resources or to stop violence once it begins. Although there is a centralized force in Chicago—the police—they rarely intervene in gang violence because they are unwilling or lack the resources to do so, or because local residents are afraid or reluctant to report violence.

Creating the Conditions for Violence

Napoleon Chagnon characterized Yanomamö warfare as a "truly primitive cultural adaptation … before it was altered or destroyed by our culture." It was, he said, the normal state of affairs before it was suppressed by colonial governments. There is, however, considerable evidence that Yanomamö warfare and aggression were less a product of their existence or nature than they were consequences of Western contact.

Brian Ferguson (1995) maintains that the period of Chagnon's fieldwork (1964 to 1972), on which he based his best-selling ethnography, *The Fierce People* (1968), was one of the most turbulent in Yanomamö history. Violence and aggression, writes Ferguson, were a product of three major changes: (1) the presence of new outpost settlements of government agents, missionaries, and researchers; (2) competition for Western manufactured goods, particularly steel cutting tools, and (3) a breakdown of social relations brought about by epidemics and the depletion of game and other food resources.

The Yanomamö, Ferguson points out, had been in contact with outsiders for centuries. Europeans began raiding Yanomamö villages for slaves as early as the mid-17th century and continued to do so until around 1850. In the late 19th century, the rubber boom in the Amazon—a horrendous period for indigenous groups, who were forced to collect rubber under the threat of torture and death—brought the Yanomamö into increased contact and conflict with other indigenous groups. After the Amazon rubber boom collapsed in the 1920s as a result of competition with Asian rubber

plantations, the area in which the Yanomamö lived was relatively peaceful until the 1950s and 1960s; then, influenza and measles epidemics swept the area, leaving only one-quarter of the children with both parents. More disruptive yet was the presence of new Western outposts.

The new outposts made available to the Yanomamö desired manufactured items, such as steel knives, machetes, aluminum pots, and shotguns. Steel cutting tools, for example, were ten times more efficient than the stone cutting tools they had long been using. Shotguns were effective both for hunting and for raiding.

The Yanomamö could obtain these items in various ways. They could relocate their villages near the outposts, they could send trading parties on long voyages to get them, or they could raid other groups for them. But the greatest advantage went to what Ferguson called "anchor villages," those that relocated near outposts. The result was a hierarchy of settlements ranging from anchor villages whose members were able to monopolize the new desired goods to more isolated settlements whose members had fewer and lower quality goods.

Yanomamö in anchor settlements traded Western items to distant groups for local handicrafts such as cotton hammocks, spear points, or manioc flour. But trading parties were also targets of raids by groups desiring Western goods. To protect themselves and their monopoly on Western trade goods and to discourage raiding, Yanomamö groups found it advantageous to cultivate reputations for violence and aggression. A reputation for fierceness was also an advantage in negotiating for desired goods. Thus, one man told of the number of people he had killed on raids just before demanding a machete.

Proximity to Western outposts incited violence in other ways. For example, once people relocated their village near an outpost settlement, they were reluctant to move. One way that small-scale, mobile societies such as the Yanomamö avoid conflict is by moving villages away from enemies when conflict is threatened. But since moving would mean giving up access to and a monopoly on Western goods, members of anchor villages were reluctant to move and, hence, needed to protect themselves and the goods they obtained from Westerners. In addition, more permanent settlements quickly depleted game resources: resources that had been used in reciprocal exchanges with other people and groups. Thus, sharing patterns, which as we noted earlier are crucial for maintaining peaceful relations, began to break down, leading to more conflict.

In these ways, deaths from disease and war disrupted traditional social relations, the depletion of game weakened traditional patterns of sharing and cooperation, and access to Western technology provided new sources of conflict. Furthermore, the new technology introduced a new way of ordering society and enhanced the ability of people in anchor villages to make war.

Access to Western goods also explains the aggressive attitudes of Yanomamö men to women. Traditionally, Yanomamö practised brideservice; grooms were obligated to work for their bride's family for up to four years. But families of grooms in anchor villages were able to substitute Western goods for brideservice, one result being a movement of wives to villages with greater access to Western goods. This, combined with the Yanomamö practice of female infanticide and polygamy, resulted in a shortage of and greater competition for females and the more frequent raiding of other villages for women. In addition, Yanomamö wives go to live in their husbands' family villages, particularly where Western goods take the place of brideservice. The result is that women are removed from the protective influence of their families and are more likely to be victims of abuse.

In sum, many of the patterns of Yanomamö warfare, violence, and aggression cannot be understood without knowledge of their history of contact with Western society and the contact conditions that increased the likelihood of violence and war. Even the power of chiefs, whose feast giving played such an important role in Chagnon's descriptions of alliance formation and aggression, was largely a function of Western contact. Outsiders, following traditional customs, brought gifts to local leaders. But the gifts that outsiders brought were far more valuable. Thus, Chagnon gave one chief a gift of 25 machetes, providing him with items that he could use to enhance his power. And thus, as Ferguson (1992, 225) says, "if villages were not anchored to outposts but were able to move freely, if long-established marital alliances were not disturbed by massive mortality, if communal sharing of meat were still the norm, and, above all, if necessary technology were widely and equally available, my theoretical expectation is that there would be little collective violence among the Yanomami."

EXERCISE 9.2

Some anthropologists have explained the tendency toward violence of both Yanomamö and the Vice Lords of Chicago as being the result of competition over, and protection of, resources. Brian Ferguson, however, contends that violence among the Yanomamö must be understood within the broader context of colonialism and its attendant physical and structural violence. What kinds of broader societal forces, and forms of structural violence (as discussed in Chapter 7), might apply to the context in which the Vice Lords struggle to protect their resources?

Sexism and Violent Conflict

Another difference between peaceful and violent societies that has been suggested has to do with gender roles. Among the Ju/'hoansi, the Xinguano, and the Semai, men and women are relatively equal and there is little institutionalized violence against women. In contrast, the Yanomamö and the Vice Lords are characterized by male dominance, and both sanction violence against women.

Several reasons have been advanced to support the link between sexist values and violent conflict. First, it is men that make war, though women may fill certain positions in the armed forces.

While there have been societies in which women engage in armed combat, these instances are the exception rather than the rule. During the Sandinista rebellion in Nicaragua in the 1980s, women took an active role in combat, but they were banned from active combat once the Sandinistas gained power. Second, there is a strong cross-cultural link between patriarchy and violent conflict. After examining information on more than one thousand societies, William Tulio Divale and Marvin Harris (1976) concluded that the intensity of collective violence is significantly higher in societies characterized by a strong male bias—patrilocal residence, patrilineal descent, polygyny, postmarital sex restrictions on females, male secret societies, and men's houses. Finally, there is evidence that societies characterized by sexual violence against women tend to be more warlike and prone to collective violence. Peggy Sanday's 1981 study of 95 societies in which there was evidence of frequency of rape supports this conclusion. The question is, does a sexist ideology promote violent conflict, or does the incidence of violent conflict promote sexism?

Those who claim that sexism promotes violent conflict make that connection in various ways. Betty Reardon (1985) and Leslie Cagan (1983) suggest that societies that relegate women to an inferior position explicitly or implicitly sanction violence against women. Moreover, violence toward women serves as what they call a "primal" paradigm for violent warfare against other peoples; once violence is allowed as a means of domination of one group such as women, it can serve as a model for dominance and violence against other groups.

For Peggy Sanday, and for many others, sexism and violent conflict both have their roots in competition over scarce resources. During periods in which resources are not scarce, males and females are valued equally. When there is an imbalance between food supply or distribution and needs, or when groups are competing for resources, males become of greater value, females become objects to be controlled, and sexual violence becomes one way that men demonstrate dominance. Among

cattle-herding people in East Africa, for example, raiding for cattle was common and sometimes led to violent conflict between groups. Violence was defined as a manly activity, leading East African societies to place great emphasis on masculinity and manliness. Manliness, however, was tested not only in battle but in male–female relations as well, for sex was a way of demonstrating strength.

In sum, factors such as a lack of centralized control, competition over scarce resources, private property, and sexism may lead societies to construct an ideological bias toward violence. Examining the effects of violent conflict to see if they produce changes in societies may provide insights into the factors that promote violent conflict.

EXERCISE 9.3

There is some suggestion of a link between militarism and competitive sports; that is, societies that are prone to collective violence are more likely to value games in which men aggressively compete against other men. How does this apply to North American societies? Which sports in North America most closely resemble or promote the values of militarism and war? Does the language of these sports reflect militaristic values? Do gender roles reflect these values? In what ways does Canada differ from the United States on these issues?

QUESTION 9.4: WHAT IS THE RELATIONSHIP BETWEEN VIOLENCE AND THE NATION-STATE?

Violence and the Nation-State

As we discussed in Chapter 8, the symbolic barriers of excluded Others, infrastructure, and

RESOLVING CONFLICT

education are essential for nation building. The use of violence or the threat of armed force is another key instrument in creating and maintaining the nation-state. Killing is the ultimate tool of nation-states. In fact, some anthropologists, among them Pierre van den Berghe, Leo Kuper, and Carol Nagengast, view the nation-state as a genocidal or ethnocidal institution, one that conspires to kill or remove those citizens who fail to (or refuse to) conform to the dictates of the imposed national culture. "Ethnic cleansing" is not only a phenomenon of the late 20th century. For example, the United States, through policies of either aggressive extermination or benign neglect, attempted to kill all Native American indigenous peoples and assimilate those who remained. Between 1975 and 1979, the government of Cambodia, the Khmer Rouge, systematically murdered 2 million of its 7 million citizens, and in 1994, the Rwandan state slaughtered 800,000 of its citizens. According to Carol Nagengast (1994),

the numbers of people worldwide subjected to the violence of their own states are staggering. More than a quarter of a million Kurds and Turks in Turkey have been beaten or tortured by the military, police, and prison guards since 1980; tens of thousands of indigenous people in Peru and Guatemala, street children in Brazil and Guatemala, Palestinians in Kuwait, Kurds in Iraq, and Muslim women and girls in Bosnia have been similarly treated. Mutilated bodies turn up somewhere everyday. Some 6000 people in dozens of countries were legally shot, hung, electrocuted, gassed, or stoned to death by their respective states between 1985 and 1992 for political misdeeds: criticism of the state, membership in banned political parties or groups, or for adherence to the "wrong" religion; for moral deeds: adultery, prostitution, homosexuality, sodomy, or alcohol or drug use; for economic offenses: burglary, embezzling, and corruption; and for violent crimes: rape, assault, and murder. (119–20)

Pierre van den Berghe (1992) contends that what is euphemistically called "nation building" is nothing but a blueprint for at best **ethnocide** (an attempt to destroy the culture of a people) and at worst **genocide** (an attempt to exterminate a people). Social scientists, he writes, tend to ignore the genocidal character of the nation-state because of the widespread assumption that nation-states are necessary for maintaining peace and economic stability. Instead, he says, nation-states are, in effect, mafias or gangs that, through the use or threat of violence, extract booty for themselves or their elites from rival "gangs" and extract "protection money" from their own citizens.

Other anthropologists share van den Berghe's view of the nation-state as an instrument of force and violence. Nagengast (1994) examined not only state killing but also the use of torture, rape, and homosexual assault to draw the boundaries of the nation-state. State-sponsored violence, she says, serves not only to inflict pain but also to create "punishable categories of people"—that is, people whose existence creates and maintains an Other. These punishable individuals represent an ambiguous underclass believed capable of undermining the accepted order of society. Arrest and torture, she says, stigmatize people and mark them as people no one would want to be. Arrest and torture provide a way to symbolically mark, discipline, and stigmatize categories of people whose existence or demands threaten the idea, power, and legitimacy of the nation-state. Because torture and violence are committed against only "terrorists," "communists," or "separatists," these methods become legitimate. "We only beat bad people," said a Turkish prison official in 1984. "They are no good, they are worthless bums, they are subversives who think that communism will relieve them of the necessity of working."

ethnocide
The attempt to destroy the culture of a people.

genocide
The attempt to exterminate a people.

The official described with apparent pride the order that he had given that "all prisoners should be struck with a truncheon below the waist on the rude parts, and warned not to come to prison again." "My aim," he said, "is to ensure discipline. That's not torture, for it is only the lazy, the idle, the vagabonds, the communists, the murderers who come to prison" (Nagengast 1994, 121).

Nation-states, and national identity, can also be an integral, if complicated, part of the process of creating and maintaining peace. For instance, since the 1994 genocide in Rwanda, the Rwandan government has embarked on a "deethnicization campaign." Ethnic labels on national identity cards are outlawed, and to identify as Hutu or Tutsi is to "risk accusations of 'divisionism' or genocide ideology" (Eramian 2014, 96).

Violence, the Nation-State, and Peace in East Timor

One of the most recent instances of state violence against its own citizens occurred on the island of Timor on the southern edge of Indonesia. East Timor had been colonized by the Dutch and the Portuguese and was granted its independence by the Portuguese in 1975. Five days after a state visit by then U.S. Vice-President Gerald Ford and Secretary of State Henry Kissinger, Indonesia invaded East Timor. Over the following two decades, Indonesians, especially members and friends of the ruling family, invested millions of dollars in various enterprises there. And, as many other countries have done, Indonesia embarked on a campaign of violence and terror in its effort to integrate the East Timorese into the Indonesian nation-state.

Indonesian anthropologist George Aditjondro (2000), who faced an indefinite jail term for criticizing Indonesian leaders, described the campaign of terror, violence, and torture embarked on by the Indonesian state against its most recent citizens. It included, among other things, a "pacification war," which lasted from 1975 to 1979, and repression

that continued even after a 1999 UN-sponsored referendum in which 80 percent of the population voted for independence from Indonesia.

Torture, says Aditjondro, was a standard method of subjugation. Techniques included physical beatings, the use of cigarette butts to burn holes in the skin, electric shock, the crushing of hands and feet with chair or table legs, the poking of the mouth with bamboo sticks, the infliction of pain on the genitals, the rape of women, and immersion in a metal tank filled with water charged with electricity.

Torture was used for five reasons, according to Aditjondro. First, to obtain information from victims. Second, to crush the fighting spirit of freedom fighters. Third, to weaken the political power of the Catholic Church by obtaining "confessions" of church complicity in pro-independence politics or in sacrilegious or criminal acts. Fourth, to protect the business interests of Indonesians in East Timor. And finally, to minimize critical press reports from East Timorese newspapers.

But torture was not the only technique of state terror used by Indonesia. There was, for example, physical terror, including mass killings of guerrillas along with women and children that took place during the first decade of the Indonesian occupation.

Some 200,000 people—around one-third of the population—were killed or died of deprivations brought about by the terror. Prisoners were thrown to their death from helicopters; people were killed by napalm bombings that also destroyed crops, and thousands died from resulting famines. Many people died in overcrowded prison barracks, some of which were covered with black canvas to turn them into human ovens.

There was also a campaign to "depurify," as Aditjondro calls it, the bodies of East Timorese women through rape and forced fertility control. Rape was often committed against the wives or daughters of men suspected of being involved with the resistance. In other cases, rape was committed against women who failed to produce identity cards or who refused to accompany or submit to the sexual demands of soldiers. Other women were forced to spy on resistance forces while serving as sex slaves of Indonesian troops. In still other cases, East Timorese women were forced into brothels for use by Indonesian troops. Rape, says Aditjondro, was also a way to destroy the East Timorese resistance by biologically depurifying their ethnic constituency.

Another way to biologically depurify the population was through forced contraception. Family planning programs were used as means to discipline the population; they symbolically represented state control over human bodies. Thus, high-school girls were injected with Depo-Provera, a birth control drug, without being told of its function.

Other forms of symbolic violence included erecting pro-Indonesian monuments and forcing citizens to participate in Indonesian political rituals (flag raisings, parades, and parties), subjecting them to arrest, interrogation, and physical torture if they resisted. Language itself was modified, with new linguistic expressions for torture and execution becoming common. *Jalan-jalan ke Jakarta* ("taking a trip to Jakarta") and *Berangkat studi lanjut ke Jawa* ("going for further study in Java") were euphemisms for executions. *Mani laut* ("taking a sea bath") referred to the practice of weighting the

© Supri Supri/Reuters

The brutalization of East Timor by the Indonesian military and by Indonesian-supported militia from 1975 to 1999 is but one example of how nation-states use force to control their citizens. Here, East Timorese youth are staging a drama portraying the killings of some 271 unarmed protesters by Indonesian troops at the Santa Cruz cemetery on 12 November 1991.

bodies of people with rocks and dumping them from a helicopter into the sea. *De-Santa Cruz-kan* ("Santa Cruz-ified") was an expression used by mothers to threaten their children with the sinister connotations of a notorious 1991 massacre of East Timorese high-school students who were protesting Indonesian occupation. Finally, 200,000 people were taken from East Timor and relocated to other parts of Indonesia.

Many East Timorese became **refugees**—forced to flee their home country to seek protection in another. Refugees that comprise a **diaspora**, or dispersed population living outside their homeland, escape direct violence and harm; however, the effects of living through sustained, everyday violence are long-lasting. Amanda Wise

refugees
Groups of people who have left their homeland due to warfare, forced expulsion, acts of terrorism, or other factors.

diaspora
A population whose members are dispersed and living outside their homeland.

(2006) conducted fieldwork with the refugee diaspora in Sydney, Australia. She found that the experience of shared violence and trauma was a key element in the collective identity of the refugees, who came together to create what she called a "community of suffering." The embodied memories of pain and suffering drew the community together. The Indonesian military inflicted violence on the East Timorese, and "such practices symbolically and affectively bind the pain of the individual to the fate of the ethnic collectivity." The shared memory and common suffering became the foundation of solidarity among her informants (2006, 15).

East Timor finally regained its independence from Indonesia in 1999, but the break did not come easily. Eighty percent of the population voted for independence in a UN-sponsored referendum; however, before they withdrew from East Timor in September 1999, the Indonesian military and military-trained and -supported militias laid waste to virtually the entire country, killing thousands of people and driving 200,000 people out of East Timor and into Indonesia, where many remain under the control of fleeing militia members.

For Wise's informants, living in exile in Australia, independence opened up the possibility of a return to their homeland. But many of them, having spent so many years in Australia, had mixed feelings about where they belonged. They had developed a sense of identity based on collective suffering. An exiled journalist described these mixed feelings: "Perhaps the worst condemnation of all is to watch our country recede from our reach like a foreign, distant, indecipherable tide and to witness how indecisively our bodies begin to seek stability after many precarious years; our bodies, unconsenting and perhaps irremediably, grow accustomed to a country which they did not choose of their free will" (in Wise 2006, 163).

Canada's part in the tragedy of the East Timorese is documented in the video *Bitter Paradise: The Sellout of East Timor*, by Elaine Brière. Probably the last tourist to visit East Timor while it was still a peaceful, welcoming society in 1974, Brière dedicated her life to making the genocide public. The video followed Brière's journey into the business world, where she was told that Canadians who were commercially involved in Indonesia did not know about the genocide or believed that it was an exaggeration; to the world of the media, where she was told by the host of a talk show that Canadians didn't "connect" with the killing of East Timorese; and to Ottawa, where her questions were ignored by the External Affairs minister. Canada continued to give enormous amounts of economic aid to the Suharto regime in spite of the killings and in spite of cutbacks in social programs at home; and Canadian businesses, such as Inco and Bre-X, continued to see Indonesia as a haven for international investment.

The tactics used by Indonesia to subdue people who resisted integration into the Indonesian nation-state are not unique. In fact, virtually all these tactics have been used by most, if not all, nation-states at one time or another. You can get some idea of how nation-states today sponsor violence against their citizens by going to the Internet, where information is readily available from organizations such as Amnesty International and Human Rights Watch.

EXERCISE 9.4

Protesting the Genocide in East Timor

Many Canadian students protested Canada's continued financial support of Indonesia with international aid. What do you think would have happened to Canada's ability to do business in Indonesia if Canada had stopped the aid? Do you think Canadian businesses should have continued to operate in Indonesia in spite of the genocide? Do you think that if Canada had taken a stand against the genocide (stopped the aid, withdrawn all businesses), the rest of the world would have followed? Defend your opinions.

QUESTION 9.5: HOW IS IT POSSIBLE TO JUSTIFY THE CREATION OF WEAPONS OF MASS DESTRUCTION?

Anthropologist Hugh Gusterson, who had been an antinuclear activist, wanted to know how nuclear weapons scientists could justify conducting research on and testing of weapons of mass destruction. What could create a worldview that enabled people to justify performing that kind of work? To answer that question, he set out to study the culture of the Lawrence Livermore National Laboratory in Livermore, California.

Gusterson (1995) suggests that those who justify nuclear weapons and who question nuclear disarmament make four assumptions about the world. First, they claim that anarchy characterizes international relations. Second, they assume that states must rely on self-help since no one else is going to offer them protection. Third, they assume that nuclear weapons are the ultimate form of self-help, because they vastly increase the cost of aggression against them. And fourth, they assume that relatively little can be done in the short term to change the anarchistic nature of the international system.

Critics of nuclear weapons make very different assumptions. They argue that international relations are not as anarchistic as they are made out to be and that rules and norms that control aggression exist. Many critics see the nuclear arms race as "objective social madness." People who work in the area, they assume, must be in denial and must demonize the Other to justify their work.

Gusterson wanted to find out not so much who was "right," but rather how people came to hold such divergent opinions about ways of resolving conflict, especially when the stakes are so high. Nuclear weapons scientists did not, says Gusterson, avoid the ethical concerns of their research. Most, however, accepted the central axiom that nuclear research is necessary to make the world safe. To some, working on nuclear weapons was more ethical than working on conventional weapons, since conventional weapons were more likely to be used. Nuclear weapons, the scientists assumed, were simply symbolic chips in a game, the goal of which was to avoid using them. When asked if he could ever foresee a circumstance in which nuclear weapons would be used, one scientist said, "No, even if we were under attack." In other words, deterrence was the only reason to develop nuclear weapons; if you were attacked, the whole enterprise had failed. Others rationalized their work more baldly, saying they were not responsible for how what they designed would be used. "Are automobile designers," they ask, "responsible for deaths caused by drunk drivers?" (Gusterson 1995, 58)

When Gusterson asked people why they chose to work at Livermore, most cited the intellectual freedom they enjoyed working in a weapons laboratory. Almost all compared Livermore favourably to working in universities (which they characterized as "stodgy," "cutthroat," or "high-pressure") or in private organizations. Some also cited the challenges of weapons research and the opportunity to work with state-of-the-art equipment. Beyond those attractions, Livermore paid about twice as much as a university position.

Once a person was hired, secrecy played a major role in forging a person's identity. Livermore employees were investigated before being given security clearance to laboratory facilities. Personnel were divided into different security categories and given coloured badges indicating their level of clearance. "Q" clearance (a green badge) was necessary for classified research; "L" clearance (yellow badge) allowed access to classified areas but not to classified information. The labs themselves were divided into areas of lesser and greater security. As Gusterson (1995, 70) put it, the laboratory was "an enormous grid of tabooed spaces and tabooed topics."

Without a green badge, a weapons scientist was not considered a full adult in the lab. The process of getting "Q" clearance was elaborate and could take six months to two years. Virtually every aspect of a person's life was subject to investigation in search of clues that he or she was unfit to handle classified material. Most people passed, though, and because secrecy was not so well guarded in practice, the security clearance process functioned mostly as a rite of passage that added to the mystique of weapons research and that disciplined the initiate.

Secrecy was one of the principal ways that the lab's diverse population was brought together. Knowing secrets, regardless of how mundane they might be, marked a person as a member of a special group and lent an air of drama and importance to one's work. Secrecy also served to limit discussion that could change people's views of the work that they were doing. As Gusterson (1995, 68) put it, "the laboratory's culture of secrecy does tend to produce certain effects in its scientists: it segregates laboratory scientists as a privileged but somewhat isolated elite; it inculcates a sense of group loyalty; and it thrusts on laboratory scientists an amorphous surveillance, which can become internalized."

The process of testing nuclear weapons was, in many ways, the critical step in creating the nuclear scientist. Any Livermore scientist could propose a weapons test, but reviewers (senior scientists at the laboratory) selected only about one out of 20 ideas for testing. Nuclear tests had elements of myth and ritual. Approval of an idea for testing reaffirmed the scientist's membership in the group, not unlike a rite of passage. Testing produced not only weapons but also weapon designers. It was a way of creating the elite. The more tests one participated in, the greater the prestige and power that accrued. A successful test validated status and credentials and brought forth congratulatory support and reinforcement. Tests provided a symbolic simulation of the reliability of the entire system of deterrence: "Each time a nuclear test is successfully carried off, the scientists' faith in human control over nuclear technology is further reinforced. Seen in this light, the 'reliability' the tests demonstrate has an expandable meaning, extending out from the reliability of the particular device being tested to the entire regime of nuclear deterrence" (Gusterson 1995, 161).

The Language of Nuclear Destruction

Carol Cohn (1987, 1991) spent one year studying the culture of a strategic studies institute, or "think tank," for government defence analysts who plan nuclear strategy. She began her study with this question: How are people whose job it is to plan nuclear destruction able to do it? As we discussed in Chapter 4, language is one of the key ways in which members of a particular culture come to understand their shared worldview as true and natural. One of Cohn's conclusions was that the planners used language to distance themselves from the consequences of the actions they were planning. The language they used obfuscated and reassembled reality in such a way that what was really being talked about—the destruction of human lives—was hidden behind metaphors and euphemisms.

During her first weeks at the centre, as she listened to the participants talking matter-of-factly about nuclear destruction, she heard language that she labelled *technostrategic*. This language included terms such as *clean bombs* (fusion bombs, which release more energy than fission bombs), *penetration aids* (technologies that help missiles get through enemy defences), *collateral damage* (human deaths), and *surgical strikes* (bombing that takes out only military targets). Domestic metaphors were common in the technostrategic language: missiles were based in *silos*, piles of nuclear weapons in a submarine were *Christmas tree farms*, bombs and missiles were *re-entry vehicles* or *RVs*, and massive bombing was *carpet bombing*. According to Cohn, the domestic images were more than a way for people to distance themselves from the grisly reality they were discussing. Calling the pattern in which a bomb would fall a "footprint" removed the speakers from any position of accountability for the acts they were contemplating.

Cohn also discovered that the language and metaphors of those working at the institute seemed incapable of expressing certain realities. The aftermath of a nuclear attack was described in technostrategic language as "a situation bound to include EMP blackout, brute force damage to systems, a heavy jamming environment, and so on" (1987, 707). She contrasted this with eyewitness accounts of the bombing of Hiroshima. There was, Cohn wrote, no way of describing this experience in technostrategic language. It removed the speakers from having to think about themselves as victims of nuclear war.

Cohn also discovered that she could not use ordinary language to speak to the defence analysts. When she tried, they acted as if she were ignorant or simpleminded. To communicate, she had to use terms along the lines of *subholocaust engagement* and *pre-emptive strike*. The word *peace* was not a legitimate part of the vocabulary; to use it was to brand oneself as a softheaded activist. The closest she could come to *peace* in technostrategic language was *strategic stability*.

To an anthropologist, the fact that people are limited by their culture, their language, and their worldview is, of course, no surprise. All cultures give a characteristic meaning to violent conflict, and to peace, whether it is viewed as the act of an animal in possession of a human body, or as the will of God, or as a game. The more serious implication of Cohn's observations is that scientists, academics, and nuclear planners give weight to their claim that their perspective is "objective" and therefore has greater truth value than other perspectives. Moreover, says Cohn, if one can speak to defence analysts only in technostrategic language, and if the language is constructed in such a way as to be incapable of expressing different realities, then there is no way for these analysts to appreciate or understand the other realities involved in the use of nuclear weapons.

QUESTION 9.6: HOW DO ANTHROPOLOGISTS DO FIELDWORK IN THE MIDST OF VIOLENT CONFLICT?

As often as possible, anthropologists try to learn about and understand various social and cultural phenomena through fieldwork and participant observation. However, striving to understand violent conflict firsthand can be difficult at best and dangerous at worst. Often, it is contentious as well. Should anthropologists place themselves in danger in the name of fieldwork? What if, through our very presence, we put others at risk or promote the conditions for further violence? Can we use ethnography to understand war from a soldier's perspective? Below, we discuss three different examples of the possibilities and pitfalls of studying violence and conflict, either directly or indirectly.

The Endangered Anthropologist

The risk of injury, disease, or hostile reactions has always been a feature of anthropological fieldwork. As anthropologists increasingly work in areas where human rights violations are common, these risks are intensified. At least four anthropologists have been murdered because of their fieldwork. In 1982, South African anthropologist and anti-apartheid activist Ruth First was killed by a mail bomb in her office at Maputo University in Mozambique. In 1984, Melanesian anthropologist Arnold Ap was tortured and killed by the Indonesian army, his body dumped by helicopter into the sea. In 1989, South African anthropologist David Webster was shot and killed by members of a pro-apartheid death squad. And in 1990, Guatemalan anthropologist Myrna Mack was stabbed to death by a soldier, ostensibly for her work with Mayan refugees and their experiences in the government's counterinsurgency war of the early 1980s, through which hundreds of thousands of people died. In addition, at least two anthropologists,

Ricardo Falla and George Aditjondro, went into exile under threat of assassination because of their work. These real dangers that anthropologists face may provide insights into how the people with whom they are working experience the threat of violence.

In 1989 and 1990, Linda Green was doing fieldwork in the Guatemalan community of Xe'caj. Like many similar communities, Xe'caj was only beginning to recover from some 35 years of violence. Beginning with a military coup orchestrated largely by the Central Intelligence Agency (CIA) against a democratically elected government in 1954, Guatemala experienced regular violence as the militarized state tried to suppress attempts to overthrow the military regime. Hundreds of thousands of Guatemalans were killed, mostly by the government, in an attempt to suppress the revolt. The late 1970s and early 1980s were particularly brutal as the government embarked on a campaign to destroy peasant villages and relocate people to government-controlled towns. In addition, paramilitary groups, largely supplied and supported by the regular military, embarked on campaigns of terror and torture in an effort to control the peasant population.

The people of Xe'caj lived in a state of constant surveillance from the military encampment located above the town. Many of the residents had husbands, fathers, or sons taken away by the military. There were rumours of death lists. People had difficulty sleeping and reported nightmares of recurring death and violence. Soon, said Green, "I, too, started to experience nighttime hysteria, dreams of death, disappearances, and torture."

Green interviewed women who had been widowed by the conflict. Without prompting, the women recounted in vivid detail their stories of horror, the deaths and disappearances of husbands, fathers, sons, and brothers, as if they had happened last week or month rather than six to eight years earlier.

Then, one day when Green arrived to continue the interviews, the women were anxious and agitated. When she asked what had happened, they told her that the military commissioner was looking for her and that people were saying she was helping the widows and talking against other people in the community. When Green told the women she was going to see the commissioner, they pleaded with her not to do so, telling her that they knew of people who had gone to the military garrison and never returned. Green decided to visit the garrison alone, and that visit would provide a vivid experience of the fears confronted by the villagers. As she approached the garrison, she noted the following:

> I saw several soldiers sitting in a small guardhouse with a machine gun perched on a three-foot stanchion pointed downward and directly at me. The plight of Joseph K. in Kafka's Trial flashed through my mind, he accused of a crime for which he must defend himself but about which he could get no information. I didn't do anything wrong, I must not look guilty, I repeated to myself like a mantra. I must calm myself, as my stomach churned, my nerves frayed. I arrived breathless and terrified. Immediately I knew I was guilty because I was against the system of violence and terror that surrounded me. (1995, 116)

Fortunately, the *commandante* said he knew nothing about why she was being harassed. He assured her that she could continue with her work, and everything went smoothly from there. But Green had gained a fuller understanding of the experiences of people who must live under the constant threat of violence.

Is There a Place for Anthropology–Military Collaborations?

In 2005, Montgomery McFate, a military adviser with a background in anthropology, published an article in *Military Review* arguing that there was a "culture gap" in our understanding of the conflict in Iraq caused by "the almost total absence of anthropology within the national-security establishment." She argued that successful counterinsurgency requires a total understanding of local culture. To achieve victory, the United States needed to understand Iraq's traditional authority structure and the competing interests of different groups such as the Shia, Sunni, and Kurds. In a second article, co-written with Andrea Jackson, McFate outlined a proposal to establish an "Office for Operational Cultural Knowledge," which would train teams to provide battlefield commanders with knowledge of local culture, or as it was being called, the "human terrain."

The need for cultural knowledge was echoed by retired Major General Robert H. Scales, Jr., (2005, 43) who argued that these new conflicts required not technological superiority but "an exceptional ability to understand people, their culture, and their motivation."

One outcome of this interest in cultural knowledge was the development of the Human Terrain System (HTS), which ran from June 2006 to September 2014. The centrepiece of the program was Human Terrain Teams (HTTs), each of which had a staff of five: an army officer serving as team leader, a cultural analyst, a regional studies analyst, a Human Terrain (HT) research manager, and an HT analyst. Each team studied the local culture, interviewed local people, and provided valuable information to the battalion commander.

Anthropologists who joined the HTS project explained their service as an effort to do something meaningful. Marcus Griffin wrote: "I have an obligation to use my skills to learn about people and to share what I learn." Working as a member of an HTT in Iraq, Griffin saw his job as finding out what Iraqis needed and helping them meet those needs.

Not everyone, however, shared this positive assessment of the Human Terrain System. In 2007, the American Anthropological Association issued a formal statement condemning the project, arguing that it would lead anthropologists to violate ethical standards and that it posed a danger to both anthropologists and the people they were studying. Another notable critic, Roberto Gonzales (2009), pointed out a number of dangers of the Human

Terrain System. First, was it possible for informants to *consent* to their participation? Second, what type of information was being gathered by anthropologists, and how would it be used? Third, how well would informants be protected from retaliation by hostile groups or political rivals?

Despite such reservations, in 2008, the Canadian Forces began a program of "white situational awareness teams," or WSATs, which are similar to HTTs. In military terminology, "white" refers to the civilian population (as opposed to the "red" and "blue" of enemy and friendly forces, respectively). Each WSAT included two military intelligence officers and three civilian Department of Foreign Affairs employees, and aimed to provide a more nuanced understanding of the cultural terrain for military leaders and advisers (Fenton 2010).

Maximillian Forte, an anthropologist at Concordia University, expressed concerns about the Human Terrain System, WSATs, and the potential militarization of anthropology in general: "Their [WSATs'] job seems to be no different from that of HTS, except that for now the civilians they use are government employees, not academics. They have breached a barrier however: the idea that social and cultural knowledge can be useful for counterinsurgency, at least that door has now been opened in Canada" (in Fenton 2010).

What bothers many critics of the Human Terrain System, in particular, is that regardless of the efforts of the military and others to put a humanitarian face on the contributions of social scientists, the information gathered by HTTs was clearly going to be used for military purposes. HTS advocates wanted to make whatever information was gathered available to other agencies and to the governments of Iraq and Afghanistan, to "enable them to more fully exercise sovereignty over their country" (Gonzalez 2009, 74).

This idea reminds many anthropologists of the disastrous CORDS program, implemented during the Vietnam War. Like the Human Terrain System, CORDS was designed to gather cultural knowledge in order to win "hearts and minds." Using information from social scientists, military

© U.S. Army photo by SSG Michael Castell

A U.S. soldier takes notes as he talks and drinks tea with local Andar District Special Needs School administrators during a cordon and search of Nani, Afghanistan, in June 2007. Can anthropological expertise be put to (good) use in a war zone?

personnel exploited Vietnamese superstitions and religious beliefs to frighten and terrorize civilians. When CORDS data were given to the South Vietnamese government, they were used to target political opponents and dissidents. This experience points to the need to take precautions to ensure that the Iraqi and Afghan governments do not use HTT information to target political rivals or to create blacklists for personal vendettas.

The use of social scientists for HTTs in Iraq and Afghanistan raises a larger issue: the responsibility of anthropologists and other social scientists to be aware of how their data may be used. The Pentagon, for example, is using information collected by social scientists to help identify dangerous neighbourhoods in Baghdad and Kabul. This knowledge allows the military to predict which neighbourhoods are at risk for riots, gun violence, or bombings; it also helps them develop lists of possible participants and their relatives, friends, and associates.

Perhaps more ominous, the military is awarding grants to social scientists to forecast human behaviour. The U.S. Department of Defense is developing a project called Human Social Culture Behavior (HSCB) Modeling. Much of this work will be contracted out to private corporations eager to secure lucrative government contracts. One corporation, Aptima, in conjunction with Carnegie Mellon University, has developed Social Network Analysis, or SNA, software. SNA has been used by the U.S. military "to predict a state's potential for instability or civil unrest in terms of nine key factors," which range from "lack of essential services" to "corruption level" to "tension."

One danger, of course, is that the philosophy of the Human Terrain System, as well as the development of elaborate surveillance technologies using vast quantities of information now available on citizens, will move from military applications in places such as Iraq and Afghanistan to domestic uses that seriously undermine democratic freedoms. Gonzalez (2009, 123–24) concludes his critique of the Human Terrain System as follows:

> *What comes across from the accounts of many social scientists supporting counterinsurgency initiatives in Iraq and Afghanistan is a fundamental acceptance of modern warfare in general and the U.S.-led occupations in particular. Furthermore, they generally accept the false notion that counterinsurgency—the "graduate level of war" to quote one military enthusiast—is more antiseptic, more humane, less damaging than conventional warfare. As technicians of power, some adhere to Machiavellian principles: do not question the prince or his war, but instead use the most efficient means to help him achieve victory. War's inevitability is taken for granted. Basic assumptions are left unquestioned. Missing from these accounts is the question of whether war is appropriate at all today.*

Making Sense of Combat: Canadian Soldiers in Kandahar

Throughout this chapter, we have explored the ways in which people in various societies and cultures make sense of violent conflict, or alternatively, create meaningful, peaceful solutions to conflict. As we have seen, language and ritual are both employed, quite successfully, to make nuclear proliferation and the subsequent possibility of mass destruction seem both feasible and meaningful. As noted at the outset of the chapter, until recently, pride in peacekeeping was a key part of Canadian national identity. For the first time since the Korean War, however, Canada had soldiers in active combat (in Afghanistan) between 2001 and 2014. In her work with Canadian Forces soldiers stationed in Kandahar, Anne Irwin analyzed the ways in which they use storytelling and ritual to make sense of their experiences in combat.

A former member of the Canadian Forces, Irwin spent many years studying Canadian soldiers, both while they trained for peacekeeping operations (Irwin 2002) and, more recently, with a unit that would undertake "full-spectrum operations," including combat (2012, 61). Irwin spent several months with the unit during its tour in 2006, living with them both at Kandahar's air force base and "outside the wire," on patrol and in combat. Irwin found that whereas time and routine on the base were quite structured, time outside the wire

was completely disrupted—"there was no day-to-day routine for sleeping and eating, not even predictable shifts" (64). Even when there was no engagement—"troops in contact," in military parlance—the soldiers experienced all time outside the wire as being in combat, not least because of the omnipresent danger of IEDs (improvised explosive devices). Soldiers who spent time outside the wire together seemed to go through a rite of passage and shared a liminal period together during combat (69). However, Irwin is reluctant to cast combat as a rite of passage that turns boys into men. Indeed, she argues that although combat has some of the elements of a rite of passage, soldiers who return to Canada seem to be both permanent adolescents (referring to themselves and their fellow soldiers as "the boys") and, at the same time, old men: prematurely aged, grief stricken, and often scarred or disabled (76).

Irwin has also collected and analyzed soldiers' narratives about the war in Afghanistan. Often, these address and link individual morality to social and political debates about Canada's combat role. One soldier, in telling the story of his experiences, said that "a lot of people in Canada think that we

should not be here in Afghanistan, but those people don't see the remarkable changes happening here. One interpreter told me, 'Because Canada is here, our people are happy again.' So to all those Canadians who continue to harp about what they don't know—here's your straw, suck it up" (Cpl Sanders, in Pengelly and Irwin 2011, 52).

Here, the soldier has turned his combat experience into a morality tale, one that takes the qualities of a good solider—responsible, tough, and uncomplaining—and transposes them onto the Canadian public. Moreover, he is attempting to show the moral justness of the war by drawing on "the moral character of a helpful and caring Canada" (2011, 53). By examining these kinds of narratives, we can see how their circulation helps soldiers understand and justify their participation in this violent conflict. Moreover, when such combat narratives draw on a sense of national identity and pride, of Canada as "helpful and caring," we can begin to make sense of the rather rapid (though contested) shift, at the turn of the 21st century, of Canada's role from peacekeeper to warrior nation.